THE LABYRINTH OF MEMORY

Ethnographic Journeys

Edited by
Marea C. Teski
and
Jacob J. Climo

BERGIN & GARVEY
Westport, Connecticut • London

Library of Congress Cataloging-in-Publication Data

The labyrinth of memory / ethnographic journeys / edited by Marea C.
  Teski and Jacob J. Climo.
      p. cm.
    Includes bibliographical references and index.
    ISBN: 0–89789–409–X (acid–free paper)
    1. Ethnology. 2. Memory. 3. Communication in ethnology.
  4. Personal narratives. 5. Oral tradition. I. Teski, Marea C.
  II. Climo, Jacob.
  GN307.5.L33   1995
  301—dc20   94–39209

British Library Cataloguing in Publication Data is available.

Library of Congress Catalog Card Number: 94–39209
ISBN: 0–89789–409–X

First published in 1995

Bergin & Garvey, 88 Post Road West, Westport, CT 06881
An imprint of Greenwood Publishing Group, Inc.

Printed in the United States of America

The paper used in this book complies with the
Permanent Paper Standard issued by the National
Information Standards Organization (Z39.48–1984).

10 9 8 7 6 5 4 3 2 1

Jacob J. Climo dedicates this volume to the memories of Jerzy Kosinski, David Miller and Joseph Guzik, who inspired his own work.

Marea C. Teski dedicates this volume to the memory of her uncle Donald Osborne, whose radiant presence still glows in her memories of childhood.

Contents

Preface

The ideas for this volume emerged from a session at the 1992 Annual Meeting of the American Anthropological Association, where Jacob J. Climo and Marea C. Teski cochaired a panel—Memory, Generation and Culture. Sharon Kaufman, University of California, San Francisco, and Jonathon A. Boyarin, New School for Social Research, were discussants for the panel. We thank them for their insightful comments at that time. Additional thanks go to Sharon Kaufman for her useful input in regard to producing a book. We also wish to thank Lynn Flint of Greenwood Publishing Group for her encouragement and patience, and Production Editor Elisabetta Linton for her excellent work with this manuscript.

Introduction

Marea C. Teski and Jacob J. Climo

There is a territory of ethnographic investigation that lies beyond both space and time. It is the most precious possession of both individuals and groups as they strive to make sense of the living, yet often amorphous, material of their experience and to speak about it. That territory is, of course, memory: the changing, elusive locale of our past, present, and future lives. For all of us memory is a labyrinth that takes different turnings each time we come back to it. Moreover, whenever we return to our memory labyrinth we emerge with a slightly different view of what is actually there. Its treasures are inexhaustible and we can never find the same treasure twice, because we ourselves change constantly, as do our purposes in searching for memories.

In this volume we do not seek to chart the huge array of kinds and purposes of memory. Rather, we seek to open a few windows in the vast labyrinth in order to shed some light on its paths and turns. We suggest some categories of memory journeys that we believe point to ways of clarifying the ethnographer's use of memory documents and narratives. Ours is a traditional goal of ethnography applied to the past: to journey with our informants through time as they conceptualize it and to allow them to reflect on their views of their own individual and collective past. In a sense we are showing some of the things that happen when individuals and groups embark on a variety of quests into their distant and recent pasts.

Memory is part of nature and, in this biological sense, a part of every species. It is, however, extensive, varied, and multifaceted only in the human species, and like everything else that is human, memory is informed by culture. Individual experience is mediated by memory and culture. We have experiences of events, emotions, people, things, and settings, but the meaning of such experiences gets interpreted in the cultural language we have learned for encoding such remembered reality.

Memory is not recall. Rather, it is a continuous process based on rumination by individuals and groups on the content and meaning of the recent and more distant past. In some ways the past is almost as unknown to us as the future, because, as we live and change, the past also changes. Ownership of memories is an important issue. They may be "owned" by an individual, a small group, or a very large group, and a right of review and reformulation can be claimed at any of these levels.

To an important extent the purposes and uses of memories are determined by who it is that voices them. The "who" of the memory voice is often a question of power. In some cases individual memories may struggle with other individual memories over matters of who is correct and who has the right to produce the official version of the memories. Groups may struggle with other groups, and institutions (e.g., church versus state) may vie with one another for the last word or the last version of how things were. Official memories may be anything from the imposed "correct" version of a power elite to the communally emergent shared tradition of an old and consistent culture.

Culture itself may be seen as memory in action as we live and enact our versions of the real living world. Habitual ways of doing things are almost automatic, for we act as we have acted before, and ultimately as we have been taught to act. We learn through actual instruction and also through imitating patterns we have observed as they surrounded us at all stages of life. When an anthropologist asks an informant about his or her culture, that informant is being asked to recreate the recent and more distant past—in other words, to give the anthropologist some memories. How was an initiation ceremony carried out yesterday? How was it done fifty years ago?

Memory seems to be the main place where culture exists, and it is also the locus of interaction between the reality of the individual and the reality outside the individual. Thus, memories are both intensely personal and also reflective of a culture at a given time and place. Memories show cultural continuity and cultural change as well as idiosyncratic information concerning the rememberer and his or her life.

In the process of recalling and retelling memories, the desires and needs of the present act upon both the style and the content of the narrative. Memory seems to be paradoxical, in that it is our major link to the past while it essentially serves the present in creative, political, and instrumental ways. Memory plays an important role in forming, altering, and enhancing the set of experiential events we call the present. And it is also paradoxical because it maps the future while it claims that it is describing the past.

Curiously, even as a memory serves the present and forms the future, it is sometimes, particularly in nonliterate cultures, the only means by which we can access the culture of the past. Cultures with written and electronic records have large inventories of objects and a greater selection of versions of the past. Although written and visual accounts and artifacts greatly stabilize versions of the past, they are also subject to changing interpretations of their meaning.

The past, then, is difficult for us to reach. It is a cultural world that can only be revealed through artifact and memory, but it is susceptible to constant change as its appearance in the present varies. Therefore, we are always using fragmentary and partial data in trying to piece together a past world where people lived and died, a whole culture that has disappeared, a vanished reality.

The definition of culture that we are using here is one that considers a culture to be a whole way of life of a group of people: their artifacts, technology, customs, ideas, and mental images of reality. Memory is an important means of preserving all this. Changes in interpretation and selective forgetting may alter the form of the past culture to which individuals and groups refer. This leads to questions of conflicting memories and interpretations of the past and the struggles at all levels from the family to national and even international levels over whose memories are the "true" ones.

Individual and group or collective memories are alike in that each tries to validate the view of the past that has become important to the individual or group in the present. Forgetting or changing memories is done to serve the present; it makes the present meaningful and also supports the present with a past that logically leads to a future that the individual or group now finds acceptable.

This volume will bring together diverse ideas about the ethnography of memory and will explore some of the approaches that enhance our understanding of the usages of memory. We present five different paths to the ethnography of memory: Remembering, Forgetting, Reconstructing, Metamorphosis, and Vicarious Memory. These categories are not meant to be an exhaustive treatment of all possible uses of memory. Rather, they suggest a variety of ways to begin classifying various kinds of memory for ethnographic purposes.

The first aspect we will consider is Remembering. This is probably the most straightforward, least distorting kind of memory, although in all varieties of memory, present needs are paramount. Remembering is the process of connecting with the past, trying to preserve it and understand its echoes in our present world. When we think about the past and try to bring forth, for example, the name of our first grade teacher, the guests at our tenth birthday party, or what we wore to the high school prom, we are trying to flesh out our remembered past in a fuller, more satisfying way. We are looking for details of the past, not consciously trying to change it but to see it as it was. The question of what we are able to remember and why we want to remember certain things relates to our present needs. But the purpose of straightforward remembering is to preserve something that really happened. We want to have access to scenes that were real in the past and to somehow preserve these things in our present experience; it is the search for the truth of what has come before.

In his chapter, "Leaving Home: Memories of Distant-Living Children," Jacob J. Climo focuses on the memory of individual experiences to explain a variety of current emotional attachments among adult children who left their parents and natal homes in early adulthood to set up their own, distant households and families of procreation. That they experience feelings of ambivalence toward parents is the only universal theme to emerge. Yet Climo reveals three distinctive voices in the present that are shaped by memories of the past: the displaced voice is not satisfied with distant living and expresses a desire to reunite with parents; the well-adapted voice accepts distant living as a normal result of occupational and educational mobility and maintains strong ties of affection with parents without desiring to change the situation; the alienated voice is glad to live away from parents because relationships are not satisfying, filled with memories of unresolved conflicts.

Climo's chapter demonstrates an aggregate memory, a cultural continuity of experience, in that all the informants grew up in America and most of them left home for the first time to attend college. Such aggregate memories, though not the memories of ethnic or group identities, nevertheless help explain the various attitudes these adult children hold toward their current relationships with distant-living, aging parents.

Rakhmiel Peltz's chapter, "Children of Immigrants Remember," describes the contemporary social settings in which aging American-born Jews use the Yiddish language to revitalize their memories of early childhood and their ethnic identity. Born in the first decades of this century to Jewish immigrant parents from Eastern Europe, these aging Jewish "children" were mainly exposed to Yiddish in their preschool years, in their early childhood relationships with parents and family. While personal memories of Yiddish run the gamut from feelings of pride, ambivalence, and shame (as a foreign language), most identify Yiddish as the quintessential quality of Jewishness in its association with both Jewish religious observance and cultural heritage.

As a participant-observer, Peltz documents the personal and collective delight and profound association with memories of the past as these aging Jews attend Yiddish conversation groups, write and perform Yiddish plays and musicals, and reenact the American Jewish experience. Peltz claims that ethnic identity should be seen as flexible and changing over time. Like other aspects of cultural identity, language is closely linked to collective memory, and living languages are those in which the speakers agree to remember them.

Marea C. Teski's chapter is based on interviews with pre–World War II Polish government officials exiled in London. Teski considers memory as their desire to preserve the past and, at the same time, to help carve out a future. Her informants experienced physical, cultural, spiritual, and existential separation from their homeland for forty-five years. Their memories focus on events and meaning in Poland's past which resist cultural changes that threaten Polish survival and reaffirm their fundamental nationalist convictions that Poland is a distinct nation and culture regardless of its fate. Themes of betrayal, hardship, suffering, and martyrdom underlie their memory model for patience and tenacity in maintaining the idea of a nation that could potentially exist.

Their memories not only involve individual but community processes of using historical and cultural metaphors to build an understanding of the past and the present. Their shared experiences during forty-five years outside Poland make them different from Poles who never left. For example, they still find strength in the Polish literary tradition of the nineteenth century and they do not identify with national guilt, a post–World War II phenomenon. Because of their exile, these people perpetuated the old Polish culture longer than possible in the homeland.

Our second category, Forgetting, deals with individual group attempts to change the past. Some memories cannot be accommodated in the present life and situation, therefore they are repressed and written out of history. We are not referring here to the psychological mechanism of repression of painful memories in which a person actually loses all recall of a painful past event or events. We are talking here about a conscious suppression of memories that challenge present identities and actions of individuals and groups. When a group is involved, forgetting can be a profoundly political act, a rewriting of history to make it support present power relationships and the imposition of a new version by those in control.

In her chapter, "Social Memory and Germany's Anti-Foreigner Crisis," Andrea L. Smith stresses the importance of social forgetting. Popular and social scientific representations of Germany's current crisis of anti-foreigner violence and ambivalent government policies regarding guestworkers misrepresent this crisis and reproduce several myths: that Germany has only recently relied on foreign labor, that Germany is an unusually "homogeneous" nation, that Germany has experienced little integration of foreigners, and that it is not now and cannot become an "immigration" country. These myths hinge on a widespread forgetting of much of German labor history.

Smith's paper outlines this "forgotten" history of foreign labor importation. When these early experiences are contrasted with modern practices and policies, a pattern emerges suggesting continuity in Germany-foreign worker relations. An examination of modern German citizenship and naturalization law suggests that the current crisis is one phase of a longer unresolved conflict between economic goals and the definition of the German nation. Recognition of this pattern of conflict is blocked, however, as earlier periods of conflict are erased or forgotten. Research on the invention of traditions and the construction of special national histories must consider the interrelated problem of collective forgetting.

Reconstructing, the third category, happens most often in situations in which cultural memories have not been written down or have been lost in some way. When this is the case a conscious effort is made to build memories to support present culture. It can also happen when individuals or members of a group have been separated for a long time. Coming together, they need to recalibrate their disparate versions of the past. This happens at family reunions and serves to improve communication and to validate the occasion. Sometimes a new tradition results, supported by reconstructed memories. The process of reconstruction may vary from a barely conscious restructuring of the past to a fully self-conscious activity of tradition-building. Other groups may do it in seeking to create or construct a national cultural identity. This identity is highly political, because it seeks to build memories needed to sustain present political identities.

In his chapter, "Mau Mau and Memory Rooms," Richard Swiderski claims that people find and organize social spaces to recall their memories in an emotionally safe environment. Swiderski's discussion guides the reader through a series of memory rooms, both individual and collective, and across a variety of cultures: memory rooms in Marx brothers films, memory spaces in poetry and literature, memories of religious ritual objects and dramas in the sitting room of a Syrian Catholic leader in South

India, personal "homeland" memories in the study of a European-born professor long residing in Kenya, and an "Elvis" room organized by a family in Tupelo, Mississippi. The tour ends with an inquiry into the contemporary Kenyan nationalist struggle to ascribe ethnic memory space and meaning to the memory of the Mau Mau freedom movement of the early 1950s.

Swiderski distinguishes memory rooms from museums, noting that museums are more rigid in architecture and contain lists of objects and schedules of display, all of which can exist apart from people. In contrast, memory rooms need to be places where the past is recalled; such rooms often include important symbolic objects but can only exist when a rememberer and his or her community is present, when people interact with each other. Regardless of the variety of their spatial arrangements, human beings construct and recall memory socially, as an emotion, and in intensely local spaces.

In her chapter, "Chaptering the Narrative" Donna O. Kerner addresses the question: How do oral and written histories intersect in the construction of collective memory at a time when oral traditions have been eclipsed by written narratives? Focusing on contemporary Chagga culture in Kilimanjaro, Tanzania, Kerner notes that indigenous historians are standing at the crossroads of two distinctive paths to remembrance: oral narrative and literate history.

To answer this question she elaborates the meaning of the Chagga revival of *mregho*, a mnemonic device traditionally used in the formal initiation of adolescents becoming adults. Local historians have reinstated the mregho stick, which was inscribed with notches in various combinations of vertical, inclined, or wavy lines, circles, and dots that served in a schematic way to preserve the memory of how experience was to be interpreted and understood. Thus, the elders taught Chagga children the rules of etiquette required for community life, particularly regarding the secrets of sexuality, procreation, and growth.

Kerner offers two explanations for the revival of mregho rituals. First, the AIDS epidemic has brought a new and critical need to instruct the young about appropriate sexual conduct and reproduction. And second, in the current multiparty political system, a village's reputation as progressive and successful influences the distribution of scarce economic resources. Indigenous historians, often representing local "improvement associations," use mregho to prove that the Chagga had developed a written language in the precolonial period, thus legitimating their claims to past and present intellectual achievements and furthering their village's claims to resources in the political competition.

In her chapter, "It Only Counts If You Can Share It," Molly G. Schuchat suggests that people create culture by sharing common experiences, then communicating their memories of such experiences with each other. Thus, in dialogue with others the reality of our personal memories finds meaning in social life. As an undergraduate in the late 1940s, Schuchat's class visited the Tennessee Valley Authority project. There she witnessed firsthand the "horrors and outrages of segregation" in "colored" water fountains and bathrooms. On returning to the project forty-five years later she notes with satisfaction the absence of segregated facilities and later enjoys sharing this information with a classmate who was with her on the original visit. For Schuchat the meaning of the present is too vast to grasp by one's actions alone, but can be understood only by anchoring one's images to others in a continuing dialogue. Hence, old meanings are brought up to date by new events, and to enter culture memory requires an interactive process. Moreover, it is not just the changed perspective from the present for the remembrance of things past, but the opportunity to have the past interact with the present, that creates culture.

Metamorphosis of memory, our fourth category, is the evolution of memory from one form to another. In this process new meaning emerges through time. In metamorphosis, new forms are not built but seem to emerge spontaneously in changed versions. This happens to some extent in all remembering, but this category refers to memories that, more than most, seem to have a life of their own and to be capable of great variation as time passes. Unlike restructuring, metamorphosis does not involve a conscious tinkering, but instead fuels change in the way things are remembered in almost subliminal social action.

In her chapter, "Memories of Violence, Monuments of History," Antonella Fabri considers the oral testimonies of Mayan refugees, victims, and witnesses of Guatemalan state violence and torture. Their reconstruction of history both challenges and resists the official state version of history, which attempts to erase and forget the repression while reducing the Mayans to stereotypic caricatures of history. In remembering the mutilated bodies of their loved ones, defying the silence demanded by a regime of fear and terror, and reconstructing their individual and collective pain, these survivors can recuperate the physical, psychological, and political body of their own history.

Brian Leigh Molyneaux's chapter, "Representation and Valuation in Micmac Prehistory," presents the case of an ancient Micmac rock painting discovered on the coast of Nova Scotia. His discussion illustrates that social memory always serves present political and economic interests, regardless of its cultural origins. Molyneaux, an archaeologist called in to conduct a seemingly straightforward survey, finds himself, "the expert," holding somewhat different perceptions of the site from those of the "natives" and those of the "developers," who are embroiled in conflict. Reaffirming that collective memory is always subjective rather than objective, he suggests the importance of a concept of negotiated memory, in which various interest groups living in a pluralistic present are aware of and tolerate their differences. Molyneaux proposes that near-future technological advances may help reconcile different memories of the same past by bringing them together into computerized and other high-tech presentation formats that respect different stages of time equally and encourage students to tolerate different interpretations of the same past.

Vicarious Memory, our final category, happens when the memories of others become a part of reality for those who hear the memories but have not experienced the events to which the memories refer. They are memories that are passed from generation to generation to become the social and cultural memories of a group, or the traditions of a family. Events, situations, even emotions and thoughts are passed from one person, generation, or group to others who "inherit" the pattern of reality contained in the memories. Thus, the sins, pains, happiness, behavior, and realities of those who raise and enculturate us become a part of our repertoire, and we live according to patterns that are not our own personally. Cultures and nations use vicarious memories to retain loyalty to a way of life by uniting people in collective occasions of shared vicarious memory.

Jacob J. Climo's chapter, "Prisoners of Silence: A Vicarious Holocaust Memory," calls attention to a generation of American Jews who grew up in close personal attachment and association with Holocaust survivors, as teachers and friends' parents, people who were burdened by personal memories of pain and torture but in the years immediately following the war communicated their feelings through silence, mood, gesture, and body language. Although American Jews born after World War II did not experience the Holocaust personally, they developed deep emotional feelings about the Holocaust and learned to accept the collective responsibility of remembering.

Iwao Ishino's chapter, "Memories and Their Unintended Consequences," deals with the memories of third-generation Japanese-Americans of their incarceration in California during World War II. Though their memories are vicarious through their parents' experiences, in some important ways their passionate involvement in this collective memory has led to recognition of and redress for this misdeed in the larger context of national politics.

Memory is as multifaceted as life itself, and, as we have said, this is not an exhaustive set of categories for accessing it. Nevertheless, these categories address important aspects of the individual and group social and cultural use of memory, and may serve as a basis for the continued exploration of the complex meanings, usages, and interpretations in the labyrinth of memory.

REMEMBERING

According to the elderly Jews who are experiencing a romance with the language and culture of their parents, what is remembered is not especially events of childhood, but emotions and sensations of identity, of closeness to self and family. These are feelings they had as children.

Rakhmiel Peltz

Leaving Home: Memories of Distant-Living Children

Jacob J. Climo

INTRODUCTION

For more than a century, memory has been a primary tool in anthropological field research. Yet anthropologists have neither classified its various uses systematically nor clearly outlined its limits for reconstructing the past or for understanding the present, for societies or for individuals.

Early anthropologists used the memory of aging Native Americans to reconstruct entire cultures. Perhaps those elders who shared their memories of past events were engaged in a life review process, integrating their past into their present lives. Yet this was not distinguished from the historical reconstructions of their institutions; societies reconstructed from those interviews were presented as if the ethnographers had observed them directly. No attempt was made to distinguish the role of the past in an individual's life from the life of his or her culture.

Anthropologists still use memory to reconstruct social histories as well as individual life histories and to explore the limits of human relationships in specific cultures and cross-culturally. We are aware of the power of the past to influence present events and processes, as historian Collingwood (1961:294) has remarked, "Historical knowledge is that special case of memory where the object of present thought is past thought, the gap between present and past being bridged not only by the power of present thought to think of the past, but also by the power of past thought to reawaken itself in the present."

And we have learned that memory can illuminate the processes that bring men and women to their present cultural and individual realities. Contemporary anthropological literature contains several examples of ethnographies written from memory, such as *Political Systems of Highland Burma* by E. R. Leach and *The Remembered Village* by M. N. Srinivas, because the authors for one reason or another lost their field notes (Sanjek 1990:36–41).

We know that memory is self-serving and that some, if not all, memory requires its corollary, forgetting. As Levi-Strauss notes at the beginning of *Tristes Tropiques*, "Time in an unexpected way has extended its isthmus between life and myself: twenty years of forgetfulness were required before I could establish communion with my earlier experience, which I had sought the world over without understanding its significance or appreciating its essence" (Levi-Strauss 1955:44).

In spite of such insights, however, we are left guessing about memory, and its variations in cultural context, until we make a genuine effort to distinguish collective memory from individual memory, to differentiate a culture's interpretation, its collective meaning of the past, from the self-serving purposes of the individual in the present.

In this chapter I use the memory of individual experiences to explain the variety of current emotional attachments I found among adult children who left their parents and natal homes in young adulthood to set up their own, distant households and families of procreation. They moved to other parts of the country and never returned to live with their parents.

I asked them to describe leaving home as an event in their memory and, on the assumption that memory serves present needs, I attempted to see if their narratives could help explain their current relationships with their distant parents. I investigated what I shall call an aggregate memory rather than a collective memory because I elicited the facts from each individual in interviews. A commonality of categories arises from the fact that they grew up in the same cultural milieu and most left home originally to go to college. But the memory is not collective because it does not ascribe meaning to certain historical events that the group identifies with and wants to remember in a ritual or cultural way.

The most universal and dramatic theme to emerge was the expression of ambivalent feelings toward distant parents. Regardless of the specific life events or incidents that daughters and sons chose to describe, they consistently represented their distant relationships in three distinct voices, constructed to characterize their emotional attachments to distant parents. Of forty distant adult children, eight (20 percent) presented a displaced voice, twenty (50 percent) a well-adapted voice, and twelve (30 percent) an alienated voice. The displaced voice is not satisfied with distant living and expresses a desire to reunite with parents. The well-adapted voice accepts distant living as a normal result of occupational and educational mobility, maintaining close contact and strong affection without desiring to change the situation. The alienated voice is glad to live away from parents because relationships are unsatisfying, filled with unresolved conflicts from the past.

When adult children recall their experiences, it becomes clear that their decisions to live far away were made with an awareness of many influences on different levels, including the conscious and unconscious, rational and emotional. Some children made decisions alone; others decided in collaboration with parents or peers. Some decided after much deliberation and planning; others decided impulsively with no consideration of the consequences.

Such decisions are influenced by both external and internal forces. External forces include economic and social circumstances that encourage distant living as a desirable and attainable prerequisite to upward mobility. Internal forces include factors related to individual psychological growth, the self, life-cycle development, and the need for young adults to prove they can be self-reliant, self-supporting, or live alone.

This early adult decision lays the groundwork for the development of distant relationships many adult children will maintain with their aging parents, including visit and telephone patterns, feelings of frustration and satisfaction, the ability to give and receive assistance and to express affection, and family solidarity.

Several external forces in contemporary life influence a child's decision to move away from parents and the natal home. Such forces include (1) core cultural values that encourage American young adults and their parents to accept distant living as normal, and (2) social and economic circumstances in contemporary America that pressure individuals to move great distances for educational and occupational advancement, marriage, and other individual opportunities. Each young adult who decides to live far away from parents must reconcile the relative influence of these forces on his or her life.

Clearly, external factors such as higher education and career opportunity play a considerable role in the decision to leave. But external factors do not operate in isolation. Rather, they must be seen in combination with internal forces that consider the decision to move away in purely psychological terms. Internal forces deal with questions of internal growth, the self, and individual life-cycle development.

In my recent book, *Distant Parents* (Climo 1992), I elaborate the impact of both external and internal forces for displaced, well-adapted, and alienated adult children. In this chapter, however, I focus on some of the internal forces that reinforce alienating and negative attachments with distant parents.

Life-course development theorists believe the major task in young adulthood is to develop role identity, to find adult social roles that are both psychologically satisfying and socially acceptable. In making the decision to stay or live far away, the individual's place within the family setting is of primary importance. Birth order, family dynamics, sibling careers, parents' age and health, the nature of emotional attachments to parents, and roles in the family all play a part in the decision. Decisions of this kind often culminate in adolescence, the stage of development that focuses on the search for autonomy (Thornburg 1982) and that is often the source of much parent-child conflict.

In some cases the individual decision to leave may be made long before adolescence. It is only actualized in adolescence because that is the time when it is socially acceptable to leave. The decision to leave may be connected to many aspects of the parent-child relationship. Sometimes an adolescent is a helper to the parents in the practical requirements of everyday life, or an emotional confidant to one or both parents. Distant children constructed three significant internal forces in their narratives: (1) parental support and expectations toward the child, (2) the kinds of conflict parents and children engaged in, and (3) the resolution or persistence of conflict after adolescence.

PARENTAL SUPPORT AND EXPECTATIONS

Most distant children recall parental support during their process of separation. The way they express it reflects their varying voices of emotional attachment to their parents. Displaced and well-adapted children remember a great deal of parental support, both financial and emotional, when they were establishing distant households for the first time. A well-adapted son recalls the importance of his parents' confidence in his ability at this critical moment in his career. Their support meant a great deal to him since his parents were uneducated and initially reluctant to have him leave for graduate school.

Well-adapted daughters freely acknowledge their parents' emotional support for their careers. Another son from a well-off family also needed and received his parents' emotional support to break ranks and leave the family business. Well-adapted and displaced children express gratitude for the financial difficulties and sacrifices their parents made to help them in their careers. A daughter notes that without their financial support she would not have been able to obtain her Ph.D.

A son remembers proudly, "My father really sacrificed to put me through school. In my family one never talked about it. I noticed after I graduated from Hopkins that all of a sudden my father started buying clothes. And he could never afford clothes. He bought these sport jackets and I was shocked. It took me a long time to understand he hadn't been able to do that. So he was very generous in that way."

Some well-adapted children call attention to assistance their parents gave them when they moved to begin their academic positions. A well-adapted daughter from a very large family explains that her mother and stepfather created a system of financial support to help all the children in their careers with loans and at the same time develop financial independence in the children. As one of the older siblings she had a moral obligation to repay because the education of her younger siblings depended on it.

In contrast, alienated children typically claim that their parents were not supportive of the college they went to or the subject they wanted to study. One alienated daughter stresses her parents' inability to help and lack of emotional support for her career. Another daughter's narrative is worth examining because of the guilt she feels about her career choice: "If I feel guilty about anything, it dates back to my career choice, and the fact that my parents were unhappy about my career choice, generally. They wanted me and my sister to be lawyers. She's an economist. We both got Ph.Ds. But they wanted us both to be lawyers."

Alienated children express more independence from parental support even when they acknowledge that they received such support. They also often mention parental inconsistencies about financial support. One son complains that his father gave him money whenever he said he needed it but never showed him how to budget it. An alienated daughter complains that her father promised to supplement her grant, then suddenly withdrew his support. Another alienated daughter acknowledges parental support but even then she understood that her relationship with her mother was not healthy.

CONFLICT BETWEEN PARENTS AND CHILDREN

Turning to the second issue, conflict between parents and children, well-adapted as well as alienated children recall significant conflicts focusing on issues of independence and autonomy in their adolescent-parent relationships. A common area of adolescent conflict that well-adapted daughters recall is social relationships, dating, and sexuality. An unmarried daughter mentions sex as an area where she could not talk openly with her parents, referring to it as a generational gap. Another well-adapted daughter remembers a serious conflict with her mother:

There were conflicts about normal things that I wanted to do like date. I could never bring up sex. I really think they did an excellent job of raising me on guilt. I felt guilty about everything I ever thought I wanted to do. I'd been told a million times this is wrong. My mother had this wonderful saying about whenever you're out with a boy anything that you think you want to do just ask yourself, if Jesus were in the back seat would you do it? So you can imagine what I felt like with this thing on my shoulders.

Frequently, well-adapted children call attention to conflicts their older siblings had with their parents. Having witnessed such conflicts vicariously, they and their younger siblings did not have to experience them directly. One son, a younger brother, resolved at an early age to become financially independent by getting fellowships to study.

Another son remembers that his father forced him and his brother to run their farm and was very critical of their work. Several children remember that their parents accused them of taking drugs. A few claim their mothers were domineering and controlling. Well-adapted informants often recall one main conflict before breaking away from their parents' authority. The eldest daughter of a large family remembers:

My last big conflict with my father came when I was in college. It was about where I was going to work for the summer. When I said what if I work in the summer resort anyway even though you say not to, that was a major step. Do I run the risk of not going home if they say, "Well then you're out." They didn't say that. They said they'll call me back tomorrow. Until I could make adult decisions I accepted their authority but with lots of kicking and screaming and back talking.

In contrast, alienated children remember angry conflicts with their parents that surrounded their separations and made them miserable. An alienated son recalls an old conflict with his parents about distant communications:

I remember that conflict had gone on forever, when I was an undergraduate too. I did my graduate work at Berkeley and when I drove out there they didn't hear much from me for the first two months. Finally I got this panic telephone call. My father sounded like, well I thought somebody at home had died. He said, "Oh my God we've finally found you. You really are OK."

It was crazy. They could have called three or four weeks before they did. They waited for me to call because as far as they were concerned I was supposed to keep in touch. They did the same thing with visiting. They had a lot more time and leisure. But they sort of wanted me to pack up the family and come and visit instead of coming here. They did come but that was an extraordinary event.

Recalling their separation experiences and careers, displaced children often mention problems and difficulties. But such conflicts are never with their parents. A typical displaced son reports, "No major conflicts in adolescence. It was the kind of conflict any parent and child might have then but it wasn't substantive. As an adolescent I was quite independent. I had a tremendous amount of trust as far as my parents were concerned. They did not restrict me very much. I suppose it was a relationship that worked because I didn't give them any reason to doubt me."

THE RESOLUTION OR PERSISTENCE OF ADOLESCENT CONFLICTS

The final internal force involves the resolution or persistence of adolescent conflicts. Generally, both well-adapted and alienated children recall difficulties with their parents during separation. The chief difference between them is that well-adapted children relegate such conflict to the past whereas alienated children feel such conflicts persist in their present relationships. Typically, a well-adapted son in his middle fifties notes, "As you grow older there's a kind of forgiveness in the relationship. And you forget the problems of your youth. You go on with your life. I think the question pertains to adult children who are younger. Can you imagine somebody in their fifties still having these kinds of problems with their parents?"

Many well-adapted children speak of conflict resolution with their parents, a period in their adult lives in which they consciously set out to resolve adolescent conflicts with their parents. In their narratives both they and their parents have changed for the better. One son reports that his father is more mellow now, not as critical as in the past and more willing to consider an alternative view.

An unmarried, well-adapted daughter claims her mother is pleased with her because her life has not been filled with trauma or tragedy so she does not have to worry about her anymore. The theme of independence appears again and again as well-adapted sons and daughters report that their relationships with parents have resolved or improved now that they are on their own and grown up.

Well-adapted daughters often note that their parents have changed for the better or that they are able to accept their children's point of view now even when they couldn't in the past. Speaking of her father, a daughter says:

He's a lot more easy going. My Dad thinks other people should grant their children more freedom. He claims that he was too strict with us. And he feels sorry that he didn't let up a little bit. I feel really great about this. I agree they should have done it forty years earlier.

I was an adolescent in the sixties too and there was an awful lot going on. For example, when I went to march on Washington I had a lot of conflict with them. Now looking back on it my Dad says: "I really admired you for what you did even though I didn't understand it then and I gave you such a hard time about that."

The most important point is that for well-adapted children such conflicts did not persist into their adult relationships. A well-adapted daughter typically says:

I remember much conflict but none of it has remained. I think also at one point my parents were rather strict with us. In my home they never gave us enough personal freedom to go with our friends. They were afraid. They always wanted to know where are you going and who are you going with? It isn't always easy to explain because you may not know where you're going with a group of kids. . . . But I really feel like I got past that and it hasn't survived as a problem.

In contrast with the conflict resolution well-adapted children express, alienated children complain that past conflicts persist in their present relationships with parents. Their problem brings to mind a line from one of William Faulkner's novels, "The past isn't dead," he said, "It isn't even past." Frequently, alienated children trace conflicts to a time when, as young adults in transition, they decided to separate themselves from their parents and establish a distant household for the first time.

Alienated children have a major problem distinguishing the past from the present relationship because there are fewer opportunities to reinforce status transitions and new identities, and to keep parents in tune with changes in their lives. Memories of the past may be confusing and sometimes painful for everyone. In conversation with an adult child anticipating new employment, an aging parent may recall the child's behavior on the first day of kindergarten or the child's early attitudes toward certain new foods. Or in anticipation of a transition an adult child may recall how her mother treated her when she was angry, successful, sad, or sick. If the distant parent-child relationship is not continually renewed and reinforced through adequate communication and contacts, it can be dominated by memories.

In one conversation an adult daughter complains that her mother's Florida condominium contains no photograph of her beyond her seventeenth birthday. She sees the symbolism, and is somehow aware that her absence all these years was partly responsible for her mother's inability to permit her to grow up. For this woman the issue of being absent, of her mother being unable to watch her grow as an adult, calls attention to the negative impact of distance on their relationship. A shy, introverted child may become an outgoing, sociable adult, or a child whose room was always a mess may become a compulsive housekeeper, but those changes can go unnoticed because of distance and infrequent communication.

By the same token, parents may change dramatically in adapting to old age (Cohler and Lieberman 1979). Children who believed their parents had a stable marriage may be shocked when their parents divorce twenty years after they have left home. A mother who never joined organizations or became involved in activities outside the home when her children were little may become active in organizations or return to college after the children leave home. Significant personality and behavioral changes take place throughout life; they must be communicated and understood so that children and parents can put the past in perspective. Throughout these changes parents and children continue to feel ambivalent about independence, dependence, reciprocity, and exchange.

One theme that often remains from adolescence is parental disapproval of the choice of male and female friends. One unmarried, alienated daughter recalls:

I think the one conflict that has survived is their idea of appropriate male friends. I clearly never found their appropriate ones. When I was living with them they were very strict. They just didn't want me to go out at all. As soon as I left for the university I was encouraged to bring people home. But it didn't seem to work out practically. I'm not sure why. I had one friend who was in the Navy so he was fine because my father had been in the Navy. The others were more questionable. I think in fairness it was in part because my parents wanted to be sure I just didn't fall into a pattern that so many girls fall into: they just marry quickly and get stuck in the town. They wanted to be sure I left home, got a University education and had choices.

And an alienated son says, "The conflict that survived most fully from my adolescence might be described as the conflict surrounding the significant female-other in my life. Or, to put it another way, my mother seems not to get along with my female companions. That goes beyond my two wives, to my earlier girl-friends as well."

Another central theme alienated children raise is the fear that past conflicts with their parents will transfer to their own children. A daughter remembers that her mother imposed unattainable standards, then worries that she may be doing the same thing to her own adolescent son:

My mother always had very high expectations for me. But I never met them. Somebody could always do it better. I mean I was a very good student in high school. I'd be excited and I'd say, "I got 98 on my Chemistry test." And my mother would say, "That's good, what did Kate get?" And my best friend Kate always got 99. She was always just a little bit better so I was always compared to her. The greatest conflict is just knowing that you never quite measured up. I've decided that my mother is a very insecure person. And if she doesn't feel good about herself how can she feel good about something she produced?

My older son accused me of the same thing, having too high standards. He'll say he just had a great interview and it really went well and he's really excited. And I'll say, "That's wonderful and I'm glad to hear it. Now remember to write a thank you note." And he'll say it's never enough. No matter what, you're always asking something else.

Another alienated daughter has resolved to respect her adolescent son's privacy as a result of her mother's intrusiveness when she was an adolescent:

One of things she was really oppressively notorious for was every time I had any sort of reading material that I could have learned anything from about sex she pried in my things, found those things, and promptly made me take them back to wherever I'd gotten them or throw them away. So I didn't read much because my mother was a real snooper.

As a result, I am incredibly determined not to pry in my own children's things. When my son brought his middle school annual home I wanted to look at it. And he said, "No Mom, there are things written in it. You know, people sign it and I don't want you to read that stuff." So I didn't. He put it in his room and I never looked. Then one day recently I was having a conversation with my husband and I said something about things kids Ryan's age know and my husband said, "He knows these things, I've read his annual." And I said, "What? You read it. You snooped in his things after he asked us not to do it?" He said of course so I told him how I never would do it because I was so infuriated when my mother snooped in my personal things. It can really be detrimental. At least it was with me.

An inability to communicate effectively with parents or solve problems as a family may linger to undermine the possibilities of comfortable relationships between distant parents and children in the later years. Since they did not develop skills to address these problems in adolescence, the problems continue.

Some alienated children have found help through therapy, which encourages them to seek the sources of their dissatisfaction by reconstructing their adolescent relationships and perhaps trying to communicate their insights to improve relationships with parents. An alienated daughter in her middle fifties believes her conflict with her mother began in early childhood:

Many of my adolescent conflicts survive in some form. I've always had real negative feelings towards Mother. Even when I was a little girl if she would hug me or kiss me I can remember turning away. I always felt real guilty about it but I couldn't understand why. I think it went all the way back to when I was born.

Six years ago we spent a year in Japan. Just before we left I found out from my mother that Dad was headed to be a missionary in China which I didn't know. And they didn't go because they had a sick baby: me. She said we had to stay home and care for the baby because there was no medical care for it in China. The sense I got from the discussion was that she had been very frustrated with me for having been born and for having stopped Dad from doing that. And it helped me realize where my anger came from. I can remember as a little girl being really frustrated and angry, and never trusting my mother. I'd like her to understand this. Perhaps she could.

Memories of adolescent relationships are packed with deeply felt emotions, among them uncertainty and guilt. An alienated daughter remembers why she lacks a confidential relationship with her parents:

I remember feeling aggrieved, being blamed for doing something I hadn't done. And they wouldn't believe me when I would explain it to them. I could not explain myself. I had a sense that I should have been doing more and different things and trusted them more. I was not a popular person in school. I was very studious and didn't have any dates. In some ways I never became fully engaged with adolescence. I just had this sense of feeling dissatisfied and misunderstood.

Parental dependency clearly has some influence on an adult child's decision where he or she will live. Parental dependence on a college-aged child may take many forms, including emotional dependence. In fact, the death, disability, or chronic illness of a parent, or divorce, remarriage, or widowhood may constrain or provide an added incentive for a young adult child to leave or stay. A college-aged child whose parent needs him or her to work or perform domestic services cannot consider distant career opportunities in the same way as someone whose parents are well and independent. Any family trauma of significant proportion would more often deter an adult child from considering a career and life in a distant location, though such traumas may have the opposite effect and become an incentive to leave.

Alienated children report memories filled with emotional trauma, sad family lives, and feeling a great need in early adulthood to escape from an emotionally dependent parent. Invariably, children who describe their parents as emotionally dependent are alienated from them. As a result of the past, present relationships are characterized by a lack of emotional closeness to parents.

An alienated daughter explains how her mother's alcoholism has created emotional dependency in their current relationship and an inability to be emotionally accessible on a regular basis. An alienated son traces his conflict with his parents to his father's abandoning him and his mother when he was very little and the neurotic relationship that developed afterwards between him and his mother. He describes her as emotionally dependent. By the time he left his home in a Texas city to go to graduate school, his relationships with both his mother and father were very poor:

My mother depends on her spouse for many things. But she is basically very self-sufficient even though her heart is not good. My mother is currently living with my step-father who is her ex-husband. She divorced him formally but they continue to live together. It was a significant step in their relationship for them to be divorced officially but go on living together. She is not capable of breaking away from that dependency.

She is psychologically counter-dependent. She attaches herself to people who are dependent on her as a way of assuring her control over them. Once you get that concept down it changes the way you see people's relationships. She assumes this posture of kind of sublime self-reliance and gives the impression of self-sufficiency. The reality is that she is compulsively dependent on people who are dependent on her like my step-father for example, like my brother, but not like me. I was the one who walked away from her.

Alienated children also suffer from the long-term dysfunctional effects of conflicts between their mothers and fathers. Such conflicts contribute to a lack of emotional closeness with parents. One alienated daughter draws a connection between her parents' conflict and her own emotional repression in childhood:

We were socialized as children to be emotionally repressed. As adults we learned it's better not to repress our emotions. Then we either can come closer to our parents or not. I always perceived my father as undermining my mother, picking on her, as kind of cruel to her in public. I think it camouflaged his own feelings of social inadequacy. She was a classic victim. Now I noticed the last few times they were here that she does that to my Dad. I had no idea that she had always done that. I hadn't noticed it before.

When I was a child I identified with both of them: the victim and the victimizer. I mean I would side with my father sometimes when he would pick on her. But at the same time in seeing her victimization I learned what it meant to be a female. I learned that role of being victim.

Anger and emotional conflict with parents tend to survive, especially when alienated children remember a deteriorated home environment. As an alienated son recalls, "I went to the University to get as far away as possible. They fought so badly that the police had to be called several times. Physical distance was a way of getting away emotionally as well. I have no regrets. I left deliberately."

What seems similar about teenage runaways and young alienated adults who leave home in anger is the clear linkage in their minds between geographic distance and their growing need for emotional autonomy. One does not know for sure whether teenage runaways will later leave permanently or stay when the decision is made later in young adulthood. It is interesting, however, that none of the well-adapted or displaced children ran away from home during adolescence, but several alienated sons and daughters ran away or reported that their siblings ran away during adolescence. One alienated son ran away as a result of the tragic circumstances of his mother's divorces from his father and stepfather. An alienated daughter whose mother is an alcoholic did not run away herself, but remembers her younger sister running away to have a love affair with her high school teacher during their first years at college. She and her sister have kept this secret from their parents all through the years. This reveals one of the most important characteristics of alienated children: they cannot trust their parents. For alienated children, memories of adolescent relationships with parents spill over into the present.

CONCLUSIONS

In this chapter I presented data from the memories of distant-living adult children about leaving home for the first time in young adulthood to establish a distant household. The materials represent what I call aggregate memory rather than collective or generational memories, in that the narratives are personal. There is some cultural continuity in that all the participants in the study grew up in America and most of them left home for the first time to attend college. When analyzed, the aggregate memories help explain the various attitudes these adult children hold toward their current relationships with distant-living, aging parents. They support other attitudes and behaviors that emerged within the larger study, such as feelings of emotional attachment, ability to assist parents in times of need, patterns of long-distance telephone use, and seasonal, routine, and crisis visits. Further investigation of such aggregate memory will probably reveal great conformity to present needs. But it seems appropriate for anthropologists to classify the uses and limitations of memory for collective, aggregate, and individual life histories. Aggregate memories are not collective memories, but will be found increasingly as anthropologists venture into studies of complex societies where collective memories require shared traditions and symbols that are often lacking.

Children of Immigrants Remember: The Evolution of Ethnic Culture

Rakhmiel Peltz

INTRODUCTION

Living in the present is always accompanied by experiencing the past, even in the most future-oriented groups and societies. Whether consciously or not, human beings are involved in the continual adjustment to and reinterpretation of the lessons and treasures of the past. It is these processes of remembering and reintegrating that I will address in this chapter. What follows is a discussion of children of immigrants and the accommodations made by that generation to the ethnic language and culture they encountered as children and young adults.

FROM IMMIGRANT TO ETHNIC JEWISH CULTURE

The concept of ethnicity, at least as it has come to be understood in American society, usually refers to cultural legacies inherited from immigrants that then appear in various reincarnations.[1] In the case of Jews in American society, historiography has often neglected an essential dimension of ethnicity that pertains to most Jews: those activities and emotions that inhabit the private sphere, the domain of primary institutions, namely the family. Thus, scholarship about the experience of the mass of Jewish immigrants who arrived at the beginning of the twentieth century and the lives of their descendants often focuses on institutions, such as the daily press, or on individual leaders. When the research approach is mainly by way of demography and institutional history, without emphasis on the thoughts and emotions of the people themselves, the picture that emerges is necessarily a limited one. The story that is told typically begins with movement out of the neighborhoods of primary immigration to eventual settlement of the children of immigrants in the suburbs, accompanied by a blossoming of Reform and Conservative congregations and community centers, depleted of traditional *yiddishkeit* (Jewishness) and of Yiddish. But is this picture an accurate one? We now have evidence for a more complex portrait. The immigrant generation, for example, was itself distanced from Eastern Europe. And for that matter, we must exercise caution and do more than simply count an inventory of items, remnants from the old country, in order to truly comprehend the culture of immigrants. For one thing, as my research has confirmed, such a view will most definitely not hold for the case of American-born children of immigrants.

My research on elderly children of immigrants reveals this generation as crucial interpreters of the immigrant culture of their parents' homes within the context of the multiethnic society of the United States in which they have lived since birth. In ethnographic research on four generations of Jews in South Philadelphia, of whom children of immigrants constituted the preponderant majority, as well as on newly founded Jewish senior citizen cultural groups in Northampton and Holyoke, Massachusetts, in analysis of archival autobiographies of children of Jewish immigrants and of literature from the realm of belles lettres—in these four arenas, I have found that the evolution of ethnic culture is strongly linked to developments over the life cycle of the members of this generation.

Although I began with a sociolinguistic orientation, the disciplines of anthropology, psychology, gerontology, and family and neighborhood history helped me formulate ultimately richer research questions for understanding language and ethnicity in the United States. As a result, I have concluded that the continual reinterpretation of memories of the culture of the first years of life constitutes a vital force in how an immigrant or ethnic group develops. As stated by McGoldrick, "To understand ethnic norms, one must maintain a developmental perspective on both variations in family life cycle patterns and the impact that immigration has on families over succeeding generations" (1993:342).

THE CONTRIBUTION OF LIFESPAN STUDIES AND GERONTOLOGY

The function of memory and remembering is obviously dependent on the time when the individual or group invokes the processes of recall and interpretation of the past. This view has largely been accepted as a result of discussions of memory as a socially constructed phenomenon (see, for example, Halbwachs 1992 [1925]; Connerton 1989; Schuman and Scott 1989; Middleton and Edwards 1990). Erikson (1968; 1975:17–22; Erikson, Erikson, and Kivnik 1986:13–53), who pioneered a model that views life as a cycle of discrete developmental stages that turns on itself and is linked to previous and future generations, should also be credited for the concept that past stages of the life cycle are always connected with and serve as the bases for the present stage.

Recently, critics have preferred the term *lifespan* rather than cycle, for the original model is thought to stress inaccurately the existence of identifiable separate stages (Coupland, Nussbaum, and Grossman 1993:xiv–xx; see also Woodward 1991:21). Giddens (1990:120–24; 1991:14, 52–55, 74–80, 145–49, 215), in charting a theoretical construct for contemporary identification of self, has underscored the notion that discrete stages for identity development do not exist, but that identities are always being renegotiated. Coupland et al. (1993:xxvi, xx) have similarly highlighted the significance of studying the discourse of identity development throughout the life course: "Identity is inherently a lifespan concern, so that studies of language and discourse within a lifespan frame are arguably the primary means by which to carry forward the analysis of personal and social identity."

The analysis of my fieldwork with the elderly involves the contrast and linkage of different life stages. Since I am focusing on their discourse with themselves, their contemporaries, their parents, and their children, both on symbolic and conversational levels, matters of identity play a central role.

The gerontologist Butler (1963; 1970), who underscored the life review as a normal and healthy part of aging, has also been a critic of a static view of identity. According to Butler, because people change at all ages, they can never know who they are. The continuous, life-long search for self-understanding, as opposed to the process of defining and consolidating one's past identifications, is thus a sign of health. Shotter (1989:146) has identified "the possession of a developmentally susceptible identity . . . living of a life susceptible to a biographical account" as an essence of being human. From this viewpoint, the life review process of the elderly would not redefine their being in terms of their youth or resolve old conflicts; rather, it would allow a reintegration of past experiences and emotions into their ever-changing lives.

From her anthropological research on elderly Jewish immigrants, Myerhoff (1980) insisted that the processes of remembering during old age were vital for the integration and reintegration of self. In other words, the elderly person was "re-membering," constructing a life, composing a whole. I would argue that this is a vital imperative of the present, and a much more complicated phenomenon than merely looking back. From her work with the elderly, Myerhoff (1988:283) learned to appreciate their need for others to witness their story and their life. In my own fieldwork with this age population, my use of Yiddish helped to induce their remembering and "re-membering." Since I was of a younger generation, both akin to and different from them, I served as a witness who helped them bridge the generations and regain connections to the language and culture of their youth. Remembering and reconstructing, at various times in one's life, invokes the emotion and experience of different moments. The power of the first years at home remains formidable, however, and in my work with the elderly I was impressed by their involvement with "re-membering" the cultural legacy of their childhood.

INSIGHTS FROM LITERARY SOURCES

The German writer Christa Wolf (1984:1), upon embarking on a visit to the Nazi Germany of her youth, as a middle-aged woman, reminds her readers that, "What is past is not dead; it is not even past. We cut ourselves off from it; we pretend to be strangers." Other authors, too, have insightfully underscored the power of childhood experience as a focus for a dialogue with the past, in later life, and as a resource for interpretation and integration. In my current research, in which the first years of life are viewed most often through the prism of the last years, I have found language to be at the center of strong identification, a living vehicle that engenders memory within its own structure and use.

Henry Roth's novel *Call It Sleep* (1991 [1932]) has been acclaimed as a classic portrayal of urban immigrant life in the United States during the early twentieth century. It is a novel mostly about an immigrant child, David, who arrives in the United States at age two and narrates his saga through age eight. The work is a linguistic marvel because Roth builds a complex but consistent code. The major language of the immigrant home is Yiddish, portrayed by Roth as standard English. The children on the street and between themselves speak in a New York dialect of English, sometimes with a few borrowed Yiddish words, transcribed in the text to reflect pronunciation. Adult immigrants, Jews and non-Jews, speak to people outside their group in an accented English that is influenced by their mother tongue. Added to these are the Hebrew and Aramaic of the religious school, and the Polish that David's mother uses to keep secrets from him.

At no point does this well-tailored language system break down in David's mind; he controls all parts and knows their place. Language is present in the foreground as intense, mind-boggling events and emotions confuse and overwhelm David, as we follow his education in matters of sex, love, family relations, physical abuse, and violence. Yet in this passionately psychological novel, language does not appear as a threat or puzzle for David, even though the different components seem to push against each other. As the processes of becoming American ensue, language is hearth and home for the immigrant child.

This does not mean that the rest of his world adjusts to David's delicately balanced language system. Right off, when the immigrant couple—David's parents—is reunited upon the wife and child's arrival in America, marital conflict and cultural disintegration are clearly presaged in the symbol of a broken Yiddish, one of the few times that standard English is not used by Roth (1991:16).[2] Not only is there disorder in David's family and its culture system, but the outside, non-Jewish world does not accept his language system. In a frightening scene in which David gets lost, this English-Yiddish bilingual boy cannot make the name of his street understood (1991:97–100). He seems relegated to be a prisoner of the Jewish street, able to communicate only with those who speak Yiddish and Jewish English. For little immigrant David, or for that matter, Henry Roth, writing at age twenty-four, himself an immigrant child who came to America at age two and grew up on New York's Lower East Side, the prospect of being fettered by the language of his youth is terrifying.

No one has better articulated how the supportive and caressing nature of the language of the hearth can, at the same time, impede growth and development in the larger society than the writer Richard Rodriguez. In his book *Hunger of Memory* (1983), Rodriguez poignantly and powerfully analyzes his own life story in terms of the bittersweet decision involved in divorcing the language and culture of the home from his public voice. This child of Mexican immigrants gave up the nurturing aspects of his childhood as he gained participation in the larger arena of American intellectual circles.

Writing at age thirty-nine, Rodriguez conjures up the boy in him to relive the shamefulness of his first language and the hope that his second language provides for him. He argues for a distinction between private and public culture. For him, the memory of his ethnic and religious roots is strongly embedded in his personal identity, but separated from his maturation as a thinker and writer in contemporary American, English-language culture. The saga he relates of a Mexican American boy is similar to the stories I hear from elderly Jewish Americans:

It is not possible for a child—any child—ever to use his family's language in school. Not to understand this is to misunderstand the public uses of schooling and to trivialize the nature of intimate life—a family's language. Memory teaches me what I know of these matters; the boy reminds the adult I was a bilingual child. (Rodriguez 1983:12)

The turning point for young Richard and his family in their quest to maintain an intimate world at home and to conquer the larger culture outside comes when his parents decide to speak only English at home (Rodriguez 1983:21). Richard reports that English unsettles the family and upsets any hope of communication between children and parents. As a child, the Spanish sounds had said to Richard, "You belong with us. In the family." Spanish had "become the language of joyful return" (Rodriguez 1983:16). Richard loses the ability to speak Spanish fluently, but after not being exposed to the language, what remains associated with the language is memory, feelings of warmth and family: "Laughing intimate voices. Bounding up the front steps of the porch. A sudden embrace inside the door" (Rodriguez 1983:71).

For the middle-aged child of Mexican immigrants, as well as for the elderly children of Jewish immigrants, the immigrant language signals memory of emotion, of a young child's warm feelings of hearth and home, of parents and family who embrace, envelop, and nurture.

YIDDISH DURING THE LIFE CYCLE OF CHILDREN OF IMMIGRANTS

Although there is a danger in depicting any group as a uniform generation or cohort, several common themes relating to language use and attitude are indicated for many children of Jewish immigrants who are alive today.

Children born of immigrant parents report that the most intensive time of exposure to Yiddish was during their first years, before entry into school. Their Yiddish was restricted to the domain of house and family, used with other immigrants, relatives, friends of parents, and neighbors. If they spoke Yiddish with their siblings, it was at home, not on the street. This crucial period of initial language contact was followed by compara- tively little use in later years. When active Yiddish speech did continue, it was typically with a parent. However, this must be qualified: sometimes the parent spoke in Yiddish and the child responded in English, or else both reverted to English in these later years. When the child initiates involvement in a Yiddish-related activity, it is often during a period when parents are no longer alive to serve as interlocutors.

A variety of data confirm these patterns, including autobiographies of Jewish communal leaders that illustrate these trends and elaborate on the embeddedness of language in ethnic culture and religion. For example, we read of the intimately private Yiddish world that enveloped a young child in Brooklyn:

I knew no English, mine was a Yiddish speaking house. When I got into public school, for the first time, I began to understand that the language of this country was not Yiddish but was English. And I had a few difficult years in accommodating myself to what was happening in public school. But obviously I made it. (Sol B. Kolack, Anti-Defamation League 1987, vol. 6, B 2–3)

In South Philadelphia, a concentrated neighborhood of primary Jewish immigration, this generation's experience with a widespread Yiddish language and culture may perhaps be best illustrated by the experiences of Moyshe. A Sephardic Jew whose parents came from Greece and Turkey and spoke and read Judezmo (Ladino) at home, with no Yiddish in his family background, Moyshe can understand and even speak Yiddish. Where did he learn it? He claims that when he was growing up, he learned Yiddish not from his friends, but from his friends' parents and grandparents. Staying in the neighborhood, he later learned more Yiddish from his customers when he peddled neckties and aprons, as well as from marrying into the Ashkenazic, Yiddish-speaking family of Rive-Rukhl.[3]

Moyshe's experience points to an overall trend in language use that appears in the accounts of his Ashkenazic contemporaries: Yiddish was reserved for interaction with the older generations. Among themselves, the children and grandchildren conversed in English. "We mainly spoke Yiddish to my mother, but between ourselves we spoke English" (translated from Yiddish), Sure recalls. Feygl-Asye refers to English as *Amerikanish*, and says that she spoke Amerikanish to her brother and sister, but not to her parents, her aunt, their friends and neighbors. At home when they sat at the table they spoke Yiddish, but she and her siblings did not feel that they had to hide Amerikanish from their parents. In other families, such as Ester-Sosye's, talking English at home was strictly prohibited. Breaching this rule was met with punishment: a slap in the face. Her parents were convinced that Yiddish was the only language of discourse befitting a Jewish household.

The domains for talking Yiddish are clearly delineated by Rive-Rukhl, who remembers that all of her friends spoke Yiddish with their parents. Public school, even if attended mostly by Jewish pupils who were taught by Jewish teachers, was viewed as a non-Jewish atmosphere. Playing on the street was part and parcel of the children's own world of activity, and hence the realm of English ruled here. Language choice was determined by these larger domains and not by specific situations. School and street required English discourse, whereas the home signalled Yiddish.

However, the ambivalence and shame that American-born children of immigrants felt should not be neglected. In part, these emotions account for the attenuation of their involvement with Yiddish. The immigrant language, after all, was a badge of peculiarity, and a child might choose to reject this distinctiveness, as this memoir of childhood in Altoona, Pennsylvania, relates:

At the end of every afternoon Mama rested briefly, cleaned up, put on a fresh apron and sat on the front porch on the swing, reading the *Yiddish Daily Forward* in full view of the neighborhood. What an agonizing experience that was for us kids, to have our mother flaunt her differentness! I used to cringe at the sight of the Jewish paper that proclaimed to the world that we were not exactly like our neighbors, that we were not quite Americans. (Karp 1983:30)

Being reminded of this difference was often painful, as we see in another autobiographical account. Although possessing an English name, Lionel, this child was called Leybele by his parents, the loving diminutive of his Yiddish name.

But all others—Jews and non-Jews alike—called me, until I went to public school, simply "Laby." Imagine being called "Laby" in a town like Waco, Texas. I recall being unmercifully teased with taunts like "Laby, the cry baby," and much worse. (Lionel Koppman, "What I Remember," p. 1, Biographies File, American Jewish Archives)

THE MIDDLE YEARS

While I investigated children of immigrants during the end period of their life cycle, they did share with me their memories and evaluations of their middle years; our conversations concentrated mainly on their careers, on marriage and children, on relations with their parents. Little was said about their involvement with Yiddish language and culture during this time. In South Philadelphia, where residents remained physically close to the immigrant generation, as members of this generation died, less and less Yiddish was heard. In the smaller cities in Massachusetts, the fewer numbers of Jews meant less of an opportunity for social interaction in Yiddish than in Philadelphia. This makes sense, given that Yiddish usage for the second generation was reserved mainly for conversation with their parents, and since most of the children did not remain under the same roof as their parents in the Massachusetts communities I studied. Notwithstanding the greater or lesser active involvement with Yiddish conversation, in the realm of their psychological being my interviewees consistently and prominently associate Yiddish with things Jewish. For them Yiddish is yiddishkeit, that is, the overall feeling of being Jewish, including religious belief, ritual practice, concern for other Jews, and other matters of personal and group identification (Peltz 1987).

The memories of their involvement with yiddishkeit during their middle years reveal a variety of choices. Izhak, a South Philadelphia storeowner, donned *talis* (prayer shawl) and *tfillin* (phylacteries) every morning. But as he worked longer hours, he decided to eliminate his daily prayers. He and Lena spoke English at home, although Lena wanted to speak in Yiddish to their daughter. Izhak disagreed, and said that she would not know English when she went to school. Their daughter understood more Yiddish than their younger son, however, who now reproaches his mother for not speaking Yiddish with him. Lena, however, switches the blame back to her son for having answered in English when she did use Yiddish. Lena and Izhak's children represent the third generation, now in their thirties and forties. This group encountered more difficulty in learning Yiddish than the children of immigrants who had come at the beginning of the century, since, by the 1950s, the number of Jews and Jewish institutions in South Philadelphia had diminished.

As opposed to the case of Izhak's rejection of daily prayer, Ester-Beyle felt a need to practice Judaism more intensely when her children were in junior high school. She had not provided her daughter with a Jewish education, although she herself had studied at the Talmud Torah on the high school level. Her own return to traditional practices began with attending synagogue on Friday night. Her renewed religious activity drew in her husband, Shmuel Arn, and now both are involved in synagogue life. Their own children, however, never experienced the exposure to Yiddish and yiddishkeit that both Ester-Beyle and Shmuel-Arn had known so intimately as children.

In a third example, Basye illustrates a move toward traditional ways as an adult that were more stringent than those that she experienced as a girl. Her father had strayed from his original Orthodoxy. The family maintained a kosher household, but he would declare any food he enjoyed in a restaurant, especially fried oysters, as kosher. Basye, who lived with her mother-in-law after her marriage, insisted that her children observe *kashrus* (Jewish dietary laws). When they were babies, a meal consisting of chicken and baby food vegetables was accompanied by juice. They would have to wait a few hours for their milk bottle. Thus, the prohibition of mixing meat and milk was followed, and she would tell them, "this is the yiddishkeit." In high school, however, when they started to eat outside of the house, they learned nonkosher ways of eating.

Of all the American-born couples, only Basye reports that she and her husband spoke Yiddish to each other, especially because his mother lived with them, and they wanted the children to understand, to learn from hearing Yiddish spoken. Not that Basye heard Yiddish while growing up; her mother was born in the United States and spoke Hungarian and English, but no Yiddish. Instead, Basye learned Yiddish when she worked as a secretary in a synagogue. "I used to think in Jewish," claims Basye. But today, because of disuse, she complains, "I don't think in Jewish like I used to."[4]

The elderly Jews in South Philadelphia typically report that their children can understand Yiddish, but generally do not speak it. Basye's son, who is thirty-four years old, lives across the street from her. He tries to speak Yiddish to his grandmother and the rabbi, but he "murders the language," according to Basye. Her daughter "understands like I do, but she wouldn't begin to answer anybody in Yiddish."

The third generation, to be sure, had much less exposure to Yiddish at home and in the streets of South Philadelphia. Yiddish, after all, was the main language and culture of the immigrants, and fewer and fewer survived as time progressed, with only a few still present in the neighborhood during my fieldwork. In the smaller cities in Massachusetts, most of the second generation never spoke Yiddish, but only understand the language they heard as children. In their middle years, there was little contact with the language, other than the limited Yiddish their parents still used while they were alive. It was never the language of the shopping street, as in South Philadelphia. Thus, the third generation learned very little Yiddish in the smaller Jewish communities. The children of immigrants in these communities, however, throughout their life, including the middle years, maintain close friendship ties with their Jewish contemporaries, with whom they share a common past.

Kelly, more than the other second-generation South Philadelphians, maintained a high level of Jewish religious and organizational commitment and leadership throughout the middle years. He and his brothers joined his parents' *landsmanshaft* (hometown fraternal organization), and Kelly eventually became an officer. He became active in Jewish branches of the Masons. In addition, in the years following World War II, Kelly helped establish a Young People's Congregation and taught Sunday School. Throughout the years, he lived and worked in South Philadelphia.

Kelly's parents mainly spoke English in their business and at home, and it was only Kelly's grandmother who used Yiddish with the family. His parents limited their usage to when they did not want the children to understand. But Kelly managed to learn the language, since it was all around the neighborhood. Although I heard Kelly occasionally speak Yiddish in his luncheonette, it was not until I recorded a conversation with him and his wife that I realized how fluent he is in the language. His wife Sure, a native speaker who arrived from Ukraine at age ten, although talking according to her native dialect and intonation, speaks more haltingly. After coming to America she claims that she and her siblings stopped speaking Yiddish, except when talking to their mother. In fact, one of Sure's sisters-in-law learned Yiddish in order to talk to Sure's mother. Kelly, on the other hand, used Yiddish with customers. Their children, they say, did not learn Yiddish and did not want to learn the language.

During my fieldwork I saw the pleasure with which Kelly responds to the children's renditions of Yiddish songs at the Sunday School he directs. He himself enjoys opportunities to speak Yiddish and tells a story of a phone call from a man who could only speak Hebrew and Yiddish:

I had—in fact I had a strange experience. A man calls us on the phone speaking Yiddish. My wife answers the phone. She said, *"vel shteln mayn man tsu redn."* ("I'll put my husband on the phone to talk.") I got on the phone and uh—we— un—his father told him, after about a half hour conversation, if your name was Israel, and his name was Israel, he came from uh—he hardly could speak, uh, Y-Yiddish, he y—only could speak Yiddish and uh Hebrew. If your name was Is—second name was Israel, you had to be related. So he was going down the whole phone book, we got pages of—years ago there was only two of us in the phone book by the name Israel. And I spoke to him for about a half hour, I really enjoyed speaking Yiddish. I enjoy speaking it anyhow every opportunity. And at the end of the conversation was, *"Kum tsi un mir' n hobm a glezl tey un a shtikl keyk un mir veln redn."* ("Come over and we'll have a glass of tea and a piece of cake, and we'll talk.")

Talking is a vital activity in South Philadelphia. The "glass of tea" symbolizes a way of talking and getting to know one another better that belongs to the past. In my work, I offered elderly children of immigrants an opportunity to share that glass of tea, to encourage communication about and among themselves, in Yiddish.

CURRENT YIDDISH LANGUAGE USE

In my research in various cities, I located very few instances of spontaneous Yiddish conversation in public and residential settings. I have documented this for South Philadelphia, the community that has retained the most Yiddish (Peltz 1987), where such impromptu speech is found among a few of the remaining immigrants. Although fluency varies, most resident children of immigrants speak Yiddish with ease. Among the children of immigrants, only two sisters that I encountered have continued to speak both Yiddish and English with each other.

In South Philadelphia today, the children of immigrants vary in age between sixty and ninety. Their parents are no longer alive. The opportunities for speaking Yiddish are no longer available, since they generally did not communicate in Yiddish with their peers. They delight in viewing a Yiddish-language performance or in singing and dancing along to a popular Yiddish melody. Such cultural events are organized by the neighborhood Jewish Senior Center. At the center, I initiated a weekly Yiddish conversation group, called a *Gleyzele tey* (Glass of Tea). Members responded enthusiastically to this opportunity to gather in this relatively unstructured group meeting, where participants generally determined the topics for discussion. From the beginning, the participants indicated that the Gleyzele tey meetings were different from other center activities, that this was a program in which they felt particularly at home. Poor attendance was a problem at the center's other morning classes, but this was not the case with a Gleyzele tey. Sharing conversation over a glass of tea and, indeed, the very name of the group was designed with the purpose of facilitating comfortable talk.

If members who normally do not talk Yiddish to each other are willing to congregate weekly to do so, there must be special motivating factors. The immigrants' habit of conversing over a glass of tea was a memory that came alive in a new form on Friday mornings in South Philadelphia. The use of their Yiddish names in the session was also a resurrection of things past, since very often only their parents addressed these South Philadelphians by that name. The element of joy associated with speaking Yiddish and with congregating for this purpose secured the group's existence and its further development.

On many occasions, neighborhood residents would automatically associate speaking Yiddish with the quintessence of being Jewish, yiddishkeit, and with traditional Jewish observance (Peltz 1987). The local Jews use the term *yiddishkeit* to connote not only the fundamental state of being Jewish, but also the conglomeration of traditional Jewish ways that they once knew. People would assume that because I speak Yiddish I had to be religiously observant. On two occasions, residents called me "Rabbi" upon meeting me. This association, however, was not restricted only to the way in which I was viewed. On many occasions, Yiddish was associated with the traditional customs residents remembered of their parents' homes. Time and again, when we would discuss speaking Yiddish, the conversation would shift to talking about yiddishkeit. For example, when I asked Roze, 73, to name the people with whom she spoke Yiddish after her grandmother's death, she replied, "Any way I could I never wanted to forget it, yiddishkeit" (translated from Yiddish). Dveyre, 84, described how she is the only one of her American-born siblings who preserved Yiddish and "who observes Jewish law at home and in the synagogue" (translated from Yiddish). Surele, 86, said she learned Yiddish from her parents, but immediately followed by describing how her brother built a synagogue in the town to which he moved.

Speaking Yiddish, along with keeping kosher, that is, observing the dietary laws, is part of a constellation of memories and ongoing practices that constitute living like a Jew for these South Philadelphia residents. Even though they might not observe these practices, it is these practices that still symbolize true yiddishkeit for them. According to Reyzl, 73, the Gleyzele tey conversation group stimulated essential emotions within the participants. It touched their inner being, the heart and the soul of personal identification. "You reminded them of that which they had, and they don't have now. That is their heart" (translated from Yiddish).

Although the main thrust of the Gleyzele tey activity was Yiddish conversation, its nature and evolution were shaped by the special history of the neighborhood, the Senior Center, and the residents. Similar experiments have taken hold in the United States during the past fifteen years, whereby elderly Jews, largely children of immigrants, have formed hundreds of Yiddish cultural clubs in a variety of institutional frameworks.[5] Some of these are connected to synagogues, Jewish community centers, and residential centers for the elderly. Others take on the form of adult education courses or informal meetings of friends. This largely spontaneous grass roots endeavor, usually utilizing no professional staff, but rather volunteer facilitators, involves telling stories and jokes, singing songs, attending guest lectures and films, and reading and speaking Yiddish.

The inception and evolution of the Northampton Yiddish cultural group provide another case study that epitomizes the recent shift of elderly children of Jewish immigrants to their ethnic mother-tongue, Yiddish. Northampton, Massachusetts, home of Smith College, is a city of thirty thousand, with a Jewish population that numbers about two thousand. The one synagogue has a membership of three hundred families. Most of the older members were born in Northampton or Springfield, as children of immigrants. None of the original East European immigrants is alive. Unlike South Philadelphia, a concentrated neighborhood of primary Jewish immigration, children of the original East European Jewish immigrants to Northampton were raised largely among non-Jews. Yet here, even more than in South Philadelphia, social networks of these elderly children of Jewish immigrants are preponderantly Jewish. While many South Philadelphia–born children of immigrants could speak Yiddish fluently because until recently they spoke with their parents in the same house and neighborhood as in their childhood, in Northampton people of the same age had rarely spoken Yiddish in their lifetimes, but Yiddish had been the first language they heard at home. However, in 1986, for the first time in the history of the local synagogue, Congregation B'nai Israel, a group of members mostly between the ages of sixty-five and seventy-five established a Seniors group. Most of the members had recently retired from their businesses, although a few still work. At first, it was difficult for them to conceive of themselves as senior citizens, as elderly. At first glance, even more improbable was the decision to relate all their activities to the Yiddish language, a language most of them had hardly ever spoken. And yet, so it happened. At the monthly meetings, one hears the calls from those who have been silent in Yiddish for their lifetime: *red yidish* (speak Yiddish).

In May 1988, the B'nai Israel seniors presented an original musical, "*Vos geven iz geven*" (What Used To Be Used To Be), in honor of the twenty-fifth anniversary of the new synagogue building. This newly formed group, which had not yet crystallized its own identity, decided to organize a performance about the history of Jews in Northampton, with the participation of all generations. They planned to retell and create anew their history through Yiddish, which they themselves had just donned, like a newly found old coat.

As a participant observer, I was able to follow the development of the performance of this new-old ritual from behind the scenes. They worked a full year in preparing the mini-spectacle. At first, it was not clear that the performance necessarily had to concentrate on their own story—but they adamantly wanted to do something in Yiddish. Some of the members had seen the staged Yiddish productions of *My Fair Lady* and Gilbert and Sullivan; others were acquainted with the bilingual musical pageant on American Jewish life, *The Golden Land*. Possessing home-bred talent, they reveled in the energy of creating something original, lively, and joyous, with music and dance.

A sixty-two year old member, on the verge of retiring as a teacher of English in the local high school, wrote the play together with two assistants. Serving as the backbone were familiar scenes and personalities from Northampton Jewish life, accompanied by popular hits from Yiddish stage and film, such as "*Mayn yidishe meydele*" (My Little Jewish Girl), "*Abi gezunt ken men gliklekh zayn*" (As Long as You're Healthy You Can Be Happy), and "*Vos geven iz geven un nito*" (What Was—Was—and Is No More). The show opened with a scene of immigrants disembarking from a ship and ended with a contemporary cocktail party at the synagogue. The author understood Yiddish, her grandmother in Philadelphia having spoken it to her, although her American-born parents had not spoken Yiddish. Her husband is a child of one of the first immigrant families to Northampton. But the group determined that in order for the younger people in the audience to understand the play, both English and Yiddish had to be side by side in the production. The planners also understood that the retelling must appeal to everyone in such a way that they would view the story as belonging to them. Accordingly, they drew the actors from youngsters who were twelve and fourteen, as well as from adults in their thirties, forties, and fifties, in addition to recruiting from their own "seniors" ranks.

The group attracted a professional choreographer who volunteered her services, as did a local band. Lights, decorations, and costumes were arranged. The actors played their roles with great verve and the audience was ecstatic. From that time on, the Jewish community associated the group with the Yiddish language. Subsequently, they were invited to perform other Yiddish material for holidays, and to speak about Yiddish and memories of times gone by with children in the synagogue school. In other words, the group of elderly children of immigrants was serving as a force for intergenerational ethnic education. The older members found a focus for their developing Jewish identity, that is, Yiddish language and culture, and would struggle gleefully at meetings while trying to converse in Yiddish, tell Yiddish stories, sing Yiddish songs, and write Yiddish letters to members who travel to Florida during the winter. If such a phenomenon can develop in Northampton, the seeds have surely been sown in other Jewish population centers.

Indeed, in Holyoke, Massachusetts, during the summer of 1993, a group of elderly members of the Orthodox congregation Rodphey Sholem, with the enthusiastic support of their new young rabbi, formed a group devoted to Yiddish culture. Rivke, the initiator, a life-long synagogue member, has taken part in local seminars and courses on Yiddish, including study at the neighboring University of Massachusetts. She is a volunteer at the office of the National Yiddish Book Center. She makes the group aware of a network of Yiddish clubs throughout the country, and the Holyoke group subscribes to a newsletter for Yiddish clubs that is published in Northern California. Rivke sends in reports of the Holyoke club's activities and receives correspondence and program materials from across the land.

The group deliberated long on choosing a name. By an overwhelming majority, the name *Di gantse mishpokhe* (The Whole Family) was selected. Yiddish, for this group and others like it, is a family matter. The attempt to establish links with like-minded contemporaries widens the family connection and confirms the existence and validity of their culture. They are attempting to recreate a feeling for family that harks back to the first years in their parents' house. Yiddish evokes passionate emotions regarding family for the elderly children of immigrants, whether in Philadelphia or Holyoke, that are allied with powerful feelings relating to both personal and group identification.

REFASHIONING AN IDENTITY FOR THE PRESENT: LANGUAGE AND MEMORY

I have brought evidence from a variety of sources to identify the language of the family as a formative influence in the socialization and acculturation of children of immigrants. Members of immigrant groups see themselves as different from the dominant culture and are viewed as such by other groups, dominant and minority. Language is a symbol of both self-ascription and imposed stereotype. Language is a focus of identity just as it is an act of identity (Le Page and Tabouret-Keller 1985:140, 248).

Fieldwork with elderly children of Jewish immigrants reveals the emotional intensity engendered by renewed use of a language that was largely relegated to their youth and to their parents' generation. The ethnographic data indicate that the memory conjured up of the past and the experience of bringing that past into the present and future have meaning for personal and group identity. Within the communities I have studied, different though they are, the residents report intense interaction with the immigrant generation and high levels of exposure to Yiddish culture during their youth. This relatively common characteristic of the early years was followed by a more varied pattern of religious and cultural involvement in the middle years. Some distancing from the parental household did occur, usually accompanied by an attenuation of exposure to Yiddish. The increased association with Yiddish during old age was strikingly uniform, including for the elderly individuals who had themselves never spoken Yiddish. The populations I studied were dominated by participants who affiliate with Jewish organizations. Whether members of the ethnic group and age cohort who do not affiliate with Jewish groups demonstrate this renewed association has yet to be examined.

The significance of the shared cohort experience should not be under-estimated. the insight of Halbwachs (1992 [1925]:40) is quite enlightening: "Collective frameworks are . . . precisely the instruments used by the collective memory to reconstruct an image of the past which is in accord, in each epoch, with the predominant thoughts of the society."

Yiddish provides a special community for these elderly children of immigrants, as well as a way of communicating that is attractive, supportive, and genuine. Since they know it well from their youth, it belongs to them. Thus, Yiddish helps to construct community and communication for the isolating times of old age. The last years of life are often a period when people are living alone, far from family, still grieving parental loss. Yiddish conversation recovers a piece of the parents' culture. In addition, in the face of their own sickness and imminent death, sharing Yiddish provides a symbol of endurance, transcendence, and joy.

Coupled to this hope is the fear that they may be the last generation of speakers, that "the 'collective memory' for . . . (the) language may be lost to future generations" (Padden 1990:190). These native Yiddish-speaking enthusiasts use language to spread roots to the past, to strengthen their social connections, and to join a generationally extended cultural chain.

As Padden (1990:190) claims, "living languages are those in which the speakers agree to remember them." These speakers have agreed and the language they have conceded to remember transforms their individual pasts into collective memories. The widespread phenomenon of a return to Yiddish that is expressed in the formation and flowering of hundreds of clubs across the nation locates the process of remembering and recovery in a group setting. As with much of the process of memory, this phenomenon is socially facilitated and constructed, but the process is seldom individu-alized and isolated. The identifiable group is actually a large one, on the macro level: the generation of children of immigrants. For one thing, the concept of generation needs to be reconfigured to more accurately include the situation of, for example, South Philadelphians who came to America as young children along with parents and grandparents, and children born in the United States, whose adult parents and in some cases grandparents had immigrated.

The city or town of their parents' birth, for the South Philadelphia and Northampton sample alike, is indistinct. To them it is Russia. Rather than where and when one was born, behavioral choices and emotional loyalties are linked more to age upon arrival in America, extent of education in American public schools, socioeconomic status, and neighborhood of residence. The foundations of Jewish continuity, for these people, are located within the oral culture transmitted at home by immigrant parents: the ambience of the kitchen, holiday celebrations with relatives, hearing Yiddish at home and on the street.

The mediation of memory by way of language use, besides being a shared experience, also signifies a relationship to time that warrants further explication. According to the elderly Jews who are experiencing a romance with the language and culture of their parents, what is remembered is not especially events of childhood, but emotions and sensations of identity, of closeness to self and family. These are feelings that they had as children. They experience a merging of a moment in the present with the past, creating identity, as ephemeral as this confluence may be. Once again I am reminded of a scene from the literary imagination, highlighted by Woodward (1986:141–42), who analyzes the memoir written by the Japanese novelist Yashusi Inoue. His elderly mother, suffering from Alzheimer's disease, disappears from home in search of her infant son. Two images merged for the author, the sixty-three year old son looking for his eighty-five year old mother, and the twenty-three year old mother searching for the one year old infant: "the years 1907 and 1969 came together and the sixty years converged, then diffused in the light of the moon." Woodward rightly stresses the power of the emotion, a "magical . . . moment of both dread and wonder," when Inoue finds meaning in what it is to be a son to a mother and at the same time to reverse the roles. It is this level of illumination and bewilderment that seems to possess the elderly children of immigrants who realize that they are their parents' children, who retain the memory of their culture as they use the language of their past in the present.

In searching to understand the tie to the future that the elderly Jews yearn for in their last years, I once again gained insight from the discussions of literary depictions of aging by Woodward (1991:136–45). Drawing on the psychoanalytic theory of the transitional object put forward by Winnicott, Woodward analyzes *Malone Dies* by Beckett. Of all the objects collected around him, Malone is left with only his exercise-book, a tangible object, but also a receptacle of language. According to Winnicott, the transitional object helps reduce the anxiety of the infant in separating from the mother and entering the objective world. It is the materiality of the object that is stressed, its tactile nature, not only its symbolic value. At the end of life, Woodward is postulating a transitional object that practically eases us into the next stage, death, and at the same time reminds us of our childhood.

Yiddish, it seems to me, facilitates and supports the changes of the last years of life for the elderly children of immigrants.

Just as Butler (1963), Kaminski (1984; 1992), and Coleman (1991) have understood reminiscence and story-telling on the part of the elderly as life-affirming activities, so too is ethnic language use a stimulus for growth and renewal for those seeking the pleasure and meaning associated with their ethnic identity. Western society has shunned dealing with old age and death (Lowenthal 1985:125–84; Woodward 1991:4–8). Yet, if these components of the life course are indeed progenitors of creativity, we should recognize them as such.

Our evidence supports the theory that ethnic identity is flexible, changing with time and situation. Children of immigrants exhibit multiple identities that influence one another. There is choice (see Waters 1990) and creativity (Sollors 1989) in the ongoing process of ethnic identification. And, as Kellogg (1990) contends, the maintenance of this malleable ethnicity is based in private and family domains.

Another important piece of this multidimensional approach to ethnicity is what the anthropologist Simic (1985), a colleague of Myerhoff, has underscored as the cyclical nature of ethnic identification—intensive during the first years, followed by an eclipse, and strengthening in the later years. Rempusheski's (1988) study of second-generation Polish Americans in Arizona, Doi's (1991) work on the ritual of the sixtieth birthday celebration among children of Japanese immigrants in California, and, especially, Weibel-Orlando's (1988; 1991) analysis of Native Americans who return to the reservation during old age or who remain in Los Angeles, corroborate this model. As Holzberg (1982:254) reminds us, "Ethnicity is a resource—an identity that older people can turn on or off as needed. When ethnicity is called into play, it sustains a familiar cultural setting that provides opportunities for continuity with the past and instrumental contributions to the present."

What is the symbolic power of ethnic language in all of this? De Vos and Romanucci-Ross (1975) and Eastman and Reese (1981) argue that all aspects of culture, particularly language, can be used emblematically. One does not have to understand or speak a language in order to identify with it, to feel connected to it. My various informants confirm this finding.

The second generation serves as a crucial bridge between the culture of the immigrant parents who had been nurtured in the old country and the world of their own American-born children who have little contact with the European-born grandparents. The ambivalence that characterizes the second generation's approach to the language and culture of the immigrants vacillates throughout the lifespan, influencing the ethnic culture that is transmitted to the third generation and that emanates from this generation. These processes of influence and ethnogenesis have yet to be adequately examined. The active memory of the immigrant culture, which is interpreted and reinterpreted throughout the lifespan of children of immigrants, is an essential ingredient in the history of the ethnic group.

Very few elderly children of immigrants embrace Yiddish as a means of daily communication. Rather, we have seen that Yiddish is ritualized as a focus for periodic expression of ethnic identity and culture in a group setting. Since this phenomenon of renewed use of the language of child-hood is occurring in diverse locations, institutional settings, and Jewish communities throughout the country, such ritualization of language is an identity marker for this generation. Rituals link the past, present, and future. Involved in this use of language as ritual is social and cultural performance, which often takes the form of everyday stories that we tell ourselves. The most elaborate and complex performance of group story-telling that I observed was the original autobiographical play by and about the Jewish community of Northampton. Using Yiddish in a format that could be understood by the community's youngest members who know no Yiddish, the elderly children of immigrants created a story that portrayed continuous transmission, from the time of their parents' initial settlement almost a century ago to their grandchildren's participation in the drama itself.

Anthropological theorists of the role of ritual have pointed to the absence of dichotomy between ritual that is sacred and symbolic and that which is practical and profane (Skorupski 1976:173; Geertz 1973:113). Kertzer (1988:9) stresses the socially standardized, repetitive nature of symbolic behavior, but reminds us that a given activity can have both ritual and nonritual aspects. The shared ritual of speaking Yiddish provides symbolic strength through social drama and public identity for a group of aging Jews whose alterity vis-à-vis American society might otherwise marginalize them further at this time in the life cycle and in history (Geertz 1983:64). The dramatic performance of "*Vos geven iz geven*" in North-ampton shows that the children of immigrants see themselves as an active link in cultural transmission. As Geertz (1973:114) has demonstrated, such cultural performances are "models of what they believe" as well as "models *for* the believing of it."

To understand the changing meaning of life to individuals and to a generation, we should examine "how people develop rhetorical redescriptions of their own life" (Van Langenhove and Harré 1993:96). "They are the texts of identity, for they create the illusion of the transcendental ego" (Harré 1989:33). The remembering of Yiddish helps to convince these elderly American Jews of the veracity of the stories they tell themselves. From their vantage point, they are saying:

We are the children of our parents, even now that our parents are no longer alive.

We possess a culture at a time of life and in a place in which the elderly and their culture are overlooked.

And, if the language is still alive, that is a sign, that we, too, are still alive.

These stories are not merely a way of remembering the past; they are an active confrontation with the present.

NOTES

I thank the editors for their help: Marea Teski for her appreciation of my research work, based on an earlier presentation at the annual meeting of the American Anthropological Association in 1990; and Jacob Climo for his suggestions and valuable criticism of an initial draft of this chapter. Fieldwork in Holyoke, Massachusetts, was aided by a grant from the Columbia University Council for Research in the Humanities.

1. Because of my focus on the generation of children of immigrants, I generally neglect for present purposes the kindred research concerns of ethnic group language, culture, and identity of African Americans, Native Americans, and Deaf Americans. Historians and sociologists in dealing with the ethnicity of immigrant groups have largely adhered either to theories of assimilation into the "melting pot," which accepts the dislodging and disappearance of the group-specific heritage, or ethnicization, which postulates the alteration yet retention of group-specific culture through mixing and blending with the ways of the dominant group. For a recent discussion of these issues, see Morawska (1994). Relatively little has been done to chart a theoretical middle ground, to emphasize the similarities in the two theoretical approaches, or to integrate the analysis of multiple and overlapping identities.

2. Other instances indicate that Roth (1991:16) knew better than to use a German pronoun and an auxiliary verb that no Yiddish or German speaker would use.

3. "Sephardic" refers to the descendants of Jews who lived in Spain and Portugal before their expulsion in 1492. "Ashkenazic" Jews originated in Germany and shifted their population center to Eastern Europe by the eighteenth century.

4. "Jewish" is a common designation for the Yiddish language in the English speech of American-born children of Jewish immigrants.

5. Myerhoff (1978167–69), in an ethnographic study of the immigrant generation, reported a revival of Yiddish language upon aging, and a mixing of cultural elements of their European youth with contemporary urban practices. Jacob

Climo (personal communication) has raised the possibility that the children of immigrants in my present study, when they become old, view Yiddish as an appropriate language and culture for "old folks" and reacquire this mode of discourse and practice for this time of life. This view adds a social niche for Yiddish use, one that has evolved as life cycle stage–bound, out of a history in which the language was used by all generations at all times. I have not collected evidence of whether the elderly children of immigrants view themselves this way. However, I do not dismiss this possible factor, especially in light of research on discourse patterns of the elderly that argues that " 'elderliness' is in significant ways manufactured and modified in sequences of talk in which older speakers are involved, through the agency of elderly *and younger* speakers" (Coupland, Coupland, and Giles 1991:55).

The Remembering Consciousness of a Polish Exile Government

Marea C. Teski

Exile governments are not unusual in the late twentieth century. Change upon change leaves many with a destiny to play out but no stage upon which to play. From 1945 to 1991 there was an exile government of Poland—carrying on activities in London—a separate body from the Warsaw government. This was essentially the same government that fled Poland in 1939. Culture, history, and remembrance were the sources of vitality for this institution, which persisted for nearly fifty years.

The question this chapter addresses is that of the role of memory for exile groups in general and for this group in particular. In 1990 I interviewed the last government before the group formally disbanded after popular elections were finally held in Poland. It might be good to begin by clarifying the ways in which concepts of both memory and exile will be used here.

Past studies of memory have largely been of the mechanical sort, viewing memory as a recording of events. This view concentrates on storage and retrieval problems. Another view sees memory as narrative. In the narrative view, memories tell a story and they are more or less at the disposal of the rememberer. They may be changed, suppressed, or even invented to tell the story that needs to be told.

I propose a third model of memory. It is the view of memory as a culturally specific field, a meeting ground between individual and culture. The field is personal but communicable, and above all it is permeable by other people's memories.

It is a dialogue with limitations between cultural templates and individual and group experiences and interpretations. In this view, memory is neither a cultural given nor an individual creation, but something between the two.

Exile, too, has many aspects. We will consider three of them in relation to the London Polish government in exile. The three aspects of exile we will use are:

1. Exile of a political and geographic nature—The group is physically separated from its homeland and is not in sympathy with the present rulers of the country.
2. Cultural and spiritual exile—The group is separate from the home culture and a different language is spoken. The members are surrounded by strangers—the diaspora experience.
3. Existential exile—This is an aspect of the human condition exacerbated by the first two kinds of exile. This kind of exile entails an awareness that we are not at home and things are not as they ought to be. There is a longing for:
   a. the kingdom of God
   b. the messianic age
   c. the good society

Some colleagues have raised questions about what it was that the Polish exiles were remembering, since the experience of a modern parliamentary government lasted only a short time from 1920 after World War I to 1939 when World War II began. It is to the long and varied history of the Polish kingdoms itself that the exiles referred their memory. It is not the task of this analysis to question the validity of these connections, but simply to trace them and thus discover the cultural pattern that gave meaning to the memories of the exiles. In a sense, every memory connection is valid if it vivifies the present and gives a direction for the future.

The Polish exiles in London experienced all three senses of exile. However, it seemed to me that the second type of exile—cultural and spiritual exile—was what they felt most acutely and tried to address in the way they lived.

As they addressed the meaning of their exile, the Poles in London had recourse to their own history and traditions, and their experience in the exile situation. They analyzed their situation and found models for their own understanding and behavior in the events of the past and in their literary tradition, which had much to say about the role of the exile and the meaning of the Polish experience in history. Together these two sources gave the exiles a structure that they used to fashion lives for themselves and to make memory a basis for present experience.

The continuing sense of significance and the long-term persistence of the exile government are importantly related to the rising and falling character of Poland's turbulent history. Poland, one of the ancient kingdoms of Europe, has a history that began more than a thousand years ago when the ruler, Mieszko I, and subsequently the people with him, were baptized. This was accomplished under the auspices of the Church of Rome and had the effect of bringing Poland closer to the culture of Western Europe. In contrast, the lands of Eastern Europe that accepted Orthodox Christianity were more closely tied to the culture of Byzantium.

Following the acceptance of Christianity, Poland's history took a rollercoaster course. At one time, during the union with Lithuania in the fourteenth and fifteenth centuries, it was the largest state in Europe. However, over time, internal and external problems brought the nation to the point that it was so weak that greedy neighbors could partition it. At the end of the eighteenth century Austria, Prussia, and Russia incorporated parts of the Polish-Lithuanian Commonwealth and Poland actually disappeared from the map of Europe. The period of partition lasted 123 years, but uprisings in almost every generation showed that Poles still considered themselves a nation and did not accept domination by foreign governments. This historical experience indicates that Poles have some experience in refusing to accept what might seem to be the actual political realities. In other words, they have experienced holding memories that contradict the present state of affairs.

The truth about politics is that all power waxes and wanes, and by the end of World War I in 1918 the three partitioning powers were in no position to maintain their grasp on Poland. Conditions were such that Poland could emerge as a nation once more. The chief of state, Pilsudski, called for general elections and a Parliament or *Sejm* was elected. The new Poland consisted of the provinces that Russia, Prussia, and Austria had taken in the eighteenth century. A short war with the revolutionary Soviet Union in 1920 led to the Soviets' acceptance of the eastern frontiers of Poland. At this point, the Polish state was established in the modern world. New civil, criminal, and administrative laws were codified and the Second Republic began. There were many difficulties, but no doubts that the nation once more was a reality.

Unfortunately, the period of peace necessary for consolidating the forms and procedures of the new Polish government did not follow. Instead, the political and economic tensions in Europe as a whole, and most particularly in Germany, intensified and eventually led to World War II. Poland's geographical position was a dangerous one—located in the midst of nations that had partitioned it in the past. The danger intensified when Nazi Germany and the Soviet Union signed a Treaty of Nonaggression in Moscow in 1939. The treaty contained a secret protocol dividing Poland

and other Eastern European states between Stalin and Hitler. That same year—1939—Poland was invaded from the west by Germany on September 1 and from the east by the Soviet Union on September 17.

Fearing war and exile, the Polish government had amended the Constitution in 1939 to provide for the continuity of government in wartime. In 1939 the government fled the German and Soviet invaders, proceeding through Romania and Hungary, accompanied by sections of the military. Finally the government was reassembled in Paris with Wladyslaw Raczkiewicz as president and General Wladyslaw Sikorski as prime minister. In 1940 France fell to Germany and the Polish government and many of the armed forces fled again—this time to England. There, the permanent wartime headquarters of the government were set up and the Polish armed forces joined the British in defense of Britain. The Polish government in London was a full ally of Britain. It controlled about 260,000 Polish troops in the West which, combined with Polish forces in Eastern Europe, made the fourth largest army among the allies.

Given this wartime history, it is not surprising that the Polish government in London could not accept a Warsaw government set up without its participation after World War II. Events in Poland in 1989—including the establishment of a non-Communist government—seem to support the exiles' contention that the governments in the homeland have not been freely elected since 1945 and that the Polish people have lacked a voice in determining conditions that importantly affect their lives. This is the position that the Polish government in exile maintained for forty-five years.

History, as remembered by the Poles in exile, has two important features.

1. Poland is a distinct entity in some sense unaffected by rises and falls in fortune and changes in its borders and name.
2. Change is always imminent and it is necessary to be able to accommodate to change while still retaining Polish identity.

Constancy of "the nation" in one form or another as well as a sense of the fluctuating character of the political scene is important in the Polish exiles' view of the world and their own unusual position in it. Resistance to undesirable change combined with the conviction that Poland is always a distinct nation whatever its fate at any given time is important to the way in which the exiles remember events.

Culture is the second important ingredient in the Polish government in exile's successful persistence through time. The definition of culture given by Norman Davies, author of a comprehensive history of Poland (1982), is similar to that of nineteenth-century anthropologist E. B. Tylor. Davies says:

Culture literally is that which can be cultivated. . . . In human affairs it refers to the sum total of attitudes, beliefs, principles, values, assumptions, reflexes, tastes, mental habits, skills and achievements which distinguish one society from another, and which can be transmitted from one generation to the next. In the life of the Polish nation and others like it, it is the most precious part of the national heritage. It is the one thing that gives the promise of eternity. (1982:226)

He goes on to describe the struggles of the Poles to avoid Germanization and Russification during the period after the partition of 1795. He refers to Nalkowski (1851–1911) and others who fought against losing their culture as "cultural patriots" (1982:234). It is for the "promise of eternity" that these patriots fought. Clearly they separated the notion of the political existence of the nation from that of its cultural existence. At a time of political obliteration there was also a possibility of cultural obliteration, but *that* extinction was successfully resisted.

What, then, is the culture that was preserved through the partition period and that persisted in the present Polish government in exile?

The literary model that I believe most strongly affected the Polish exile government's behavior and view of themselves is that of the nineteenth-century exile experience—most particularly the model set by the poet Adam Mickiewicz, who fled to exile in Paris and established a powerful model of the proper role of the Polish exile.

Kramer (1988) discusses the importance of Paris as a setting for developing exile-consciousness. In the eighteenth and nineteenth centuries exile was increasingly tied to nationalism. Paris's association with the French Revolution and its hospitable reception of exiles made it the location of choice, especially for exiled writers.

The refugees of 1830 who left Poland were known as "the great immigration," and Mickiewicz was one of the most famous of this group. By 1839 there was an exile community of about eighteen hundred Poles in Paris and by 1846 the number was closer to four thousand (Kramer 1988:26). Mickiewicz established an exile role for himself that has had a strong impact upon Poles in exile ever since.

Exiles must confront the problem of the difference between their home culture and that of the exile haven. Mickiewicz felt that it was his duty to gain support for the homeland but also to explain the homeland to the rest of the world. He spent most of this time with other Polish exiles and his writing clearly states ideas of national identity that have been important for exiles well into the twentieth century:

Mickiewicz was entirely typical of the Polish emigre community in that national salvation overshadowed every other literary or social issue for him. His French experience thus became a twenty-year effort to define the Polish national identity, to defend the uniqueness of that identity against the West (and East), and to mobilize France in the campaign to restore Polish independence. (Kramer 1988:177)

One point that Mickiewicz seemed to emphasize was his feeling that Poles were different and even thought differently from other Europeans:

Mickiewicz himself made every effort to avoid this mistake, choosing instead to stress the Polish characteristics in his thought and to show how that [sic] Polish perspectives differed from the systemizing theoretical tendencies of the Germans and from the intellectual values of the West in general. As Mickiewicz explained the difference, Poles approached their problems through intuition and spiritualism rather than through the structures of western analytic thought. (Kramer 1988:221)

A different way of thinking and an ability to transcend the rational certainly seem to have been operative in the maintenance of a twentieth-century exile government in London for nearly fifty years. Like Mickiewicz, the twentieth-century exiles first went to Paris. Later, when the occupation of France made it necessary, they moved their operation to London. Under six constitutionally elected presidents the government has stated through the years that the postwar Communist government in Warsaw—established in 1945—was illegitimately imposed upon the nation by the then Soviet Union. Moreover, since the Polish wartime government was not a party to the peace agreements, the war had not officially ended for them and thus they continued to operate under wartime constitutional directives. They were, they said, the legal constitutional government of Poland until the elections of 1990 in the homeland. Their determination in maintaining this position in the face of "reality" makes us question reality itself. They truly believed that they were affirming a different reality by refusing to accept the government set up with Soviet influence.

History, culture, and precedent lay behind the decision of the London exile government to follow this course and to hold to their position for so long. As we have mentioned, the Polish allies were not included in the peace process after World War II. The Teheran (1943) and Yalta (1945) agreements that determined the form of the postwar world were signed by

Churchill, Roosevelt, and Stalin. Poland was assigned to the Soviet sphere of influence, a decision in which the Polish government in London had no part. Soviet dominance in Poland led to the establishment of a government in Warsaw that ignored the 1935 Constitution of the nation. Most of the London Polish government did not accept the postwar Warsaw government and declined to return to their homeland. From 1945 until 1991 the London government operated according to the 1935 constitutional procedures awaiting a legitimately elected government in Poland. Only when that happened did they suspend their activities.

What was it that allowed the exile government to persist for so long? Was it strong cultural memory or just stiff-necked stubbornness? Perhaps it was a little of both, but I believe that two factors were especially significant. First of all, they remembered the nineteenth-century exiles and second, they remembered that the partition of Poland ended when the modern state was established in 1920. The memory and the hope allowed them to hold on for almost fifty years. They had a memory model for patience and tenacity in maintaining an idea of a reality that did not exist but that potentially *could* exist.

In 1990 members of the government in exile considered themselves to be different from people in their host culture. The minister of information said: "Our values are not the same as Anglo-Saxon values. Sometimes they are even opposed—there is cultural conflict. We are more spiritual—less materialistic. Somehow it's hard to pass this on."

In what they considered to be the defense of Western civilization, Poles served in the British army during World War II—giving years of service to insure a free Europe—only to see Poland placed in Stalin's sphere of influence. Both the service and the betrayal are part of a cultural memory that goes back much further than World War II.

Themes of betrayal and suffering are elements of an important literary motif that is a strong element of Polish tradition—the idea of the martyrdom of Poland. The imagery of rending apart—the fate of some human martyrs—applies to the history of partitions of Poland, especially the eighteenth-century dismemberment and incorporation into Austria, Prussia, and Russia. These images are burned into personal and collective memory. Pain, the "hardening process," and the nobility of suffering are important elements of remembered hardship. These are stated and unstated parameters of existence that all Poles born before World War II learned as they grew up.

What has all this to do with the memories of the members of the Polish government in exile? The answer is that memory is not only individual but also a community process of using historical and cultural metaphors to build an understanding of the past and a remembering consciousness of the present. Because all consciousness is remembering consciousness, the past becomes part of the present and of the future, too.

Forty-five years of living a different set of experiences have caused homeland and exile cultures to hold divergent kinds of memories. Even though the cultural templates were the same originally, experiences and the understanding of experiences differ. The remembering consciousness of the exile recalls a Poland before the events of the past forty-five years had happened. All members of the exile government share aspects of this remembering consciousness. It is based upon shared culture and shared experience. Their shared experiences confirmed and strengthened it, and there was a sense among the exiles that they were now different from the Poles in Poland. A minister said analytically:

Clearly, if we go back—and we could go back freely if full elections were held and a government chosen by the nation were in charge—it would be a fine thing, but we will be visitors. Our children and grandchildren are here.

And our culture is different—he might have added. Forty-five years of living a different set of experiences have caused homeland and exile Polish cultures to diverge. The exile experience has created one kind of Polish culture in London, while the homeland experience has created another in Poland itself.

If literature is significant in creating and reflecting culture, changes in literature will certainly show changes in culture. Gomori (1972) discusses the changes in Polish literature after the experience of invasion by Germany and the Soviet Union in 1939 and the German occupation.

Before 1939, Polish literature did not know the problem of guilt, the hero of the Polish novel was always a victim of circumstances; there was always someone else, usually a foreigner, to blame for his errors and failures. (1972:58–59)

After the occupation experience, Gomori believes guilt became part of the literary culture.

On the one hand, the occupation and the Warsaw Uprising reactivated certain national stereotypes restoring the validity of Polish martyrdom born in the 19th century struggles for independence. The mass extermination of the Jews and the incredible hecatomb of the Warsaw Uprising, on the other hand, created an atmosphere in which almost everyone who survived could feel guilty for not being able to save others from annihilation. (1972:58)

Totalitarian government in Stalin's time led to a sense of ambiguity and dehumanization resulting in a literature of profound cynicism and doubt. Perhaps the most extreme of this cynicism and doubt is expressed in Hlasko's *The Graveyard*. Gomori comments:

The Graveyard is a charcoal sketch of a totalitarian society where people have lost their faith, or integrity or both. Thus the graveyards are the people themselves who buried their hopes, expectations and—decency. (1972:65)

If the members of the Polish government in London felt cynicism and doubt, they did not express them. In addition to a fairly straightforward interpretation of events, they showed a kind of ironic humor not incompatible with nineteenth-century literary culture. They had not experienced German occupation and they had not experienced postwar totalitarian government. They were living in the West and all of their experiences of Poland referred back either to Polish history or their memories of Poland before World War II.

How are we explaining the exiles here? Not as anachronisms but as people whose circumstances allowed them to maintain "Old Polish" culture for a longer time than was possible in the homeland. Their memories of experience over the years contained little that might cause them to revise their remembering consciousness. Their techniques for maintaining culture in an alien environment worked as well in the twentieth century as they had in the nineteenth. The psychologizing of memory had not occurred to this group of people. They did not analyze their motives but assumed that the deep motivation was the same as the stated motivation. Words like *honor*, *constitutionality*, and *duty* had retained deep cultural resonance, and there was agreement between them as to the meaning of these words. I do not mean to suggest that there was no cynicism or bitterness in this group. There was a lot of self-pity because of what they considered to be betrayal by the United States and Britain in consigning postwar Poland to Stalin. There was a hint of the nineteenth-century martyr image in their interpretations of this occurrence. It was a kind of remembrance in which betrayal is recognized as something that has happened before. The martyr image and memory allow acceptance of suffering without the growth of excessive cynicism, but it does involve a bitter feeling. What I do want to suggest is that there was an underlying memory pattern related to nineteenth-century memories of culture, nationalism, and exile that formed a common background for their present memories. In some sense the members of the government in 1990 had modeled their lives on memory patterns of nineteenth-century lives. These men had fulfilled themselves as individuals by also fulfilling cultural ideals—patriot, officer, cultural patriot, and exile. It was as if each person's life was *his* life but also an archetypal life. Thus these lives seemed larger than life and those living them seemed to have extraordinary vitality and they seemed to live with deeper meaning.

FORGETTING

The end result is that part of the past is omitted from public discourse and the current dilemma of anti-foreigner violence is presented as a short-term, localized issue.

Andrea L. Smith

Social Memory and Germany's Anti-Foreigner Crisis: A Case of Collective Forgetting

Andrea L. Smith

> People are always shouting they want to create a better future. It's not true. The future is an apathetic void of no interest to anyone. The past is full of life, eager to irritate us, provoke us and insult us, tempt us to destroy or repaint it. The only reason we want to be masters of the future is to change the past. They are fighting for access to the laboratories where photographs are retouched and biographies and histories are rewritten.
>
> Kundera 1980:22

INTRODUCTION: GERMANY'S ANTI-FOREIGNER CRISIS

Over the past decade, Germany has been facing what is described as an immigration, asylum, guestworker, or foreigner crisis. Violent attacks on foreigners increased tenfold between 1990 and 1991, approaching two hundred per month in early 1992.[1] The government seems unable to control the thugs; Chancellor Kohl announced that in order to check violence against foreigners, thousands of foreigners would be placed in camps.[2] Perhaps of most concern is the apparent tacit approval of many Germans for the violence. Journalists report that "sometimes people have stood by, even applauded, while thugs have terrorized asylum-seekers,"[3] and thousands of onlookers cheered rioters on during the 1992 siege of a refugee hostel in Rostock.[4] A youth from the former East Germany states, "Before, anyone who beat up foreigners was grabbed by the Stasi and thrown in jail. Now it's almost legal."[5]

In newspaper and academic accounts, terms used for individuals subject to government and thug attention vary, causing a corresponding shift in how the problem is constructed. Articles in the U.S. popular press over the past three years most commonly refer to those attacked as "asylum seekers" or "refugees."[6] The most recent of such coverage also notes Germany's liberal political asylum code,[7] suggesting that the code is a primary underlying cause of the violence. Articles immediately following reunification tended to highlight instead Germany's physical proximity to changing Eastern European states, implying that anti-foreigner unrest could be ultimately associated with turbulent changes in those countries. In contrast, many academic works on European migration focus on German "guestworkers," foreign workers recruited actively by the government since World War II. Germany has a population of some 4.7 million guestworkers and their families (Arnold 1991:278), and a political crisis surrounds the status of these "guests" as they prolong their "visit." Castles, Booth, and Wallace (1984) cite many cases of attacks against guestworkers that occurred a decade prior to reunification. Other scholars use an all-inclusive term and construct the targeted "other" as simply "foreigners." German labor historian Ulrich Herbert believes that "the foreign question remains one of the recurrent unresolved issues on the sociopolitical agenda in the FRG" (1990:1).

How can we understand this crisis, and who are its victims? Some suggest that anti-foreigner unrest stems in part from the nation's chaotic immigration policy. Herbert describes the government's approach to foreigners as indecisive, vacillating, and conflict-ridden (1990:257). Esser and Korte state: "There is such a lack of planning in the FRG's immigration policy that it could be described by the expression 'non-policy' " (1985:201). Are today's racist attacks in part a reflection of the government's inability to develop a coherent immigration policy? Or, could they be a direct result of the unusually high number of foreign asylum-seekers strapping German resources, as U.S. journalists some-times suggest? Or are today's attacks symptomatic of a deeper, longer-term problem?

This chapter argues that our confusion regarding the nature of this crisis hinges in part on the widespread collective forgetting of much of German labor history. Because this crisis is viewed in a historical vacuum, it is described in the popular press as a short-term issue, caused by sudden changes in Eastern Europe and/or easily resolvable through constitutional amendments. A longer historical perspective brings entirely new issues to the fore, however, and suggests that this particular case of forgetting may be quite intentional and even integral to the reproduction of several myths central to the definition of the German nation, especially the myth of German homogeneity. In the process of unraveling the significance of this particular case of collective amnesia, I hope to demonstrate that anthropologists and historians concerned with the construction of group memories and national histories must also consider processes of erasure and forgetting—these processes are interrelated, and necessarily occur simultaneously. But before delving beyond surface representations of this problem to the construction and reproduction of national myths, it is useful to first turn to works that provide a theoretical basis for tackling these issues related to power, knowledge, and the nation-state.

THE STATE AND SOCIAL IDENTITIES

In "Notes on the Difficulty of Studying the State," Philip Abrams provides a framework that enables us to move beyond reified visions of the "state," which he describes as really a "mask which prevents our seeing political practice as it is" (1988 [1977]:58). He distinguishes between the "state-system," the "nexus of practice and institutional structure centered in government" and the "state-idea," an ideological construct that appears to become increasingly reified and divorced from practice over time (58). Modern states are "triumphs of concealment"; the domination of state subjects and the legitimacy of the state are achieved by concealing "the real history and relations of subjection behind an a-historical mask of legitimating illusion" (77). Abrams calls for a move away from reification through historical inquiry (80).

In their study of English state formation, Philip Corrigan and Derek Sayer stress that state formation simultaneously involves projects of totalization as well as individualization (1985:4–5). The classification of individuals and groups is of fundamental importance to nation-states. In the process of state formation and in the everyday operation of state institutions, social identities are defined and controlled. State institutions also "totalize," or attempt to create a unified whole out of a diverse fraction of the human population, presenting as homogeneous what are really diverse experiences of different groups (Corrigan and Sayer 1985:4). Capitalist society, fundamentally unequal, is structured along class, gender, ethnic, and other distinctions, but the state-idea often does not allow for the expression of these differences. One powerful means of suppressing difference is the omission or deletion of conflicting or marginal memories from national histories, a central point we will return to. Corrigan and

Sayer also call for an examination of the routinized, mundane activities of the institutions of the state-system (1985:203). They believe that it is partly here where the political power of the ruling group is found, and where it is daily reestablished. The development and enforcement of immigration and citizenship regulations comprise one set of such daily, routinized activities. Not only do immigration and naturalization bureaucrats reinforce state power on a daily basis, but the exercise of this power is overtly directed at the shaping of the national body, at the control of social identities, and acceptable forms of social activity. Immigration and citizenship policies determine the state's relationship to "others," providing a cold and forceful definition of who those others are. Like many other operations of the state-system, these regulations are naturalized and mystified, presented as ahistorical and unchanging, natural elements of the eternal state. But to be functional, these regulations must remain fundamentally blunt, overt, and thus they are vulnerable expressions of the state-idea, expressions that may provide a glimpse into the real intentions behind the mask.

Germany provides a particularly interesting case through which to study immigration and citizenship policies. By examining how popular media and official and academic discourses define Germany's current crisis, we may learn if the lack of a coherent policy is related to some hidden disunity of German political power, as Abrams claims is always hidden behind the mask of the reified state (1988 [1977]:79), or if there is instead real unity behind the illusion of a seemingly chaotic situation. Let us first return to typical explanations for Germany's current crisis of anti-foreign sentiment and ambiguous immigration policy. These explanations are based on several myths, myths so frequently reproduced that they seem to present purposefully constructed ideological obstacles hiding an untold reality and present.

MYTHS

One myth found surprisingly often in popular and academic works is that Germany is homogeneous. Usually this homogeneity is not qualified. Surely, there must be class, regional, and linguistic variation in Germany. But while *these* differences are not also noted, the homogeneity referred to is implicitly racial or ethnic. A *Wall Street Journal* article entitled "Clashing Cultures: Immigrants to Europe from the Third World Face Racial Animosity," states: "As Third World people pour into Europe, the differing cultures collide." A skinhead youth is cited as saying, "If you mix races in Germany, it never works."[8] Discussing Northern European nations in his work on German guestworkers, Rist states "where they were once relatively homogeneous and their citizens *easily identifiable*, they have now become heterogeneous and pluralistic" (1978:xi, emphasis added). In these regions of presumably visibly homogeneous citizens, rising conflict and violence are attributed to the introduction of more racially or culturally distinct peoples. In an article on immigrant minorities in Germany, Schmitter states that the prolonged presence of ethnically, culturally, and linguistically different groups since World War II in "previously homogeneous countries" has resulted in recent anti-foreigner conflicts (1983:308).

In his review of European social science research on migrants and minorities, Oriol critiques ethnocentric assumptions common to this work (1982). He states that researchers from some continental European countries are "not very open to raising questions inspired by pluralism," (xii) a problem he attributes to the "fact" that these countries like "the FRG had a limited historical experience of social and cultural heterogeneity" (xii). Well, yes, perhaps we could say that Germany's historical experience of heterogeneity was limited—limited because people perceived as different were exterminated by the National Socialists. The presentation of nation-states as homogeneous is a project in constant jeopardy (Corrigan and Sayer 1985:197); making the conscience or the experiences of the dominant class or ethnic group truly collective is always a struggle against other ways of seeing: "because society is not factually a unity these (other ways of seeing) can never be finally erased" (6). A most extreme attempt to erase difference, in the guise of eliminating corrupting "elements," was the Nazi agenda toward Jews, Gypsies, and others, and one could argue that in the case of Germany, this project was largely achieved. Contemporary social scientists may unwittingly participate in this project by forgetting the history of Germany's exterminated ethnic groups, reproducing the Nazi ideology of Germany's presumed racial purity, and by ignoring the heterogeneity present there today.

The second common myth is that integration is difficult, if not impossible, and unfair to immigrants. The "Heidelberger Manifesto," a document published in the early 1980s by professors of several universities, argues that a "mixture" of cultures could be damaging to everybody (Räthzel 1990:38). This paper stated that all people should live in their "own place" (38). When a proposal for reforming Germany's naturalization policy was suggested, which would grant citizenship to third-generation immigrants at birth, it was turned down in 1986 as unnecessary. It was thought these individuals should undergo the normal (harrowing) route for naturalization. Hailbronner states, why impose citizenship on third-generation immigrants, "a status that they might resent"? (1989:77).

The third myth, so often claimed that it is rarely challenged, is that Germany is not an immigration country. One scholar notes that Germany's strict nationality law is considered by some "appropriate for a country that, by inescapable tradition, is not and cannot become a country of immigration" (Brubaker 1989:9). A *New York Times* article states that solutions to current anti-foreigner violence that would allow settlement of a limited number of foreigners are rejected as such solutions "would be accepting Germany as an 'immigration country,' something that is anathema to many citizens."[9] Immigration scholar Edye states that the government's only consistent statement regarding immigration is that Germany is not a country of immigration (1987:13). The official guidelines for naturalization officers offer this reminder: "The FRG is not a country of immigration [and] does not strive to increase the number of its citizens through naturalization" (Brubaker 1989:111).

This widespread ideology influences terminology. Immigrant residents are not called "immigrants" or "minorities," but "guestworkers," a term implying a short visit granted by gracious German hosts. Germany has no "immigration" law but instead a "foreigner's law," *Ausländergesetz* (Räthzel 1990:32). How could Germany have an immigration law if it is not an immigration country? This vision of guestworkers as a unique group, different from other previous immigrants, minorities, or foreigners, has influenced German social science research, Oriol claims. Separate theoretical approaches are used for research on "minorities" and "guest-workers": "In the FRG, there is a sharp contrast between a deep historical concern for [traditional minority groups like Gypsies or Jews] and the ways of dealing with present migrant communities" (Oriol 1982:xiii).

While many academic and popular writings frequently state that Germany has had little recent experience with the integration and assimilation of immigrants, a more detailed historical analysis finds that this characterization is partial and inaccurate, and significant challenges will be outlined in this chapter.

The final myth encountered is that the most important or only time foreign labor was imported to Germany on a large scale was during its post–World War II economic miracle. This is the myth most difficult to identify, as it is often reproduced through simple and seemingly innocent omission. Works on immigrant labor in Europe may commence their German chapter in the 1950s with little explanation; the reader assumes that migration before that time was quantitatively insignificant. But the prevalence of this amnesia in popular German discourse suggests that it is more than a result of academic oversight. German historian Ulrich Herbert states that the employment of foreign labor in Germany is "not perceived in public discussion as a *historical* topic; its earliest perimeter is generally reduced to developments since the early 1960s." He adds that the question of foreigners is treated in a historical and cross-cultural vacuum (1990:1, 3).

These four myths together construct a strikingly ahistorical vision of Germany and immigration. A generic version could be presented as follows: "Germany has a problem today with its guestworkers because it is homogeneous and is simply not prepared or able to handle so many foreigners. Integration is clearly economically impossible or simply not feasible for a non-immigration country. This problem is recent anyhow, and thus it should go away soon." But it is rarely recognized that immigrant labor has played a crucial role in the German economy since 1871, or that problems of today significantly parallel problems of earlier times. Why and how have these earlier experiences been forgotten?

THE STATE, MEMORIES, AND FORGETTING

The first step in liquidating a people . . . is to erase its memory. Destroy its books, its culture, its history. Then have somebody write new books, manufacture a new culture, invent a new history. Before long the nation will begin to forget what it is and what it was. The world around it will forget even faster. (Kundera 1980:159)

Dominant and private histories or memories are central to the symbolic constitution of social groups, particularly nation-states (Alonso 1988:40; Anderson 1991; Hobsbawm and Ranger 1983; Lewis 1975). Modern states often strive to establish legitimacy through special reconstructions of the past, or invented traditions. Many political groups, like nations, "were so unprecedented that even historic continuity had to be invented" (Hobsbawm and Ranger 1983:7). Modern nations usually "claim to be the opposite of novel, namely rooted in the remotest antiquity, and the opposite of constructed," in other words, "so 'natural' as to require no definition other than self-assertion" (14). Anderson describes this contradiction as the paradox of "the objective modernity of nations . . . versus their subjective antiquity in the eyes of nationalists" (1991:5).

The invention of national traditions or official histories is a highly selective, politically charged, and ongoing process, involving the construction of a unitary national history from multiple, conflicting, and competing group memories, what Corrigan and Sayer call the totalizing project (1985:4). Maurice Halbwachs was aware of the violence of this process early on: "The totality of past events can be put together in a single record only by separating them from the memory of the groups who preserved them and by severing the bonds that held them close to the psychological life of the social milieus where they occurred" (1950:84).

Ana Alonso examines how the memories/histories of subordinated peoples are appropriated or reworked to advance the legitimation project of the state, presenting three major techniques of such "state cannibalism": naturalization, departicularization, and idealization, and adds that an option for unpalatable histories is exclusion (1988:44–45). The process of exclusion, or of officially sanctioned forgetting, may be the process most difficult to combat or to recognize. The hermeneutics of forgetting are difficult to unravel, as one is faced with only a void, an omission, what may seem a simple oversight. But erasure is a powerful strategy, as Kundera writes in his novel *The Book of Laughter and Forgetting* (1980). When examining the construction and representation of national and counterhegemonic histories, erasures or collective forgettings must also be considered. While it is partly through special reconstructions of the past that group identities are established, challenged, or transformed, the process of choosing which events to erase or forget is as crucial and as strategic a process for individuals and state historians as selecting which ones to remember, and these processes must occur simultaneously— while selecting memories, those not chosen are relegated to erasure. While many histories may be invented, "revised from remembered history where feasible and fabricated where not" (Lewis 1975:12), similarly, remembered history may be rejected as false when the desired self-image changes and the remembered past no longer supports it (Lewis 1975:13). The politics of constructing and reproducing national and social memories are intrinsically related to the politics of forgetting.

GERMANY AND FORGETTING

Germany has a special relationship with history. The invention of historical continuity has been central to establishing legitimacy of rule in most states, but in modern Germany we have a double paradox of a state trying to present itself as born anew from the ashes of the ruined Nazi Reich, while still holding onto a legitimacy based on an earlier invented collective past. While early German governments dabbled in the invention of German traditions (see Mosse 1975), the Nazis were especially conscious of the importance of history. They used an ideology of continuity in

German history as propaganda to legitimate their regime, claiming themselves "spiritual descendants of ancient Teutonic Tribes, Luther . . . Frederick the Great" (Röhl 1970:xi). Later Soviet scholars also promoted German continuity to demonstrate that the early Prussian Junker capitalist tradition culminated in the barbarous Third Reich (Röhl 1970:xi). Postwar Western historians avoided reproducing these conclusions, and German continuity became a taboo subject. The continuity debate was reopened in German historiography in the 1960s, and many now stress continuity between early periods of German history and the rise of the National Socialists. But while World War II has been reconnected to earlier periods of German history, 1945 is a year in limbo, floating unattached to any nation, to any people. According to Räthzel, the year of the founding of the Federal Republic has been regarded as a new beginning, a time when the nation was "reborn without sin" (1990:44). In order to secure legitimacy, the government this time has had to present itself as most decidedly divorced from previous ideologies. Continuity with the past has been blocked.

This discontinuity affects our understanding of Germany's immigration crisis in several ways. The question of foreign workers is treated in a historical vacuum (Herbert 1990:3). The widely used term associated with the Nazis, *Fremdarbeiter* (foreign worker) has been replaced with *Gastarbeiter* (guestworker) (Herbert 1990:3). The official dominant ideology now is that there is no trace of fascism or racism left in Germany, thus, current strife cannot be considered racism, cannot be linked to past conflicts, and is given a new term, Ausländerfeindlichkeit, or "hostility to foreigners" (Räthzel 1990:45). This ideology of discontinuity is implicated in the widespread repression of Germany's long-term tradition of employing foreign workers, and of the fact that there has been a "so-called foreigner problem in the labor force for more than eighty of the previous hundred years" (Herbert 1990:3). It is to this missing tradition that we will now turn.

GERMANY'S EARLY EXPERIENCES WITH FOREIGN WORKERS

Early Phase: 1870s–1914: Polish Agricultural Labor

In response to increasing labor shortages caused in part by long-term local and national emigration and agricultural intensification,[10] and in an attempt to reduce labor costs, East Prussian Junker estate owners began to import Polish agricultural workers in the late nineteenth century.[11] By 1885, anti-Polish sentiment had grown in Prussia. A newspaper article of March 11, 1885, stated: "A wave of Polish immigration is inundating our eastern provinces. . . . All this forces upon us the question as to whether it is not in fact necessary . . . to close the door tightly on any further expansion of Polish culture" (*Leipziger Tageblatt*, cited in Herbert 1990:11).

In response to popular concern, the government stopped further Polish immigration and deported all forty thousand of the nonnaturalized Poles from East Prussian provinces (Herbert 1990:13). However, agricultural intensification and increased competition with New World grains led to a greater demand for lower priced labor (Weber 1979 [1894]:192). Agricultural interest groups dominated by eastern Junkers campaigned for an end to the immigration block and permission to employ Russian-Polish workers for temporary agricultural work (Herbert 1990:17). In 1890, the government responded to their demands and legislated a three-year labor importation trial period (19). Decrees allowed Poles from Russia and Galicia to work in industry or agriculture in only Eastern Prussia, fearing Polish infiltration and agitation elsewhere. Their work period was limited to April 1–November 15. A *Karenzzeit* (seasonal "closure period") forced workers home annually, and only unmarried workers were allowed, measures designed to prevent settlement (19). While these restrictions represent a compromise between government and estate owners, they corresponded neatly with estate owner needs. In 1891, these rules were extended to other parts of Prussia, although Poles elsewhere were prohibited from industrial work. The three-year trial period was renewed, and the number of foreigners in the German Reich increased dramatically. Legally registered workers increased from 206,000 in 1871 to 1,259,000 in 1910 (1.9 percent of the total population) (20).

The German immigration laws were amended in 1907. Poles had been breaking their contracts due to horrendous working conditions and employers sought government intervention to stop this practice; meanwhile, patriotic groups lobbied for a halt in foreign employment and enforced deportations (Herbert 1990:34). The government responded by establishing new rules aimed at regulating foreign labor more effectively. All foreign agricultural and industrial workers were required to obtain domestic permits (36). Workers could work only where stated on permits, which also included personal information including worker nationality. Only Poles from Russia and Austria-Hungary, 80 percent of foreign agricultural labor (Esser and Korte 1985:167), were subject to the compulsory annual rotation. Other foreign and German migrant workers could work year-round (Herbert 1990:37). These permits and the compulsory rotation system for Poles remained in effect until 1918. By 1914, one out of seven agricultural workers, 433,000, were foreign, and during summer months this proportion increased to over 50 percent in some agricultural areas (Wunderlich 1961:24).

Working conditions for foreign agricultural workers were horrible. Poles from Russia- or Austria- or Prussia-occupied Poland had few or no political resources. Threat of deportation was constant. Employers who kept a portion of workers' earnings as a deposit sometimes mistreated their workers deliberately: If workers tried to defend themselves, they were easily deported and their deposits retained by employers (Herbert 1990: 38–39). Writing in 1894, Max Weber stated, "The control over the Poles is limitless: one nod, and the local administrator—who is also an estate owner—sends him back to Poland" (1979 [1894]:199).

Polish workers were paid lower wages than Germans for the same jobs at least through the turn of the century (Herbert 1990:39). Employers saved on housing costs for Poles, who were considered satisfied with less (Wunderlich 1961:23). Lodgings included haylofts, stables, and make-shift barracks, often lacking heating devices of any sort (Herbert 1990:41).

Junker agriculturalists greatly benefited from this labor. Employing Poles helped protect them from direct wage competition with industry, as Poles were prohibited from taking industrial jobs. Their lower wages helped landowners compete with cheap overseas products, and the seasonal nature of their employment allowed landowners to convert to more labor-intensive farming methods as they could rotate out workers to lower labor costs (Herbert 1990:44).

Industrial Labor

Before the 1890s, foreigners were less commonly employed in industry. But despite increased restrictions and the 1908 permit laws, factory owners began to rely on foreigners at increasing levels by the turn of the century, employing workers from the Austrian-Hungarian and Russian empires (largely Poles and Slavs), Italy, Netherlands, France, Denmark, and Scandinavia. Illegal workers were commonly employed (Herbert 1990: 46), and industry organizations lobbied heavily for reduced employment restrictions. In response to government attempts to deport illegal workers, for example, the Association of German Jute Manufacturers reported to Prussian commerce ministers in 1898 that Russians comprised 20–30 percent of the total work force, and without them, their plants would be forced to shut down (47).

By 1907, half the Reich's foreign labor worked in industry (Herbert 1990:54). Foreigners were concentrated largely in mining, construction, and brick-making, comprising 4.5 percent of the industrial work force (22); 8 percent of mining; 10 percent of stone and earth work; and 7 percent of construction labor in 1907 (55). In some mines, over half of all workers were foreigners (59). Industrial workers suffered poor working conditions. They were segregated into the most undesirable and poorly paid positions, with extremely limited possibilities for advancement (56–60). In the steel and iron industries and mining, more than two-thirds of all foreign workers were concentrated in unskilled jobs (59). Foreigners took the most dangerous jobs as well. Two-thirds of lead-related diseases in the district of Oppeln in 1911 affected Ruthenian workers, who comprised only 25 percent of the labor force there (60–61).

Industry advertised the bifurcation of tasks as presenting a major advantage to German workers. A 1908 statement at an annual German Employer's Federation meeting argued: "Our working population has gradually risen to a higher level of culture and economic well-being, so that it may in a certain way appear desirable to hire unassuming, tractable foreign workers for the low-skill jobs" (in Herbert 1990:49). Industry and government often conflicted, however. While industrial groups advertised the benefits to Germany of foreign workers, government officials promoted nationalistic interests. Fears of *Überfremdung*, over-foreignization, grew in the early 1900s (Herbert 1990:28–29). Dangers threatening the moral integrity of the German people were associated with Poles, whose "disadvantaged status and legal discrimination were linked in the popular mind with their rejection as inferior individuals" (45); yet southern Europeans and Croatians were also targets of xenophobia (48).

By 1914, 1.2 million foreigners worked in Germany in lowest-level agricultural and industrial jobs (Herbert 1990:93). They kept wages low, were expendable during economic slumps, and did not require social benefit payments. During this period, Germany's transportation system grew tremendously, with its railroads built largely by immigrant labor (Hourwich 1922:183). Foreign labor is considered by some a primary factor in Germany's rapid industrialization during the late nineteenth century (182).

World War I

When World War I broke out, workers of draft age from allied countries were sent home. But a plan had already existed before the outbreak of the war regarding workers from hostile countries: a March 13, 1914, report suggested that these foreigners be retained for continued use as a source of labor (Herbert 1990:93). Once the war commenced, in a dramatic shift of policy toward Poles, they were immediately classified as civilian prisoners and prohibited from leaving their employer or place of employment. Poles were retained in part because they were sorely needed for troubled German agriculture. As nearly 2.7 million men were withdrawn from the labor market to serve in the war, an acute labor shortage had developed, and with one-third of the food supply saved for troops, risk of civilian starvation was severe (Wunderlich 1961:28). Laws were established restricting movement of Poles and placing them under curfew (Herbert 1990:97). They soon became prisoners of the state, losing any previous political rights, their working conditions declined, and they received little or no wages. Military officers sometimes retained half of their earnings, and employers often paid in vouchers redeemable at the end of the war. The involuntary conscription of foreign labor was illegal; a possibility for men of enemy countries unfit for service to return via neutral countries had to be kept open in consideration of international law (95). Aware of this problem, the Interior and Agricultural Ministries reported January 1914:

It does not appear to be possible at the moment to take more emphatic governmental steps than the previously instituted measures. . . . In particular, there is no legal basis for forcing them (Russian seasonal workers) immediately into concluding a contract, as requested in the petitions presented. (Communication, Prussian Ministry of the Interior and Minister for Agriculture, cited in Herbert 1990:95)

Government and local officials tried to persuade Poles to sign labor contracts voluntarily to avoid scandal. Apparently a wide range of methods of persuasion were practiced. The Saxony Chamber of Commerce reported January 1915: "Experience has shown . . . that an extension of contract went like clockwork in those areas of employment where the police proceeded with great severity when workers refused to sign the new contract" (Elsner, cited in Herbert 1990:96). A Wehrmacht regional command center ordered that conditions of arrest be made more stringent "until those under arrest promise to be obedient" (96).

As labor shortages increased, new Poles were "recruited" from occupied Poland. Poles crossing the border from Germany, if caught, instantly lost rights to return home; approximately 700,000 Poles were "recruited" and sent to work in Germany in this manner (Esser and Korte 1985:168).

In its quest for labor, Germany also turned to Belgium. Approximately 500,000 Belgians were unemployed after Germany confiscated heavy machinery in 1914–1915, and factories were closed to avoid producing goods for the enemy. Representatives of German industry attempted to recruit Belgians voluntarily, but had limited success, and began to lobby government officials for forced recruitment (Herbert 1990:102–3). At a War Ministry conference in September 1916, a chemical plant representative stated: "Open up Belgium, this enormous pool of human labor! We've brought in thousands of workers from Poland but haven't gotten a single one from Belgium. . . . There are 700,000 unemployed in Belgium, among them a sizable contingent of skilled workers. I already said that compulsion must be applied in Belgium" (in Herbert 1990:104).

On November 26, 1916, a Belgium-based recruitment plan went into effect. According to Herbert, all male inhabitants seventeen or older were forced to assemble at specified places. The local commander removed those of high social rank and the infirm, and "those remaining were ordered to report voluntarily for work in Germany. Whoever refused to obey this order was immediately bundled onto a freight train standing ready and then shipped by rail to one of the internment camps in Germany" (Herbert 1990:105). Around sixty-one thousand workers were transferred in this manner to Germany in roughly three months, and seventeen thousand "volunteered." By 1916–1917, 395,122 Poles from Russia, 8,118 Poles from Austria-Hungary, 94,135 Belgians, and 10,640 Italians were employed in Germany according to permits registered with the German Labor Agency (108).

Regional administrators and factory owners were given a fair amount of leeway during this period, and their reports suggest that workers often were treated inhumanely. The local Düsseldorf authority regularly confiscated I.D.s and documents of Polish-Russian workers to ensure that they did not leave, and stated:

According to experience to date with the Russians, they feel very uncomfortable if they are not being watched and under constant supervision. . . . Local police forces have repeatedly arrested and locked up Russians wishing to incite other workers, or who were work-shy and unruly, for 24 or 48 hours, keeping them on bread and water. The effect of this punitive measure was everywhere the same: the Russians became willing and obedient. (Düsseldorf Landrät, 1915, cited in Herbert 1990:111)

Further blurring boundaries between civilian and forced labor was the forced labor of prisoners of war (POWs) (Herbert 1990:117). Huge numbers of POWs were obtained at the outset of the war, creating problems of housing, guarding, and feeding them. Severe labor shortages and initial war defeats led the government in December 1914 to transfer housing, lodging, and supervising costs to private industries in exchange for their labor. POWs were first used in mining, and subsequently agriculture and heavy industry (90). Jobs were selected for POWs largely by nationality: Russians and Serbs were sent to agricultural positions, and Italians, French, and Belgians were sent to industries. POW workers were paid only approximately 25 percent of their gross earnings, and often through vouchers redeemable only at POW camps. The numbers of POWs working in Germany during the war are astounding. In December 1916, 14 percent of all pit miners were POWs, and in some mines this proportion approached 30 percent (90). Over 1.1 million POWs were employed in August 1916 (91), and by October 1918, nearly one million POWs were employed in agriculture alone (Wunderlich 1961:29). Problems with POW labor were similar to those with enforced civilian workers: additional manpower was needed to guard them, and there were high numbers of escapes and low levels of productivity (Herbert 1990:92). But despite these problems, the benefits from POW labor were enormous. After the war, the Reichstag Investigative Subcommittee on International Law noted its importance to the German war effort:

It was impossible to imagine any larger-size enterprise, either industrial or agricultural, that did not make use of the aid of POWs. . . . Only a future age will be able to fully and properly evaluate the accomplishments achieved by utilization of POWs as laborers and to recognize what an essential contribution their work made to the maintenance of the war economy. (in Herbert 1990:91)

The "future age" that would evaluate these "achievements" would arrive sooner than these bureaucrats may have imagined. In 1937, a National Socialist committee began reviewing the experiences with foreign civilian and POW labor during World War I, finding these "overall as having been quite positive" (Herbert 1990:131). Herbert describes the use of forced labor as a "program of tremendous economic importance," stating that this experience had "clearly demonstrated a harsh fact: forced labor was useful only if implemented in total fashion and in grand style" (119). This was the practice to be carried out during World War II.

Interlude Between the Wars

The German government quickly repatriated most of the approximately two million conscripted foreign workers at the end of the war to open up their jobs for returning German soldiers. During this interwar period, food shortages in 1919–1923 led to a mass rural exodus and severe urban unemployment (Wunderlich 1961:65). Because eastern agricultural work had been carried out by Poles for the past several decades, agricultural interest groups again lobbied for permission to import foreign labor, claiming that Germans were unsuitable for this sort of work and would never be satisfied with the housing provided by employers to Poles (Herbert 1990:122). Despite growing unemployment, these powerful interest groups again had their way. By March 1919, having closed the border to all foreigners and still repatriating remaining Polish war labor, the Reich Office for Economic Demobilization was simultaneously authorizing the employment and immigration of fifty thousand new Poles (122). As the economy weakened and the government was facing increasing social unrest, however, laws were established aimed at turning remaining and incoming foreign workers into annual migrants. Quotas were established and the number of foreign workers was reduced to seventy thousand in 1931 (Wunderlich 1961:66).

World War II

Germany's experiences with coerced foreign labor during the first few years of World War II display chilling parallels with experiences of World War I. This dark period of Germany's history of foreign labor exploitation is better known than others, and will be summarized briefly, although Nazi relationships with foreign workers were complex, constantly in flux, and merit more in-depth analysis.[12] When the National Socialists came to power and the economy was boosted with the expansion of armaments industries, increasing numbers of foreigners were imported (Esser and Korte 1985:168). Temporary labor agreements were made with Poland, Italy, and Yugoslavia. In 1933, approximately one hundred thousand foreigners worked in Germany, and in 1938 their number had quadrupled (168). Labor control was managed by a central agency for labor exchange working closely with the police and the Security Service (Herbert 1990: 129). By 1938, it was obvious that voluntary recruitment alone would not provide the country with enough workers for an expanded war economy, and the Aliens Control Decree was established, prohibiting all foreigners from leaving Germany and placing their control in the hands of the police (Esser and Korte 1985:168).

Millions of foreign workers were "recruited" by the Nazis through unlawful and outrageous means throughout the war. The experiences of World War I seem to have been closely examined. Instead of attempting an initial guise of legal, voluntary labor recruitment, involuntary recruitment procedures like those practiced toward the end of the first war were carried out immediately on a grand scale during World War II. For example, Poland-based labor offices were in operation three days after the German army crossed into Poland (Homze 1967:23). By October 1939, all Poles in occupied Poland between ages sixteen and sixty were subject to compulsory labor (29). The disciplining of such a massive foreign work force was less problematic during this war, as the nation had become the most extreme sort of police state. Horrifying work conditions are noted in many sources, including beatings, rat-infested living quarters, and extremely high mortality rates. Threat of confinement in camps was a most effective means of disciplining foreign workers (Esser and Korte 1985:168–69).

A worker hierarchy based on "racial" criteria was established. While the ideological framework for such a hierarchy was complex, the overall classification of foreigners did not stray far from the hierarchy practiced (but only partly enforced by law) during World War I, when Poles and other Eastern Europeans and Russians comprised the lowest rank, Western Europeans (Italians, Belgians, and French) were next, and Germans were supreme. The Nazi hierarchy determined not only the lifespan of foreign workers, but also minute details regarding wages, housing conditions, and food rations. Lowest on the Nazi "blood hierarchy" following Jews, Polish workers were paid the lowest wages by legal decree (Wunderlich 1961: 245). Rulings in March 1940 included special labor permits for Poles, badges indicating nationality, restriction of movement, and strict segregation from Germans (Homze 1967:40–41). To prevent intermixing of German and Polish "blood," sexual liaisons with German women were punished by execution (41).

Although nearly four million Russian POWs had been captured by 1942, their employment was avoided out of fear that they would spread communist doctrines to Germans (Homze 1967:73). When it was decided that labor shortages were too severe to continue ignoring the vast number of potential Russian laborers, only 1.1 million of the 3.9 million POWs remained; the rest had starved to death in POW camps (81). The thousands of Russians who were finally sent to Germany were so famished, and their rations so much smaller than those assigned to any other nationality, that they often died on the job (Herbert 1990:157). Company owners complained and sometimes provided extra rations illegally to keep workers alive enough to maintain production requirements.

Many stress the contradictory nature of Nazi policies toward foreign workers during World War II. A more cynical approach suggests that it was during this time that imperialist techniques for exploiting cheap labor were pushed to their bleakest yet logical extremes (Meillassoux 1981:140). Writing about concentration camps, which he stresses were *labor* camps, Meillassoux states:

They provided virtually free labor for Thyssen, I. G. Farben, Krupp and other large and still respectable industrial corporations. They were supplied with men, women and children rounded up throughout colonized Europe, exploited to the point of physical exhaustion, then physically liquidated as soon as they could no longer work. German capitalism was thus spared the cost of maintaining and taking care of its ill, weak or aged workers. (1981:140)

By 1945, approximately eight million foreigners were working for the German war effort; six million of these were coerced civilian workers from occupied regions and two million were prisoners of war (Esser and Korte 1985:169).

Early History and Myths Revisited

We have now seriously challenged one of our immigration myths: that extensive employment of foreign labor is a recent phenomenon in Germany. It should be clear that since 1871, Germany's economic growth during peacetime was based heavily on foreign labor, and that this labor was essential to the geographic and temporal extent of German aggression during wartime. The scale of foreign labor employment is shocking: foreigners comprised over half of the labor force in some industries before 1914. Germany in these earlier periods was faced with a contemporary dilemma: how to get the most out of these workers while prohibiting long-term settlement. During peacetime, solutions included mandatory short-term work permits, restricted movement, special laws circumscribing foreigners' rights, prohibitions on married workers, easy deportations to curb worker organization and agitation, and forced worker rotation, all administered by a highly organized central labor office, often in direct coordination with the police. A hierarchy based on worker nationality and class was reinforced by requiring permits and rotation of only some groups.

These procedures were elaborated during wartime. During World War I, workers' rights, wages, and benefits were stripped down to near non-existence or eliminated, movement was strictly curtailed, and workers were confined to prison-like camps. Workers' nationality was sometimes identified externally. At the end of World War I, massive repatriation of this borrowed labor was enforced. By World War II, National Socialists learned from mistakes of the previous war and quickly set up an efficient system of prison or slave labor, comprised of foreigners and German Jews. This labor was critical to the German war effort, comprising a full quarter of all workers by 1944 (Herbert 1990:153). Herbert states that without foreign workers, "the war would have been lost for Germany by the summer of 1943 at the latest" (153). The employment of foreign workers can thus be viewed as a crucial element of the German economy throughout modern German history.

While this "forgotten" history soundly challenges the popular mis-conception that Germany's employment of foreign guestworkers is a recent phenomenon, our three remaining myths at first seem unchallenged. These include the myth of German homogeneity, that Germany is not an immigration country, and that integration is a difficult if not impossible process for such a nation. Throughout this nearly seventy-five-year period, Germany seems to have prevented permanent integration of its foreign labor force, as workers were eventually rotated out, deported, or exterminated. Have any foreign workers settled at any time during this legacy? Information required to answer this question is extremely difficult to uncover, suggesting another revealing "omission." It is as if the myths of German homogeneity and inexperience with immigration are so pervasive and naturalized that the kind of thinking needed to produce such evidence is absent. It is difficult to determine what percentage, if any, of Germany's World War I labor remained in Germany. However, a substantial portion of Polish-Prussian workers, considered Germans by law during the late-nineteenth century Reich, settled permanently in the Ruhr mining region. The integration of this "ethnic" group has been considered by some to be an "American-style" model of assimilation (see Murphy 1983).

The most striking period of immigrant integration, however, followed World War II. At the end of the war, Germany's borders were reduced. After having lost some six million Germans during the war (Orlov 1987:268), the nation faced the arrival of twelve million refugees, also called expellees or displaced persons. These refugees included approxi-mately five million Germans from former German territories, several million Ethnic Germans (people of German descent) forced out of Central and Eastern European countries, two million Germans who fled from the Russian zone by 1946, several hundred thousand non-German collaborationists who "fled into Germany with the retreating German armies" (Shils 1946:3), as well as several hundred thousand children of various nationalities, roughly one hundred thousand whose parents were killed in concentration camps, another one hundred thousand who were brought to Germany and placed with German families during the war, and remaining foreign workers (3–4). What percentage of these refugees would be defined today by Germans as "foreign," and how many foreign workers remained? Sources suggest a substantial number. Esser and Korte state that one of the main problems following the war was "the treatment of former forced labor who did not return home" (1985:169). In 1946, Shils estimated that nearly one million Eastern Europeans (mainly Polish, Ukrainian, and Yugoslavian foreign workers) refused repatriation, and predicted that "many of them will ultimately melt away into the German population" (1946:15). This prediction was most likely realized: liberal Allied Forces–inspired policies following the war required recognition of all expellees as citizens, regardless of former nationality (Wallich 1955: 278), and in 1951, the Act on the Legal Status of Homeless Foreigners granted legal equality to those who had served as forced laborers and who chose to remain in Germany (Esser and Korte 1985:169). Thus, following World War II, along with millions of German refugees, at least one million foreign workers and two hundred thousand children of unknown nationality were granted citizenship status and stayed in Germany.

The integration of twelve million war refugees, of various degrees of "foreign-ness," was a colossal task regardless of the refugees' supposed racial origins. Refugees comprised one-fifth of the total population, and more than 30 percent of some regions in 1946 (Wallich 1955:273). Their assimilation was expensive; refugee expenditures during 1949–1951 are estimated at 10.8 billion marks (280). Housing had to be built quickly, and Wallich writes "not infrequently bitter rivalry developed between the newcomers and the bombed-out members of the local population who likewise aspired to new homes" (276). Thus, while not all of the over twelve million integrated were constructed as "real" Germans, all experienced similarly tremendous upheaval, expelled from quite different countries, economies, and environments (Shils 1946:4). This experience of massive resettlement of millions, a sizeable proportion of whom were "foreigners," challenges our final myths. This history demonstrates that Germany *has* received permanent immigrants, comprising at one point one-fifth of the entire population. The assimilation of at least a million immigrants directly challenges the ideology of German "racial homogeneity." And despite the scale of this process, integration did not prove impossible, but was rapidly accomplished. One can assume that the blending of foreign "blood" has caused few problems, as distinctions between foreign and German settlers from this era are not commonly, if ever, recorded. By 1955, the twelve million immigrant-refugees were so well absorbed into the economy that Germany began to look elsewhere for additional labor.

GUESTWORKERS

Having reviewed Germany's "forgotten" legacy of long-term employment of foreigners, we can compare this less-known past to contemporary experiences with postwar guestworkers. Given the importance for West German officials following the war to present their nation as a new beginning with links to the previous Reich severed, do we find a corresponding shift in approach to foreign labor?

The importation of workers during the 1950s and 1960s was carried out consciously by the government to meet growing labor needs. Unable to tap the traditional Polish labor pool (Esser and Korte 1985:175), the German Federal Labor Office (GFLO) operated a large-scale recruitment of workers from southern European countries. Labor agreements were signed with Italy, Spain, Greece, Turkey, Morocco, Portugal, and Yugoslavia (Yücel 1987:121). Recruitment was conducted in home countries. German Liaison Offices were responsible for interviewing and hiring workers (122); five hundred to six hundred offices were in operation in southern Europe during the height of the recruitment drive (Rist 1978:xii). Age limits were established: thirty-five years old was the upper limit for unskilled laborers, and forty years old for skilled laborers (Yücel 1987: 122). Workers were also screened for health problems and criminal or political records (Castles, Booth, and Wallace 1984:71), and only literate individuals meeting specific schooling requirements were eligible (Yücel 1987:122). Contracts were first short-term, usually for one year, after which workers could renew, change jobs, or return home (Yücel 1987: 123), and only single workers were recruited to prevent family settlement. The number of foreign workers grew quickly from 95,000 in 1956 to 507,000 in 1961, 1.3 million in 1966, and 2.6 million by 1973 (Castles et al. 1984:72).

To further regulate immigrants, the Aliens Law of 1965 (*Ausländergesetz*) was established, requiring that all foreigners hold residence permits (Esser and Korte 1985:184). These permits would be granted only "if it does not harm the interest of the FRG" (as cited in Castles et al. 1984:76). This broad phrase granted local or national officials wide discretion in filing permits. The Aliens Law also reduced foreigners' rights. With this law, they were granted all basic rights except the right to vote, and "the basic rights of freedom of association, and movement, and free choice of occupation, place of work, and place of education, and protection from extradition abroad" (Castles et al. 1984:77). Paragraph 10 allowed for deportation of foreigners for any of eleven reasons, including severe traffic violations and the destruction of public security, including adultery.[13] The

Labor Promotion Act of 1969 added an additional requirement: that workers obtain a residence permit before receiving work permits (Esser and Korte 1985:184). Since both permits were issued for short durations, government officials maintained notable control over foreigners. They could check the status of individuals easily, restrict the areas in which foreigners could settle, and could more easily deport individuals. For example, authorities could deport a family upon the birth of a child by refusing the newborn a residence permit (Räthzel 1990:43).

After the 1973 recession, a recruitment stop was enforced, and non-EEC individuals were (and still are) prohibited from entering the country, with the exception of privileged foreigners from countries with special arrangements with the FRG (such as the United States and Switzerland), political asylum seekers,[14] and Ethnic Germans (Räthzel 1990:34). Many workers left at this time due to unemployment or because their permits were not renewed, and the number of foreigners was reduced somewhat, although less than expected: from 2.6 million or 12 percent of German workers in 1973, to 1.9 million or 9.5 percent of the work force in 1976 (Castles et al. 1984:72). Fearing further border closings, many foreigners managed to bring in more family members, and foreign birthrates rose.

Additional measures were passed to discourage family reunification. Spouses and family members who arrived after December 1, 1974, were prohibited from working (Castles et al. 1984:78). The entry age for foreign workers' children was lowered in 1978 from twenty to seventeen (79); and again in 1981 from seventeen to fifteen (81). Foreign workers were offered a premium for return: 10,500 DM for the worker plus 1,500 DM per child if they would leave Germany permanently (Räthzel 1990:38). In response to pressure from Germans living in regions with high concentrations of foreigners, a new law was passed April 1, 1975, allowing cities with more than 6 percent foreign population to apply to the government for designation as a "congested" area. When a city receives such designation, city officials can end all further foreign immigration into the area by turning down residence permit applications. Foreigners seeking permit renewal since the establishment of this law have stamped into their passports a list of cities where settlement is prohibited (Rist 1978:78–79).

These regulations are often described as economically driven, and clearly there has been a conscious attempt to maximize the economic potential of foreign labor. Great attention has been paid to ensure that social costs typically associated with a labor force are reduced. By inhibiting family settlement and screening out sickly and elder workers, costs associated with children's schooling, workers' parents, and worker health care have been deferred to sending countries. As during earlier eras, employers continued to save money on foreign workers' housing. According to Ray Rist, workers in the Ruhr region in the 1970s lived in decrepit conditions: 84 percent had no baths and 68 percent had no lavatory in the room; in addition, 16 percent of foreign families lived in one room, 39 percent in two rooms, while Germans in the same region averaged 0.79 persons per room, although immigrants were paying on the average one-third more rent than Germans (1978:35).

In addition to savings on housing, schooling, and workers' retirement, we must also consider all the other costs associated with the reproduction of the labor pool. These costs include the market value in the capitalist economy of costs to the worker's family of raising the worker into a producer of labor power, and goods consumed by the worker when back home unemployed or between jobs, costs deferred to the sending country (Meillassoux 1981:114). Migratory movements this way can result in huge transfers of man-hours from noncapitalist or domestic economies to capitalist economies (107). German government officials were not unaware of how the nation would benefit from their manipulation of labor immigration. The state secretary in the Ministry of Labor stated in March 1966:

the foreign employees, 90 percent of whom are at their most creative age between 18 and 45, make a considerable contribution to goods production. . . . In addition, foreign workers . . . pay income tax and social security deductions according to the same rules as indigenous German workers. Given the age of the foreign workers, this has a very favorable effect, at present especially in connection with old age insurance, because far higher revenues are taken in from the foreign workers than are currently paid out in pension benefits to this category of individuals. (L. Kattenstroth, Grusswort der Bundesregierung, 1966, cited in Herbert 1990:212–13)

Herbert reports that in 1966 foreign workers paid 1.2 billion DM in social security contributions, while only DM 127 million were paid out in benefits (1990:292, note 33).

IMMIGRATION AND NATURALIZATION POLICIES: ECONOMIC OR POLITICAL INTERESTS?

Today's policies toward guestworkers are strikingly similar to—not strikingly different from—policies of earlier Reichs. The rotation of workers and initial provision of one-year contracts mimic pre–World War I policies. As in earlier periods, work and residence permit requirements and restricted rights for foreigners allow authorities to keep track of and deport foreigners easily. And now, as before, benefits to the economy have been outstanding. Throughout this legacy, temporary workers have served as a powerless working class, diminishing chances of development in Germany of a strong class consciousness, while promoting German socio-economic mobility (Rist 1978:35).

In each of the phases described, foreign workers have been considered a mobile labor pool expendable during economic downturns, and laws defining their rights and restrictions seem organized to ensure their primary definition as such. Regulations have been established for immediate problems and longer-range guidelines have never been established. Policies thus have been inconsistent, contradictory, and rapidly changing throughout this history. Many social scientists interpret the inconsistent and short-term nature of these policies as resulting from their establishment with solely economic (as opposed to humanitarian or "moral") interests in mind (see Esser and Korte 1985:179). But *have* only economic interests governed these policies? While state officials (especially since World War II) present new regulations as unfortunate but necessary measures due to economic exigencies, evidence suggests that such explanations deceive.

The German state-idea, the ideology justifying relations of domination, is presented as overtly economic. Capitalist values are naturalized, and decisions and policies presented as if they were the only possible outcomes, determined solely by rational problem-solving. Abrams finds that the presentation of the state in capitalist societies is uniquely opaque, involving the segregation of economic from political relations (1988:78), but he calls for a move beyond merely uncovering economic connections: "In seeking to dismantle that ideology it is not enough to try to rediscover the connection with economic facts *within* the general terms of the ideology as a whole, the acceptance of the reality of the state. Rather, we must make a ruthless assault on the whole set of claims in terms of which the being of the state is proposed" (1988:76).

State officials may want us to uncover economic motivations driving immigration regulations, in part to prevent recognition that regulations actually may emerge from a deeper conflict between economic and political goals. Examples of conflict between economic and political interests abound in this review of Germany's labor history. The late nineteenth-century importation of Polish agricultural workers was strongly opposed by government officials; the annual worker rotation system established was a compromise solution, meeting largely business needs. Employers of the modern era also have opposed governmental restrictions on a free labor supply. Before the 1973 recruitment stop, a debate had developed over growing costs of an integrating guestworker population, and a proposal was presented to return to a mandatory worker rotation system. This proposal floundered, perhaps as West German firms would find "no possible utility in losing trained and proven foreign workers after a period of several years due to some rigid stipulation of compulsory rotation—only to have to train new, unskilled guest workers to replace them" (Herbert 1990:233). When the government initiated the recruitment halt, not as many workers left as had been predicted. Räthzel states that this was because they were badly needed, and kept on, by industry (1990:39).

If policies throughout this period reflect a compromise between political and economic interests, how can we learn what the underlying political goals and ideology might be? Germany's naturalization and citizenship laws, in regulating who can and who cannot belong, outline plainly the social boundaries of the "ideal" German state, and by examining these laws we can reveal the underlying ideologies motivating the political sphere. These laws conflict fundamentally with the practice of importing foreign labor to Germany, and thus come into direct conflict with capitalist interests. I contend that this collision between economic and political goals has resulted in a delicate deadlock, a deadlock that drastically limits the sort of policies that can be generated toward Germany's foreigners and that neither side can afford to lose.

Germany's Citizenship and Naturalization Regulations

Citizenship requirements of most North Atlantic nations are based on two principles: *jus solis* and *jus sanguinis*. Jus solis is the granting of citizenship to individuals born on the territory; jus sanguinis is citizenship based on descent (Brubaker 1989:99). Many nations' citizenship laws are based on a combination of two principles. In the United States and Canada, for example, citizenship is granted unconditionally to those born in the territory, even to people of noncitizen parents, through the principle of jus solis, but citizenship through descent, jus sanguinis, is limited. In the United States, citizenship by descent is granted unconditionally only to the first generation born abroad, contingent on prior parental residence in the United States (105).

German citizenship is solely based on the principle of jus sanguinis. Place of birth is irrelevant (Brubaker 1989:105). German citizenship thus can be transmitted perpetually to descendants of Germans living outside

Germany (hence automatic citizenship to Ethnic Germans), while descendants of noncitizens, even if working and living there for generations, never receive citizenship automatically. Through the application of this legal principle, those with a right to join the German nation are only those related to other Germans, or those construed as being of the German "race."

Naturalization provides a route to citizenship when not granted automatically. In some countries, such as France and the United States, naturalization is a legal right once certain conditions are met (in theory). Germany operates on a discretionary model, however. With discretionary systems, naturalization is never a right, even if all conditions are met, and is considered exceptional and completely at the discretion of naturalization officials. German naturalization policy is based on the conviction that Germany is not and cannot be a country of immigration (Hailbronner 1989:67). Foreigners wishing to become naturalized must have lived continuously in Germany for at least ten years in "permanent" residences; immigrant barracks do not suffice. They must also meet several vague requirements: they must have a "good reputation," demonstrate an "irreproachable" way of life, manifest "lasting orientation" to Germany and German culture, and actively support the "free democratic order" of the FRG, and there must be public interest in the individual's naturalization. Even language requirements are vague: instead of administering a standardized test, the individual must have written and spoken German "to the degree expected from a person in his or her lifecycle" (Brubaker 1989:110). Given the imprecision of these criteria, authorities retain wide discretion in naturalizing individuals, and Germany's naturalization rates are quite low. In 1985, 13,894 foreigners were naturalized, including 4,813 married to German spouses, although by this time over 2.6 million foreigners had met the ten-year residency requirement (Hailbronner 1989: 70). Of foreigners with ten years' residence in Germany, naturalization rates are estimated at 0.5 percent for Yugoslavs and 0.167 percent for Turks (70). In Sweden, where citizenship is also based on jus sanguinis principles and where naturalization also is discretionary, Turkish naturalization rates are seventy times higher than in Germany (Brubaker 1989:120).

An important exception to the naturalization policy underscores the racial orientation of German citizenship. One group of foreigners holds a legal right to naturalization: *Volksdeutsche*, or Ethnic Germans. Ethnic Germans instantly receive all rights granted German citizens, and hold a legal right to naturalization, if they so desire. But these people may share little "ethnically" with Germans: most have lived in Eastern European countries for several generations, if not hundreds of years, and many do not speak German (Räthzel 1990:40). Some Ethnic Germans were never even German by origin, but Flemings or Frisians, such as Eastern European Mennonites (Hobsbawm 1992:5). But these immigrants nevertheless supposedly share at least one thing in common with other Germans: descent, or "race."

Over 1.5 million Ethnic Germans have arrived from the former Soviet Union and Eastern Europe alone between 1950 and 1989 (Opitz 1991: 262), and Ethnic Germans now comprise over one quarter of all foreigners entering Germany today[15] (Räthzel 1990:35). The background of many now arriving is surprising. During World War II, nearly a million Ethnic Germans were deported to Germany from Eastern Europe and were resettled by the National Socialists onto newly seized and depopulated territories in the East because Germans did not want to move there (Wunderlich 1961:189–90). Regarding these settlers, Wunderlich states that due to the lack of Germans to fill the empty east, "almost anyone willing to confess being a German could be included in the master race by certificate" (1961:246). Ethnic Germans recently have used these or similar certificates to verify their "Germanness." Räthzel states that Ethnic Germans "have to prove their Germanity and right to citizenship by presenting papers—which derive directly from the fascist period—in which they were defined as Germans" (1990:42). People were registered by the Nazis on various lists according to "degree of German blood." About half of the Ethnic Germans coming from Poland today were registered on "*Volkliste* 3," which Räthzel explains included those who had just "some German blood but had proved faithful to Germany" (1990:42).

The assumption that Ethic Germans will integrate easily as demonstrated by their instant naturalization rights contrasts dramatically with the opposite assumption regarding "foreigners": foreign integration is considered rare and exceptional, somehow qualitatively different from the process to be experienced by Ethnic Germans, and those who attempt to do so must undergo an extensive and harrowing naturalization process with a minute success rate. The need to defend these two contradictory philosophies regarding "foreign" integration has led to fancy political footwork by some German politicians. According to Räthzel, government officials argued in the 1980s that the country could no longer afford to accommodate foreigners, but politicians quickly changed their assessment of the nation's ability to assimilate newcomers when huge numbers of Ethnic Germans began to arrive a few years later (1990:40). The government provided funds for housing and German language programs and found it necessary to establish a mass advertising campaign aimed at convincing Germans that *these* new arrivals *were* welcome and would not cause economic hardship (40). Räthzel states, "after all, the [Ethnic Germans] were Germans, not foreigners, [and] to receive them was an act of patriotism not just humanity" (40).

The underlying political ideology, as encoded in German immigration and naturalization law, is that Germany is and should remain a homogeneous racial community. Germany continues to grant instant citizenship to those defined as "distant relatives," no matter how distant, how long ago they left, or how many arrive. Monies spent integrating these people only reinforce the government's commitment to a racial definition of the national body. Regarding "nonracial" foreigners, a similar consistency is found between the law's definition of these people as perpetually "others," and its application.[16] Few foreigners pass the naturalization process. Policy confusion thus arises only with guestworker living and working regulations; a patchwork of temporary provisions are instituted to meet specific needs. But no substantial or long-term policy shifts regarding guestworkers have ever been established. Today's apparently confused situation stems from an unresolved conflict between unyielding and opposing political and economic interests.

CONCLUSION: FORGETTING GERMANY'S FORMER GUESTWORKERS

Germany's current immigration crisis stems from Germany's continued reliance on a labor force substratum comprised of foreigners, a practice that is necessary to meet economic goals, but that collides with its definition as a homogeneous racial unit. In the past, this conflict between the definition of the nation and the desire for cheap labor was resolved by periodically deporting alien workers. But given the country's traumatic past from which today's politicians strive to distance themselves, this option is no longer acceptable. Instead, laws and policies are established irregularly to resolve new problems on a short-term basis. A dramatic decision to deport foreigners is avoided while efforts toward liberalization of foreigner policies, including permanent settlement and integration, similarly flounder. Critical to the maintenance of this delicate balance is the omission of this long history from public consciousness. If it were openly acknowledged that Germany has faced the same conflict between economic needs and political goals for over one hundred years, a popular movement could emerge calling for its resolution. Solutions could involve either a real immigration halt or permanent "out-rotations"—politically difficult for those distancing themselves from the Nazis, and a last resort for the capitalists, or a shift toward integration—more highly desired by capitalists than expulsion, but dreaded politically as such a move would collide with the definition of the nation. Collective forgetting of Germany's long history of employing and then deporting foreigners is essential to the prevention of such a resolution. Furthermore, politicians preparing present or future policies toward the current body of guestworkers need a German past devoid of large-scale immigration and integration to continue arguing publicly that integration of today's guestworkers would lead to economic and social hardship and has no precedent. If it were recognized that integration *has* occurred successfully in the past, some might wonder why such a process would prove difficult today.

Strategic collective forgetting is also critical to the preservation of the myth of German homogeneity. Social homogeneity on a national scale is absurd to those who consider class, linguistic, or regional variation, and notions of racial homogeneity and of distinct human races have been refuted on scientific grounds periodically by anthropologists.[17] But the ideology of German racial homogeneity persists nevertheless, institutionalized and operationalized through the workings of the German constitution and citizenship law. Those to whom this ideology is important or central would find it further shaken by the recognition that large numbers of foreigners have always comprised a substantial portion of the German population, some staying on and even "mixing in" with the rest of Germany (see Murphy 1983). Experiences of the period of integration following 1945 would prove especially difficult for "homogenists" to accept. Faced with a history that contradicts sharply the ideal self-image, the history is ignored, erased, and forgotten, and the self-image is maintained (Lewis 1975:13). Such a large-scale collective amnesia may be especially possible in this nation where public officials and citizens alike must present—and to a certain extent, believe in—a self-image disconnected from the former Reich. Due to their special past, modern Germans may be especially vulnerable to forgetting.

The end result is that part of the past is omitted from public discourse and the current dilemma of anti-foreigner violence is presented as a short-term, localized issue. Germany's long heritage of labor importation is not mentioned, current guestworkers are not considered immigrants, and numerically less significant asylum-seekers receive wide press. Integration is considered unusual or impossible, while the memory of post–World War II integration of at least a million foreigners is curiously deleted, and the current massive integration of Ethnic Germans of dubious backgrounds is dismissed as greatly different due to supposed blood ties. The overt ideology of a country driven to today's situation by solely utilitarian economic goals preserves camouflaged and unchallenged the deeper ideology of a homogeneous biological German nation, and the workers and crisis remain.

NOTES

This chapter is based on my Master's thesis, "Social Memory and Germany's Immigration Crisis: A Case of Collective Forgetting," 1992, University of Arizona Department of Anthropology. Versions were presented at the Ninety-First Annual Meeting of the American Association of Anthropology, December 2–5, 1992, in San Francisco, and at the Tenth Annual Graduate Student Conference of the Institute on Western Europe, March 26, 1993. I am grateful to the recognition provided by prizes received by the Institute on Western Europe and the Division of Social and Behavioral Sciences, University of Arizona, 1993. This paper owes much to the valuable comments by Kevin Gosner, Robert M. Netting, Daniel Nugent, Thomas Park, and Hermann Rebel.

1. *The Economist*, February 15, 1992, 21.

2. *Arizona Daily Star*, October 11, 1991, 13.

3. *The Economist*, October 19, 1991, 58.

4. *Saarbrucker Zeitung*, August 31, 1992.

5. "Youth Adrift in a New Germany Turn to Neo-Nazis," *New York Times*, September 28, 1992.

6. The following articles identify victims of violent attacks as "asylum-seekers" or "refugees." Articles listed in Group A include those that directly or indirectly link violent attacks on foreigners with Germany's political asylum code; Group B articles are from earlier months and instead highlight recent reunification or Germany's proximity to Eastern Europe.

Group A: *The Economist*, October 19, 1991, 58. *Arizona Daily Star*, October 5, 1992; October 11, 1992, 13. New York Times, November 3, 1992, A5; November 25, 1992, A4; December 8, 1992, A6. *Frankfurter Allgemeine Zeitung fur Deutschland*, September 28, 1992, reproduced in *The German Tribune*, October 2, 1992, 5. *Hamburger Abendblatt*, September 18, 1992, reproduced in *The German Tribune*, September 25, 1992.

Group B: *Arizona Daily Star*, November 18, 1990; October 11, 1991, 13; *The Economist*, October 13, 1990, 51; *New York Times*, August 11, 1990, A3.

7. Article 16, Section 2, of the Federal Republic of Germany's constitution of 1949 guarantees the right of asylum to all victims of political persecution, a liberal policy designed as a gesture of atonement for Nazi war crimes (see Esser and Korte 1985:169) or to symbolically distance the new nation from the prior regime. Chancellor Kohl's party, the Christian Democratic Union, has urged the elimination of this article from the constitution for several years, and has received

growing popular support for such action in response in part to ever-increasing anti-foreigner violence. Leaders of the Social Democratic party, which opposed this action, were finally convinced to approve a change in asylum law after polls showed that their liberal policy toward foreigners was becoming increasingly unpopular. The new law would limit those entering the country by screening out applicants at the border who are from countries not considered to have political persecution, and limits the number of foreign workers granted work permits annually to one hundred thousand (*New York Times*, December 8, 1992, A1, A6).

8. *Wall Street Journal*, August 14, 1990, A1, A9.

9. *New York Times*, April 7, 1992, A4, "Anti-Immigration Parties Rattle Bonn," Stephen Kinzer.

10. For a detailed account of Germany's history of foreign labor employment, see Ulrich Herbert's excellent work, *A History of Foreign Labor in Germany, 1880–1980*, Ann Arbor: University of Michigan Press, 1990. For additional material on German emigration, see Hourwich (1922), Walker (1964), Wunderlich (1961). Labor shortages may be partly linked to nearly a century of widespread emigration from Germany. In the province of Mecklenberg, for example, 1 percent of the population left each year from 1850 to 1854 (Walker 1964:165–66); by 1854, so many migrant farm workers had left that soldiers were sent in to help with harvest labor there (167). In East Prussia, where monocropping of rye and other grains on large estates predominated, growing labor shortages due to out-migration of German farm workers were compounded by the estates' extreme vulnerability to international price fluctuations and competition with cheaper New World grains in the late nineteenth century. To compete, estate owners turned to cheaper foreign labor, intensified farming techniques, and new labor-intensive crops like sugar beets, practices that exacerbated labor shortages seasonally, and encouraged the transition to a seasonally rotating foreign labor pool (see Weber 1979 [1894]).

11. It is difficult to determine exactly when the importation of foreign labor began. Before unification of the German Reich in 1871, the topic presents difficulties to researchers. The category "foreigner" was problematic, as there was no national state to define who was German (Herbert 1990:1). The previous political unit, the German Confederation, was an extension of the Holy Roman Empire and consisted of multiple semiautonomous entities, including regions populated by large numbers of non-German minorities (Czechs of Moravia and Bohemia, Slovenes of Carniola, and Italians), while excluding regions with sizeable German populations, particularly East Prussia, West Prussia, and Posen. In addition, foreign laborers often were not considered "immigrants," but temporary migrants, and early figures probably underestimate numbers of foreign workers dramatically.

12. For more lengthy discussions of the use of foreign labor during World War II, see Borkin (1978), Homze (1967), and Wunderlich (1961).

13. A forty-two year old Turkish worker was deported for a "public security

and order" violation: he had an affair with his landlord's since-divorced wife. Aliens Office officials asserted that he had ruined a German marriage and endangered public morals (Rist 1978:140).

14. For a summary of the current status of Germany's political asylum regulations, see note 7, above.

15. An estimated 220,000 Ethnic Germans arrived from the ex-Soviet Union and Eastern Europe in 1991 (*The Economist*, April 11, 1992, 51).

16. The anti-Jewish legislation of the Third Reich is a further example of the racial orientation of German ideas about citizenship. The Nuremberg Laws of 1935 and the "First Supplementary Decree to the Reich's Citizenship Law" of November 14, 1935, discriminated against some half million Jewish German citizens explicitly on presumed racial criteria (Schleunes 1970:128–30).

17. See for example Benedict (1943); Montagu (1942); and UNESCO (1961:499).

RECONSTRUCTING

I argue that there is something about memory that makes a room and something about a room that contains memory but that the context is neither architectural nor cognitive but emotional.

Richard Swiderski

Mau Mau and Memory Rooms: Placing a Social Emotion

Richard Swiderski

> What Ulysses preserves from the lotus, from Circe's drugs and the Sirens' songs, is not merely the past or the future. Memory really matters—for individuals, for the collectivity, for civilization—only if it binds together the imprint of the past and the project of the future, if it enables us to act without forgetting what we wanted to do, to become without ceasing to be, and to be without ceasing to become.
>
> Italo Calvino, "The Odysseys Within the Odyssey,"
> in Calvino 1987:138.

Part way through *A Night at the Opera*, Groucho Marx is in his Manhattan apartment, having just arrived from a grueling transatlantic trip that included hiding stowaways Chico and Harpo in an already overcrowded stateroom. The two are now concealed in the apartment, on the run from a bullish detective, who knocks at the door. "Anybody in here with you?" the detective demands to know. "Only me and my memories," Groucho wistfully responds as the pair duck away.

From *Animal Crackers* onward, the Marx Brothers seemed intent on reminding their American audiences of how we all got where we are. Even if they had to do so in boxy sets required by primitive sound filming techniques, and by their own stage orientation, it was in rooms that they held their memories. Groucho's mock romantic evocation of faded loves in his response to the detective echoed other memories in the lively flight of his two brothers, in their demolition of imported European culture during that night at the opera.

I argue that there is something about memory that makes a room and something about a room that contains memory, but that the context is neither architectural nor cognitive but emotional. In particular, these rooms and the memories they at least metaphorically contain are convenient containers for otherwise disconnected masses of object and feeling. Memory is a social emotion in the sense constructed by Merleau-Ponty and elaborated by Harré (1986). In its room, memory brings together the feelings and those who can or would share them.

Neurophysiologically, memory is fragile and elusive. The ability to recall and the content of recall are readily obliterated by concussion, tumor, and deterioration of the cerebral cortex. Yet even a compromised brain holds memory. The elderly in their rooms stereotypically do more recalling than sensing and reach emotion that way. Proust, who spent his days isolated in a cork-lined room, found memory in a sudden taste of petite madeleine. "Strong emotion recalled in tranquillity" was Wordsworth's definition of poetry, and many other instances come to mind, all of them demonstrating a connection between the act of remembering and feeling emotion and an interior space. Within such walls there comes a focus.

My grandmother recently was moved from her own apartment in a senior citizens' complex and brought to live with my parents in Florida. She had been telephoning other family members in the night telling them of plots against her, of people attempting to penetrate the walls of her room and blow poisonous gas inside. It was thought to be a sign of senile dementia and eventually diagnosed as such with appropriate terminology attached. Her room was full of old furniture she would not relinquish, pictures of children, grand- and great-grandchildren, and a TV set, an accumulation of all she has been and become since arriving in America earlier in this century. But her closest friends and relatives have died in a cluster and she is left with a room that must be made to correspond to the disaster as a break in its solid continuity. Why she chose poison through the wall I do not know exactly, but the violation and the threat to her show what must have happened to that room. It became the basis for a strong expression of feeling not justified in sensory experience. The assurance of memory was violated by death and so was the room, by its possibility.

I believe that my grandmother's room and (not to seem facetious) Groucho's, Proust's, and Wordsworth's rooms were what Werner Sollors (1986) calls "ethnic rooms," that is, places that display the distinct identity of their inhabitants. These ethnic rooms are memory rooms furnished with matter that evokes particular joy or sadness when displayed to (or theatrically concealed from) others. Groucho's hidden brothers, Proust's evasive loves, Wordsworth's sister Dorothy, and my grandmother's deceased husband and living children are all brought forth in these rooms through things. Encounters take place there and elsewhere as well, as if the room can make the emotion by unifying time and space in a feeling that transcends them. There even has been published a photographic guide (Hall 1992) to setting up ethnic rooms. The entire history of immigration into America (or from an African or Latin American village into a city) coalesces in the room's distinctive social act of memory. That memory is all the more social and all the more an act for seeming to take place within the inhabitant's mind.

Sollors mentions the "ultimate immigrant saga," Superman. The movie script for the most recent filming of Superman was written by Mario Puzo, the author of another immigrant saga, *The Godfather*. Superman had a gigantic ethnic room, The Fortress of Solitude, which is also a memory room of his origins on the destroyed planet Krypton. With a little more turning up of examples (from Anne Bradstreet to Henry Ford to James Baldwin) it might be possible to show that America is a condo complex of such rooms. The rooms are exactly as George Washington or Theodore Roosevelt left them.

As Frances Yates (1974) has so well recounted, finding memory in rooms (theaters and coliseums) has long been both metaphor and practice in at least European civilization. Ethnic memory rooms are not a phenomenon confined to America or Europe. They seem to form a widespread complex of enclosed space yielding recollection.

In Kuravilangad, Kerala State, South India, I sat in the parlor of a "Syrian Catholic" home speaking with the patriarch. Çri H. was seventy-two years old at the time and head of one of the prominent lineages in the area. In appearance he resembled a Brahmin elder, shirtless and in dhoti, a scapular extending between neck and left shoulder like the gota or sacred thread of Brahmin men. Inside a floor-to-ceiling glass case opposite where we sat was a collection of papers, ceramic souvenirs of fairs and foreign cities, and children's metal toys, among other indistinguishable items. Çri H. welcomed me and asked me if I had found the Munnu Numpu, the Three Day Feast and fair at the local church, to be of interest. I assured him that it was most attractive. He outlined the stages of the feast, processions from village churches converging on the plaza before the main church, and listed the saints, each associated with a different Christian lineage and sodality, exhibited in the main procession. He then removed from the case a purple velvet cushion on which an oval case rested. Inside the case was a collection of objects, the most conspicuous of which was a large, ornately worked metal key that Çri H. said was the key to the shrine at Loreto (the house of the Holy Family miraculously transported from Bethlehem to a site in Italy). Water used to wash this key is said to ease the trials of childbirth. Also inside the case were slips of paper said to be saints' relics, or at least to have touched saints' relics. There also was a tiny spherical bottle that once contained holy water from the Mount of Olives in Jerusalem, and another small case inlaid with glass rectangles. Inside this were a few old Kerala coins, two pieces of mother of pearl, and some grains of paddy the meaning of which Çri H. said he did not know. He clearly felt obliged to show these objects to a visitor and explain them as he did, perhaps with the purpose of assuring some salubrious result for the visitor and/or for his lineage on the day of the annual parish feast.

Later, a colleague who knew Çri H. and his family very well asked me if he had shown me this collection of objects, and made a skeptical reference to his beliefs about their healing powers. It seemed to me, however, that the patriarch was not so much trying to display objects to which he attributed remarkable powers but rather that the attribution of powers intensified a code that the objects expressed. With this display he energized and completed a memory room that was also an ethnic room surrounding us. If a visitor failed to respond to the emotions of this performance it was because she was not situated to link objects with context and Çri H. was not about to explain it as an anthropologist would. His presentation was for someone like him, an ideal resident of that symbolic space who did not need to stop for a refresher course on the way to acknowledging what encloses us. The magic was perhaps a repute that the objects actually had, but it had become an intensifier of memory's shared emotion all the more easily shared thereby.

Kuravilangad is a village, like others in the area, supposedly reclaimed from the sea. The main event of the second day of the Munnu Numpu, which I had just witnessed, was "vali Jonas," the "Jonas boat," in which a team of men from the same hamlet carry a large model of a Portuguese *não* on their shoulders amid a turbulent, sealike crowd on the steps leading up to the main church. Fixed on the deck of the boat is an out-of-scale statue of the Old Testament prophet Jonah (Jonas). After the craft has tipped and yawled about as in a violent storm and some people in the crowd have nearly been trampled (it has happened in the past according to local recollection), the ship turns to face the church and suddenly halts. A man mounts the deck and removes the statue. The bearers then carry the ship steadily up the stairs and back into the church where it rests near the niche where Jonas resides during the whole of the ecclesiastical year, until the next Three Day Feast.

The men who bear the ship say that its movements are beyond their control as long as the statue of Jonas is on board and the ship is faced away from the church. Only men of their hamlet and kinship group can carry the ship in procession, however; it will not "sail" for anyone else. They made a vow when the area was covered with water that if the waters receded they would reenact the prophet's ride on the tempest-tossed sea that precipitated him into the mouth of the sea creature. This also has the effect of keeping the waters from flooding back.

The Three Day Feast was originally a Syrian Christian celebration and did not include Jonas's boat ride. That seems to have been added when the parish was Catholicized under Portuguese influence (or mandate) in the seventeenth century. Processional ships with erratic behavior appear in Catholic celebrations from Guinea Bissau to Macao, as well as, of course, in Portugal. It probably appeared in the old Syrian Christian celebration as a spectacle to attract balking parishioners into the now Catholic fold. The Portuguese and their local allies were eager to provide any inducement they could to replace loyalty to the Eastern Patriarch predominant among Kerala Christians, with loyalty to the Roman Pope and the Portuguese system of ecclesiastical rule, the *padroado*. They were not above *compelle intruere*, "forced conversion" as prescribed by Aquinas, but this far inland their writ had to be slyly extended.

Jonas may have come from Syrian tradition rather than Roman, and his boat rides upon waters not entirely Portuguese. Kerala was colonized much before the Christian advent (even before the first Christian advent, from the Near East via trade routes, in the third–fourth centuries C.E.) by Brahmins from the north of India who brought with them Vedic Hinduism and the caste system, which they imposed upon (or delivered to) the indigenous (Dravidian?) population. Vedic culture became so strongly entrenched in Kerala that it is still the only area in India where it is possible to see the Classical Sanskrit drama performed in the correct ritual setting (Valiamanga Temple in Trichur) and a version of the Vedic fire ritual practiced in an all-Brahmin village. In order to rationalize their dominance and their extensive hereditary land holdings, the Brahmins concocted a story: Parasu-Rama, "Rama of the Axe," an avatar of the god Vishnu, had singlehandedly driven off the sea and awarded the land thus claimed to his devoted Brahmins. Technically, then, all land in Kerala belonged to the Brahmins in about the same way that all land in the Spanish New World belonged to the Spanish King; all residents were rent-paying tenants. As other social and caste groups entered into prominence the

Brahmins were constrained to devise fictions allowing them land under their suzerainty, but it was always necessary to pay some service to the Brahmins in order to hold land.

The Syrian Christians maintain a fiction expressed in legendary narratives that they are the descendants of Brahmins converted by the apostle Saint Thomas on his mission to India. They were convinced, says one story, when the saint caused the water Brahmins were using at their ablutions to remain suspended in the air. The Christianized Brahmins had to flee the wrath of their caste-mates and moved inland to settlements such as that at Kuravilangad. While there is no documentation to prove the conjecture, it seems at least plausible that the story of waters receding and vows made to carry a boat in procession is a Christian (first Syrian and then Roman) transformation of the Parasu-Rama reclamation story. It has the double advantage of asserting ownership of the land and the Brahminic antecedents of the avowed owners. In the absence of a community of Brahmins Çri H. and his family fulfill this image.

Image has a great deal to do with it. Indian sacred performance conveys a numinous image without any explicit indication that this is the intention. The ocean is present in the Jonas procession in this way. Others attending the festival ask if you noticed it and written sources (George 1966:184) describe it. Yet the ocean's presence does not seem conscious or planned but appears to be the result of a happy convergence of properties. Within the mass surrounding the boat or Jonas and later circling the church there seem to be waves and current. Viewed from above and far away the same mass has an oceanic spread and motion. Its surface glints with white cloth and ornaments and there are light, shivering rings which men make by striking suspended metal plates. The ocean created inductively from the movement of the boat is formed of the convergent imagery where the boat travels. Çri H.'s Brahmin status is formed in the same way, and his memory room is a manifestation of the entire process.

He shows articles themselves derived from the sea (mother of pearl), associated with water, or having a watery glint. Of course these articles might be arbitrarily associated and their oceanic qualities only a dream. They are oceanic as they come together in memory of the lineage's Brahminic right to the land through the withdrawal of the sea. Çri H.'s display of the items constitutes that room as a space in a feast similarly constituted, by things coming together to make a whole greater than what they suggest. It is not just the patriarch and his memories but the entire community in a particular and peculiar state of legitimacy, dwelling in a house as old as Christianity in India, amid fields periodically flooded to plant the paddy. The key to the house at Loreto where the Holy Family lived but which moved miraculously across the sea unlocks through the medium of water the womb that brings forth the next generation. Memory is an act of assembling images and symbols into an oceanic room that is most specially ethnic.

Çri H. constructs his memory room as memory is constructed socially and as an emotion. He does not put it together in private, out of the pieces of life already lived, like a James Baldwin protagonist (Giovanni). He assembles his memories within the arena, invariably public, of his entire lineage, which is the arena of the feast and its large-scale act of assemblage. Groucho's mock-maudlin memory room is a private session to which others are admitted only by hints. But of course that transforms it into a public secret concealed by many at the same time.

A recent American analog to Çri H.'s room is the Elvis Presley room composed by a father and son team in a small town near the singer's birthplace, Tupelo, Mississippi. The pair are engaged in the act of "living Elvis," an extreme self-immersion in the artifacts and appearances of their idol. They dress as Elvis did during his prime, wear their hair in a historically accurate replica, and collect any and all references to Elvis in the media. The walls of their small dwelling are covered with photographs; they have a bath mat that once was in the mansion at Graceland. They conduct their house as a museum recounting the works and exploits of their subject. Çri H. owes his act and appearance to a long and relatively stable imagistic process, an articulated correspondence between himself and the qualities of his lineage. The Elvis room is still in the process of formation and so its dynamic is more explicit. It lacks the formative subtlety of symbols and images in the Kerala room. The Elvis room is a small kin grouping in the act of capturing such a public imagery through the creation of a memory room, as if Elvis were a property of *their* memory construction. Of course, given the impermanence of succession in American culture (and the drifting historical content of fandom), it is unlikely that the Elvis room will survive as long as the oceanic room has, but it may well be replaced by other rooms of the same formation. Some already are a rich feature of the American landscape, partaking of media saturation just as Çri H.'s and others like it partake of ritual saturation in the Indian landscape.

The Kenya highland town of Eldoret was pioneered by South African voortrekkers who established large-scale farming in the region. It is a landscape far different from Mississippi or eastern Kerala, a high altitude mesa with complaisant weather at all seasons of the year and soil suitable for farming, a landscape already long contested. Some white farmers withdrew at the national redistribution of land that attended Kenya's independence, but new landholders, corporate and private, have taken their place. There is at least one European memory room in this place. It belongs to J. van K. and it is as casual in its presentation as Çri H.'s is demonstrational.

J. is a European by birth but has lived in Africa most of his adult life; he is now a Kenyan citizen married to a local woman with whom he has three children. His room is in a house he rents while his own is (slowly, as the money becomes available) being built not far away. There is a Kenyan-style "family" room just inside the entranceway-kitchen: there the chairs are crowded together in an almost impassable density and a color television replaces the large radio usually somewhere in such a Kenyan hospitable room. The typical profusion of doilies is restrained here though there are a few to make it clear what is meant by the space. J.'s room is in direct contradiction of this space. It is at the end of a long dark hall and is itself rather dark. A single book- and paper-piled desk dominates the front section center and further into the room there is a sofa against one wall and a few overstuffed chairs facing it over a low glass coffee table showing a few English-language magazines. This setting is closer to the idealizations of *African Homes and Gardens* (it does exist) than to the social density of the real Kenyan room toward the front. The structure seems to be that of an office with the official's desk in one section of its own and a conversational grouping for less formal meetings set off in another part of the room. J.'s office at the university, where he teaches, is not structured this way, nor are the offices of the university officials whom he emulates. They prefer a desk as large as possible for the space occupied with as many chairs as possible grouped before. J.'s room is therefore a departure both from the available domestic and official models he conforms to, and an evocation of an international office model remade domestically. This structural evocation of an alien ideal is an action of memory, a part solitude in which strong emotion is partly recalled. The design continues in the furnishings of the room.

On the wall, most noticeable of the room's contents, is a large cuckoo clock that ticks loudly and calls at the hour. This is conspicuously European in both sound and appearance. Time does not pass with such measured clarity in Kenyan houses, though wrist watches are common apparel. J. makes the point of telling how he obtained the clock in Nairobi and has been able to have it repaired there when required. The foreign is therefore native but all the more idiosyncratic for being obtained in the Kenyan metropolis. Standing on the floor is a small, erect frame displaying an embroidery showing a snow scene recognizably Dutch from the windmills and dikes. The wall to the right at the end of room is filled with row upon row of scholarly and religious books, titles in English and in Dutch. Above them is a small collection of photographs in a single gilt frame. Lingering long enough to see this, you have entered J.'s memory room.

What makes this more coherent than the thematic collection of objects it might seem is J.'s discourse, which never is given systematically or as an occasion, like Çri H.'s, nor so fully in conjunction with the contrived setting, like that of the Elvis fan. J. tells of events "at home" (in Europe) and among his family on any occasion, within this room or not, but it is only in this room that the strength of those accumulated statements as a social emotion of memory is realized. This room is not a solitary retreat where an exile relives his past. It is a gathering place for those who have through association with J. been admitted into its significance. Only a few decorations out of keeping with the main of domestic paraphernalia suffice to bring about that condition in the acquaintance. Friendship is a function of this memory and its sociability.

When J. tells of his days at school, and how he spent more time having a good time than studying, he is commenting upon similar tendencies among his students at the university and he is setting up the memory room centered around the desk, which might even be stacked with student papers ready to be read and graded (great volumes of examinations are the standard at the university). The sketchiest anecdote gives way to the modest furniture of time in which an important component is that it is not self-explanatory but requires the intermediary of acquaintance to make it memory. Far from dabbling alone in his recollections, J. invites others to attend these thoughts in the theater that requires their own recollections of his utterances. It is a sign of acquaintance to be invited into his room, as if you have known him long enough by then to be able to enter the room that really is there. When I moved to a new house he arrived one day and came directly to the room where I was working as if to communicate his recognition of our friendship in that manner, stating it by entering my room of his own accord, ready to appreciate what was there. That sensibility is the same as memory in form and awaits the content.

J. is forever enhancing and extending the perimeters of his room by adding to the realm of his acquaintances and initiating them into the responses that accord with citizenship in his space. I believe "citizenship" is the correct metaphor for his phenomenon because of the reference to the home country as a place of loyalty and belonging to which he certainly can return. He speaks of the freedom to mind one's own business on the streets of the cities there as a refreshing alternative to the public display and celebrity-hunting that take place elsewhere. He repeats the anecdote of a Kenyan sports star who was accosted by a child seeking an autograph on a street of a Dutch city. The child was reprimanded by his mother telling him to let the man enjoy his peace. The mutual respect of people as a social and civic virtue is memory becoming act becoming structure in J.'s room.

The events and externals to which J. refers are mostly in the past and elsewhere, but there is one body of associations that creates a problem for his room, especially if its fulfillment is to be as casual and unforced as he desires. That is the proximity of South Africa and its government's policies of discrimination against a racial majority. The Boers who have commanded that policy were Dutch immigrants, their religion and their language, Afrikaans, recall Netherlands Dutch. J. recounts some fond Eldoret stories of Afrikaaners and their horse-drawn wagons but he makes no spontaneous allusion to South Africa itself. He is conscious that South Africa is referred to in who he is where he is, and makes no attempt to deny that possibility. But it remains a possibility that may intrude upon the social construction of his memory. It is not congenial to the household that provides the walls of his room.

Frances Yates (1974:275) describes the efforts of one Giovanni Camillo to fashion a complete theater of memory. His final work was so elaborate that it hardly could have served any purpose, mnemonic or other. Apart from the evident absurdity, often cited in the history of memory technology, of devices more complex than anything they might serve to recall, there does seem to be a need to make a place of what is recalled, and to make what is to be recalled form a place. Memory can be taken to be constituted only in the act of remembering easily faces, facts, and figures in a systematic order and thus drawn in analogy to architecture and the planned sequence of drama. The architecture and the contained drama of a memory theater token more than the cognitive surfaces of memory; they house the feelings of those gathered who must have brought their ability to recognize this from elsewhere. The forgettability of many memory schemes may be due to their attempt to accomplish the full social act of memory by trying to encourage more cognition. J.'s room is probably stable on the brink of mechanism. It is not formed of lists, the strategy of museums and galleries, whatever else their purpose might be, having only the lists and artifacts to recall a once-living social world. J.'s room is only formed when others are there.

The memory rooms touched upon here do not form a typology; they are wildly different from each other and might not in any accurate account submit to being known by the same name. None of them exists without its rememberer and his or her community. A memory room can be imagined from an artifactual assemblage or a set of characteristics. It cannot be known in any one hermeneutic direction, from object to subject, from "me" to "my memories," in Groucho's example. At very least it is "only" me "and" my memories, implying that others might also be there, *are* there in the evident audience.

Memory is *constructed* (not simply construed) socially as an emotion in a most intensely local place. In recent years, when dictators have fallen and the suddenly liberated have forced entry into their rooms, the surprises were not so much quirks and bizarre privacy but the degree to which the deposed masters gathered and reified the aspirations and interests of those they had ruled. Fernando Marcos's exercise equipment and home transfusion center, Imelda's justly renowned shoe collection, the Ceausescus' stately bed: the objects and environments suddenly precipitated into gigantic memory rooms for everyone concerned. In the Georgian film *Repentance*, which was one of the remarkable accompaniments of glasnost, the deceased Stalin-like dictator is repeatedly exhumed by unknown parties at night and propped up on his family's patio, forcing his former supporters to reenter his centripetal presence. The entire, not-so-guiltless society is being dragged into the tyrant's boudoir. The rememberer is the daughter of his chief victim.

In the Japanese tea room (to play out this strain of variations in one more example) there is a niche called the *tokonoma*. It is bare except perhaps for a displayed calligraphic scroll and an ikebana arrangement of flowers appropriate to the season. The tea room is not a memory room. It is work of no one person and has reference to no single stream of thoughts and passions. Swords are left outside and shogun is the equal of commoner there. It is a gathering of the circumstances of memory and the place but without the society and without the emotion. The absence, then, of memory leaves an aesthetic relieved of responsibility to draw upon a dangerous outside where there are swords and shoguns and memory rooms which might exhibit the same objects. Cancellation of other emotions also cancels out memory but not its social basis.

On October 16–18, 1992, there was held at the Gulf Hotel in Kakamega, Western Province, Kenya, a conference entitled "Mau Mau: Forty Years After." Though it had indeed been forty years since the Mau Mau rising, the conferees concluded that it was too soon to assess it adequately. It was also apparent from the papers offered that the plea made by O. W. Furley (1972) at the twentieth anniversary of the revolt had been largely ignored. Furley called upon historians to search for records that might be lost and asked that they undertake interviews with surviving "freedom fighters," as Mau Mau veterans have been named. Though he did not say so at the time, he might have added that a dearth of material would lend itself more readily to political manipulation than a larger mass collected as records and not for the purpose of sustaining one particular Mau Mau image. A memory room of the Mau Mau was certain to be constructed and what was included would matter greatly to politicians.

In fact two Mau Mau memory rooms have been constructed and can be visited by the general public. One is at the Kenyan National Archives on Tom Mboya Street in Nairobi and the other is at the Kenyan National Museum on Museum Hill in the same city. These two rooms are not explicitly dedicated to the Mau Mau nor do they contain Mau Mau memorabilia alone. Nonetheless their materials configurate the public memory of that formative time now before the birth of the majority of living Kenyans. And they describe a kind of room that recurs in Kenya, establishing a relationship between place, space, and object: a memory room.

The photograph of Dedan Kimathi recumbent is common to both rooms and to many others. Kimathi was one of the leaders of the armed insurrection. He was captured during a raid, tried and imprisoned at Kamiti, where he was hanged and buried in 1958. The photograph shows Kimathi soon after he was subdued: he is lying on a cloth, shirtless, with his arms in manacles, his eyes shifted to the right, away from the flash. The image summons up the man's presence, down but still very much alive. It is perhaps the most often reproduced of Mau Mau images, possibly because it is one of the clearest, as well as a successful subversion of the photographer's intent, which was to show the Mau Mau in defeat. The photograph forms one portion of a room that Kenyans inhabit as Kenyans.

It appeared, for instance, on the cover of the September 1992 issue of *Monthly News*, one of many Kenyan political affairs magazines. Kimathi's face, dreadlocks bunched on top, is juxtaposed with a color photograph of Mr. Clement Gachanja, a KANU politician who was promoting himself as "Kikuyu community spokesman." Gachanja, according to the article inside, was implementing a KANU strategy to use the surviving Mau Mau fighters as a ploy. He was organizing a harambee to fund renovation of the house where Kimathi's widow lived, and helped organize a rally of Mau Mau veterans. The author of the article sneered at Gachanja, and asserted that the Mau Mau factor

will play a very insignificant role during the coming elections. Those using the Mau Mau veterans fail to appreciate that the majority of the voters in the coming multi-party elections are young people born well after independence. To them the Mau Mau struggle for independence is part of a gallant history of this nation but not a determining factor of the outcome of the elections. (*Monthly News*, September 1992, p. 7)

As if to underline this, an advertisement for The Silver Spoon Catering Service on page 37 of the same magazine lists its contact as Kimathi P. Muriithi.

The article and the advertisement suggest the dimensions of the Mau Mau story in contemporary Kenya. It has passed into memory and is revered in retrospect but has no direct influence on the political choices of those with no living connection with the events. Mau Mau veterans, especially "generals" of the movement, were exhibited at several gatherings in mid-1992, but each time the authenticity and political relevance of the men were openly doubted. For instance: "The MP for Kiharu, Mr. G. M. Mweru, questioned the purpose of the rallies being held by ex-Mau Mau veterans. He asked the Office of the President to give a list of the genuine ex-Mau Mau generals, saying some of those who had been addressing meetings were bogus" (*Nation*, June 22, 1992, 5).

The Mau Mau fighters ceased to be people with memories themselves, who might be interviewed (though they are interviewed for newspapers, and say they have been denied land they were promised). They were, like Kimathi, an image to be posted and juxtaposed with others, used to stress the legitimacy of a party. The particular kind of legitimacy of the surviving Mau Mau was not that of a testimonial: heroes signaling their approval. Rather, it was an appeal for continuity. Kenya was a one-party state until recently; KANU, the ruling party, was descended from the single party of the first president, Jomo Kenyatta. The Mau Mau period took place before KANU was ever formed, but Kenyatta himself was placed on trial for harboring Mau Mau sympathies. The Mau Mau presence sanctifies that single-party continuity. It is a kind of room that KANU promoters like Gachanja try to construct and which opponents like MP Mweru try to keep from being constructed.

The living proximity to the founding of the nation and the formation of a national identity in common opposition to a colonial power associates experiences with the artifacts of that founding. The Mau Mau veterans are living links with those origins and they can be brought to testify to its recurrence. Kimathi is a photograph and more easily used. They might simply be collected into a space and piously recalled. But thought there are such collections, some of them owned and exhibited by the Mau Mau generals, the memory room is unstable. Because most Kenyans were born later and yet there remain veterans, the internal space of the place made of the Mau Mau cannot be consolidated. It is memory wandering in search of a room to contain it.

During the "ethnic clashes" that occurred during the early months of

1992 where were reports of "oathing" in the forests. Oathing calls up the Mau Mau. Mutungi (1977:99) notes:

With the increased tenacity to political power of individuals and groups of individuals, it seems naive to forget that political power cares little about technical legalism. Any means to get into, and retain, political power will meet their needs. Thus, during the struggle for independence from colonialism, most freedom fighters and their supporters took oaths as a solidarity measure towards power. The Mau Mau movement in Kenya is too recent an example to be forgotten.

The clashes were eruptions of violence over disputed land. Kalenjin groups in parts of western Kenya were attempting to evict Kikuyu, Luhya, and others from land the Kalenjin claimed to be theirs. Rumor had it, and a parliamentary commission report (eventually rejected by that body) verified, that the clashes were instigated by politicians and local leaders seeking to encroach upon land owned by members of "other" ethnic groups. The oathing was clearly a recollection of the Mau Mau resistance against constituted power, practiced both by the Kalenjin warriors and their Kikuyu opponents. Its practice was doubly evocative, for whatever power it might have to fashion a mystical solidarity, it also suggested the underlying significance of the Mau Mau insurrection. It was not only a battle against colonists but a civil war among the Kikuyu, and between Kikuyu and other groups who collaborated with colonists (Ogot 1972). Oathing associated with land clashes in 1992 called up this Kikuyu particularity of the Mau Mau. It displaced the uniform national memory—the kind in those museum rooms—with a stronger, antagonistic memory of conflict between those united to form Kenya. This was while the very politicians later accused of fomenting the clashes and supplying arms were denouncing "tribalism" as contrary to the KANU motto "amaini, upendo, umoja" ("peace, love, unity"). Oathing is an image of solidarity in the forest in the presence of unsettled, un-Christian powers (most Kenyans are Christians), in opposition to the peace, love, unity motto of the nation. It was memory as action, refusing a room. Huts were burned and people massacred with arrows. Warriors emerged from the forest to attack farmers. Refugees crowded relief agencies in cities. Ironic similarities to events in nearby Somalia, Ethiopia, and Sudan were pointed out. The Ugandan authorities noted that there were Kenyan refugees in their country rather than the other way around. While oathing may have recalled the Mau Mau, the actual circumstances of the clashes were very much of the moment, and the evocation of the past was merely an attempt to divorce Kenyan events from happenings in surrounding states. The room was built to isolate, but its walls were permeable. Kenya was in the Africa of the news, whatever arguments for uniqueness were being fashioned in the museum of its own history.

In early June 1992, word spread around Eldoret, Kenya that a seventy-three year old woman in an estate on the outskirts of the city had borne a child. Opinions ranged from a renewed faith in miracles to educated skepticism. The team of reporters from the *Nation* newspaper who interviewed Lucy Njoki Njenga at her home (26 June 1992:16–17) found (and photographed) her nursing a newborn child she insisted was her own. Among other facts about her life they learned that she had been a Mau Mau freedom fighter during Kenya's war of liberation in the 1960s. Mzee Kenyatta had given her land, however, in appreciation of her performances as a Nyakinyua traditional dancer. Much of the land was later grabbed by a powerful politician, but she was able to hold on to two acres with the help of other influential parties and now lives off the rental of huts on the land. Mau Mau does not play a central role in the lady's account of herself, yet once again it seems to express a person's spirit outside of history. Njoki's tenancy of the land, granted by the founding father, was contested but affirmed, though reduced, and she now lives among her grandchildren, demonstrating her capacity not only to produce but to nurture one more child. There is a Kikuyu ethnic element in her self-proclamation and even more so an assertion of womanhood in defiance of both age and the encroachment of male deal-makers. The repute of the Mau Mau is set among these other attributes, and Njoki herself represents it in the totality of the impression she creates. She does not reminisce about her freedom-fighting days; possibly the generative symbolism of her Born Again Christian faith is more important in her presentation of the infant. A Mau Mau imagery coming about is intrinsic to the experience of those she addresses.

Njoki is clearly a Kikuyu woman living in the large Kikuyu community of Eldoret, and those ever land-grabbing politicians evidently are Kalenjin, though once again the codes are clear and do not need to be made explicit. Her story may simply be the sort of oddment that gossip and newspapers pick up and spread around, for the sake of entertainment that touches upon lively categories. But Njoki's declaration seems to be an effort to form and stabilize the Kikuyu ethnic memory room of the Mau Mau under the circumstances of the 1992 clashes. Women actually were prominent in Mau Mau fighting, and their images are on the walls of the public exhibits in Nairobi. At her age, Njoki could refer to that experience, to a gift of land from Kenyatta bestowed not because of her freedom-fighting role but because of her skill in performing a Kikuyu dance form. Her claim is precisely a woman's claim, to have brought forth new life in old age while holding on to her remaining property. Like other Kikuyu women in the area she is a good businesswoman, making a living from that property. And if, as the newspaper commentators felt constrained to demonstrate, no woman of Njoki's age has ever conceived a child, the possibility is interesting because it precipitates a desired, even needed, symbolism.

A young woman who herself has just given birth to a girl tells a story of the role of women in the Mau Mau rising. The context of her tale was a discussion of Kikuyu women and their aggressiveness. The Mau Mau fighters, she said, had only sticks and pangas as weapons and their only source of firearms was the British. An elderly woman would in the presence of soldiers try to load onto her back a pile of firewood branches. She would deliberately stumble and collapse under the weight (even though these women were and are perfectly capable of carrying such loads). A soldier, schooled in manners like all British and believing that all old women are feeble, would come to assist the woman. While he was busy helping her to remove or refasten the load, the woman would stab him with a concealed knife and quickly escape with his gun. Thus the Mau Mau gained their arms.

While these two tales of Mau Mau women are not enough to illustrate a major trend, they seem to be attempts to use the available Mau Mau materials to make a place for women, distinct from the rallies where Mau Mau generals are exhibited—locations constructed by men with outwardly political motives. It might even seem that the much-discussed "truth" about the Mau Mau is that the revolt turned around a conflict between men and women, not between colonists and natives, British and Kenyans, or loyalist Kikuyu and revolutionary Kikuyu. These battles have been absorbed with time, but a consequence of the land clashes has been to further the dispossession of women and reduce their capacity to manage households. Njoki and other women are using Mau Mau references to make a memory room that is literally a household standing against the onslaught of technology wielded by males, whether it be farming equipment or guns.

The two official rooms where Kenyans can go to commune publicly with images and artifacts of the Emergency are presented as Kenyan rooms juxtaposed to the rooms created or appropriated by the colonists. The room on the upper floor of the national archives is above a large collection of African implements and artworks made by a Kenyan collector. It is only very loosely organized and lacks the explanatory catalogues, conservation, or security of collections of comparable worth elsewhere. The historical exhibit in the National Museum is set off in a building with the Large Mammals exhibit. It is over the Lamu Room, a recreation of a Swahili house formed by another Kenyan collector. The new rooms being formed by men and women in the arena of public events, in the news, and in their recollections seem to stand in the same relation with the official rooms that those rooms stand with the colonial rooms at the museums and in private houses. Recall J. H.'s room with its evocation of a distant Europe and a rejected Afrikaaner past. Kenyans themselves make memories to satisfy immediate needs and because the national resources of memory have not been settled. What is the status of the fossils and artifacts of a Pleistocene site like Koobi Fora? Were they available for construction into a place of Kenyan memory would that stabilize the process? Memories without places and places without memories form the Kenyan present. How can the national room form while the first president, Jomo Kenyatta, is still a Kikuyu, and the current president, Daniel arap Moi, is still a Kalenjin? It is as if George Washington were only a Virginian or Mahatma Gandhi a Rajput and nothing else. Mau Mau come into memory rooms contested and variously interpreted.

Chaptering the Narrative: The Material of Memory in Kilimanjaro, Tanzania

Donna O. Kerner

INTRODUCTION

In 1989, while on a short return trip to my field site in Tanzania's northeast region, Kilimanjaro, I stumbled upon an ethnographic puzzle concerning the traditions and conventions related to an aspect of material culture known as *mregho*. The Chagga people (the primary residents of the region) conceptualize mregho as the embodiment of historical memory and cultural knowledge. The embodiment takes the material form of inscribed sticks, but mregho also refers to the set of lessons, exegeses, and performances that accompany the use of the sticks in a critical phase of adolescent initiation ceremonies.

As I began to explore the phenomenon of mregho I discovered considerable variation in the way my informants from different areas of the region thought about it. Some, mainly older informants, viewed mregho as a tradition of the past, worthy of recording and preservation, and representing a form of indigenous literacy. Others (varying in age, but with some formal school), viewed mregho as living, vital memory and moral rules and were interested in reinstating the rituals surrounding it. Yet other informants claimed ignorance about both the material sticks and the context surrounding their social use.

My exploration of the meaning of mregho led me along a number of different paths simultaneously. As an aspect of initiation, mregho can be understood as loci of key cultural symbols (Beidelman 1971, 1986; Kuper 1947; Turner 1962, 1967; Wilson 1957), processes that structure social representations of age, generation, and time (Baxter and Almagor 1978; Evans-Pritchard 1951; Gluckman 1962; Spencer 1970), and organizational forms that operate to transmit social knowledge (LaFontaine 1977; Richards 1956). Oral texts, such as those provided in mregho performance and contained in song, riddle, and proverb, have generally been regarded in the literature on sub-Saharan initiation rites as instrumental in moving ceremonies from one transition phase to another. Yet it appeared to me that a more intriguing approach was to question how and why oral texts were attached to material objects in the first place. What was the purpose of these visual, conceptual maps? Were they merely mnemonic devices or something more?

Next I was interested in understanding the flexibility in my informants' view of mregho as unchanging tradition and living process. Thanks to the growing scholarly interest in popular memory studies (see Popular Memory Group 1982), it is possible to begin an examination of mregho with the accepted dictum of Durkheim and his students, most notably Halbwachs (1950), that memory is a social fact and historical traditions are frequently invented to justify claims in the present. Several recent studies have also illuminated how memory in preliterate societies may be embodied through social transaction (Battaglia 1992; Connerton 1989). However, the phenomenon of mregho challenges us to pose a set of questions about just what types of texts or narratives are socially constituted as memory, which are viewed as static or open to interpretation, and how different types of narratives are related to each other. The Chagga cultural memory glossed as mregho is contained in three textual formats: the inscribed sticks, the oral texts, and written accounts that describe and explain the sticks, oral narratives, and rituals. Informants have different ways of understanding the interrelationship of these different textual forms depending upon their generational position, level of education and literacy, gender, and clan affiliation. For example, a number of elderly men who were formally educated during the colonial period, held salaried jobs in the civil service, and are respected as local intellectuals, are well versed in ethnographic and historic accounts of the Chagga, including some of the materials on mregho. Their reading of recorded accounts dating back to the 1920s informs their own oral history research on mregho performance. Because within their lifetimes they have witnessed the eclipse of oral tradition by written narrative as a basis for asserting historical truth claims, the way that they choose to interpret one body of memory over another on behalf of the groups they represent illuminates the broader problem of memory studies in complex modern societies:

namely, how do oral and written histories intersect in the construction of collective memory? From their particular liminal vantage point, indigenous African intellectuals may reveal to us how recontextualization, that is, the dropping or adding of historical elements or the insertion of these elements into new genres (Fentress and Wickham 1992), is enacted as historical process.

From a third perspective, I was curious to understand why there was something of a revival of interest in mregho throughout Kilimanjaro at the close of the 1980s. In other words, what does the activation of the recontextualization process signal about how different factions of a community are responding to the social problems and opportunities that confront them?

This chapter gives a preliminary answer to several of these questions and might be most productively read as structuring the research agenda for a larger, long-term collaborative project (Kerner and Mneney [eds.], forthcoming).[1] The material for the chapter was drawn from a variety of sources: interviews with Chagga intellectuals between 1991 and 1993; texts collected by these informants of reconstructed mregho performances in the 1950s and 1960s; Lutheran missionary Bruno Gutmann's German translations of mregho texts collected in the early 1920s; District Commissioner Charles Dundas's analysis of texts collected by mission converts (1924); missionary/sociologist Otto Raum's reanalysis of Gutmann's materials in the 1940s; and the late paramount chief Petro Itosi Marealle's Swahili translations of mregho texts (1947). This chapter focuses exclusively on mregho instruction for boys. Chagga girls also underwent mregho instruction, but contemporary examples of oral texts for girls' mregho have proved more difficult to obtain.

The section that follows provides a brief summary of some of the structural features of Chagga society to enable readers to appreciate the historical and contemporary context of mregho. I will then discuss the textual and performative elements of mregho in initiation ceremonies and provide two contexts in which mregho traditions are currently harnessed to contemporary social problems. In the conclusion I return to the problem of how different forms of knowledge are reconstituted as memory in the process of recontextualization.

LOCATING CHAGGA CULTURE

The Chagga people, who inhabit Mount Kilimanjaro in Tanzania's northeast, occupy one of the most favored econiches on the continent.

Historians and linguists reckon that the contemporary population on the mountain, now over one million (United Republic of Tanzania 1988), settled on the fertile mountain slopes in successive waves of migration beginning some three hundred years ago. The diverse dialects of the contemporary population indicate hybrid cultural origins from Kamba and Maasai northern dispersals and the Shambaa and Pare areas to the south. The earliest nineteenth-century explorers and missionaries to the mountain discovered thriving agricultural communities based on banana as a staple crop, with well-established links to other societies through long-distance trade. Control over the provisioning trade with Swahili caravans to the coast and interior served to shore up the accumulated wealth and power of chiefs in the approximately one hundred petty chiefdoms in the pre-colonial period (Moore 1986; Rogers 1972; Stahl 1964). In other words, these were "open" societies in which new forms of knowledge, alliances (with Swahili traders, missionaries, and later, colonial administrators), and new types of technologies could be utilized by one chiefdom over another to consolidate its power and extend hegemony over its neighbors. Thus, political fortunes of these different chiefdoms waxed and waned until achieving a relatively fixed status under first German, and later British, colonial rule.

Owing to early missionary activity, favorable climate, and progressive colonial policies in the area of cash crop production and marketing, the Kilimanjaro region enjoys a high level of infrastructural development relative to the rest of the country. The Chagga are comparatively well-educated and disproportionately represented in white collar professions and business. Close proximity to the northern safari tourist zone and the Kenyan border has provided commercial and service sector opportunities to Kilimanjaro residents and insured open transport and communication links within and beyond the region. Peasant communities on the mountain are "straddling" economies with households engaged in subsistence and coffee cash crop production, supplemented by income derived from wage labor and business enterprises (Kerner 1988a, 1988b). The Chagga are predominantly Catholic and Lutheran, the missionaries having divided the souls of different chiefdoms. Chiefdomship was abolished after independence in the early 1960s. The lands held by patrilineal clans are, at least on paper, now absorbed into the village, ward, and district system of the state. Chagga dialects are still commonly spoken on the mountain, although these days almost all are fluent in the national language, Swahili, compulsory education having served as a major homogenizing influence.

The contemporary stance projected by the Chagga to outsiders is urbane and progressive. Progress is a key word invoked with pride to indicate a long familiarity with Western religion, education, and technological advances. It also signals attitudes and values that the Chagga believe foster economic prosperity: achievement motivation, a Protestant work ethic, and a disdain for status-leveling beliefs and practices such as witchcraft and ancestral cursing. Sorcery, ancestral sacrifices, consultation with traditional healers, divination, and some aspects of initiation ritual continue to be practiced within these modern communities, but in limited secrecy so as not to incur the reprisals of church officials. Thus, while the superficial appearance of Chagga culture has all but disappeared, giving way to an image of accommodation and assimilation, the substratum of cultural values and beliefs continues, albeit in modified form. Occasionally elements of this substratum percolate to the surface, as with the current dialogue about the reinstatement of mregho instruction.

THE BESTOWAL OF MEMORY
THROUGH MREGHO

The Social Context of Mregho Instruction

Initiation constituted but one part of the continuous socialization process in the precolonial period in which children were taught the rules and etiquette required for life in the community. Texts collected by the German missionary Bruno Gutmann (1922/23) indicate that the Chagga conceptualization of the person was submerged within communal bonds and sentiment and within the larger sphere of generative forces connecting all living things. Early childhood socialization through songs, riddles, proverbs, and rebukes served to teach and reinforce the categorization of persons and things so as not to unleash potentially destructive supernatural forces.

However, the socialization of youth reached its apex at initiation, when the full knowledge of the adult community was revealed to newly circumcised boys (in the bush) and girls (inside the house) during a period of extended seclusion (Dundas 1924; Gutmann 1922/23; and Raum 1940). This training was considered part of the preliminary steps toward *wali*, the marriage ceremony. Only those provided with proper knowledge and understanding were considered fit to manage a household and enter into the life of the community as full persons (Marealle 1947).

Gutmann was particularly emphatic that mregho instruction represented a distinct phase of initiation into adulthood, following circumcision and extended lessons during the recovery period in the sacred meadow. The first two phases of initiation were organized under the purview of the chief and were designed to mystically bond the newly initiated age set (*rika*) to the chief's court. The male rika served as the military force under the chief, and his power in part derived from their good will, since they could depose his designated heir if he proved politically or magically incompetent.

By contrast, mregho instruction took place among a smaller subset of the rika and members of the next ascending age-set, and it was organized by parents of the initiates and elders of the local patrilineal kin group. Initiates might be taught singly or in small groups, but extant texts indicate that these lessons had the feel of a family affair. The parents of the initiate would contract a respected elder, the *meku* (ideally the paternal grandfather), to carve the mregho stick. The stick was approximately 140–170 cm long and divided into eighteen to twenty-three sections by bark rings that separated subsections of smaller carving consisting of inclined and vertical lines, circles, and triangles. An assistant to the elder, the *mwitsi* (interpreter/counselor), was also recruited from the rank of the next ascending age-set. The mwitsi was ideally an elder brother or paternal cousin, and he later would serve as the go-between in the initiate's marriage negotiations. An elaborate three-day banana brewing ceremony opened the mregho instruction and involved the elders, counselors, initiates, their sisters, and their parents. Gutmann's long exegesis of prayers during this opening ceremony indicates that its purpose was to awaken the life force linking all members of the patrilineal kin group, living and dead, to the vital power of the land:

I cut you banana for a teaching, for a son of this house, for the child of the old one who moved into this land and found no field but he broke the earth and brought forth his sons. For this son we are cutting so that he will prosper and grow and cultivate and bring forth sons for whom we cut here. . . . Help me to awaken the life power of banana so that banana may shoot up like the reed kiwale which is sought for the children to open up their throats so they may begin to speak. (1922/23:87)

The primary device for imparting knowledge was the mregho stick and its performance. The knowledge imparted was of two types: knowledge of *things*, which inhered in relationships (in other words, sensory experience mediated through transaction with others) and knowledge of *how to do things* (skill knowledge). The inscriptions on the stick were represented to initiates as a cosmology of the human body, and served as a schematic map that preserved the memory of how experience was to be interpreted and understood.

Knowledge of Things: The Performance of Mregho

Mregho instruction took place over several days and inverted the normal course of activities by beginning at sundown and finishing before sunrise. Texts from the chiefdoms of Old Moshi, Marangu, and Kibosho differ in length, order, and content, but all seem to have been "read" from bottom to top. Lessons from mregho recapitulate ontogeny, beginning with the bottom of the human body (the foot) and ending at the top (head hair). Ontological exegesis was interwoven with lessons concerning procreation, growth, morbidity, and death. Nested in these lessons were further lessons to insure the health of the body politic.

Mregho teaching consisted of a call and response song performed by the meku and mwitsi. The meku would begin each text by intoning the prayer, "Stillness, oh Great Stillness" (a praise feature of the Chagga God *Ruwa*, the silent listener), and would follow with a "puzzle song" to be unraveled by the mwitsi. Texts from the first two sections of the Old Moshi mregho capture the sense of the performance:

Meku (pointing at the first of five triangles): "Stillness, oh Great Stillness, the staff of the little man (initiate). Here it is. You man who are the one to teach, tell me from the staff of the little man, what is it that created you?"

Mwitsi (speaking to initiate): "When the old man sings he has created you. When God created you in your mother's body and gave you your heel, this is the first thing he created. Thus you were created in the darkness and you were given the heel in order to stand up. This is what is shown here."

Meku (pointing at the second of five triangles): "Stillness, oh Great Stillness, the youth that are apprentices here today you are growing out. The mother is the snail shell (house) of tenderness. Tell me of the staff of the little man, what is it here which created you? What is it?"

Mwitsi (to initiate): "What the old man sings he is telling you that the sole of your foot it is that which has been created for you in the darkness of your mother and you have become a human being. Do not dare to insult your mother who has brought you up so that you have become a human being. If your mother has said anything that has irritated you, that you hate, you must swallow it into your sole and remain quiet. When the old man sings, mother is the snail shell of tenderness, so it is in the mother's womb. You were entombed in liquid and you have been drawn together. Your father has put you into your mother's womb through fluid and you have developed and you have become a human being. If you had developed without a sole you would have remained like a stick and would not have been able to walk. If you are walking on this sole, you are bringing an animal to present to your mother when she is old and still she has nourished you and brought you up from a formless mass." (1922/23:89–90)

Gutmann's informants stressed that mregho instruction was a life-long lesson. Initiates would eventually serve as mwitsi and mwitsi would eventually serve as meku. Textual performance and interpretive competence improved and reinforced memory at each successive lesson as the actors acquired deeper levels of understanding. Interpretive debate and errors (for which the mwitsi owed the meku a payment) served not only to consolidate the lesson, but sometimes worked to change the text. The use of "deep" (esoteric, secret) language, designed to hide meaning from strangers and the uninitiated, also changed the interpretive texts over time. Collective memory was at one level perceived as static and unchanging, renewed in the course of each generation by the act of inscription, performance, and memorization. On another level, inscriptions and texts varied from lineage to lineage and chiefdom to chiefdom, shifting with individual memory and new social challenges.

Powerful Words and the Conceptualization of Time

What power inhered in the relationship between mregho sticks and their texts? The sticks themselves seem not to have been the locus of power that transformed young men into adults. They were not fetishes; they were carved anew for each initiate, and kept (according to informants) under the bed until the birth of the man's first son. At that time, the man's father would call for the mregho to light the cooking fire for the sacrificial animal to celebrate the cutting of the umbilical cord. The act of destroying mregho by fire completed a cycle of reproduction and linked it to the next successive cycle. Firstborn children take the name of their paternal grandparents and are thought to inherit their life force and personality characteristics. The relationship between meku and initiate reinforced this alterity by leading the initiate through a recapitulation of biological and social ontogeny. This cycle was completed with the birth of the first son and it was the father of the young man who called for the mregho to light the fire to cook (generate) the sacrificial animal to be shared by members of the patrilineal kin group and their ancestors on behalf of his new grandson. Thus, meku and initiate were created anew and it was the new grandfather who would inscribe the next family stick and "open the throat" of his grandson so that he might "learn to speak" (as an adult, knowledgeable person).

Because the stick itself represented a cosmology of the human body, a great number of its lessons concerned sexuality, the mystery of procreation, and growth. As Moore has noted (1976), for the Chagga, laws of society and laws of nature were viewed as inextricably linked in a single system of cause and effect. The proper combination of female and male elements and the proper sequencing of such combinations would insure generation and prosperity. Wrong combinations resulted in chaos, sickness, and death. Thus, initiation instruction began with teaching about each aspect of the human body, the form and function of organs of ingestion, elimination, and procreation, the proper sequencing of events that lead to healthy procreation, and then proceeded to lessons about food—its production and consumption—followed by instruction on practices necessary for healthy growth.

As laws of the human body and the social body politic were intertwined, mregho instruction extended to cover rules of internal security, chiefly rights and obligations, and the rules of warfare. Genealogical instruction, concerning the lives of chiefs and noble persons, was continuous throughout the lessons on the body politic. The memory of such notables was preserved in two shifting categories: the names of those who are remembered (because they have living descendants who sacrifice on their behalf) and those whose names are forgotten (because they have no living heirs). Those whose names are no longer remembered have shifted from a spiritual plane of existence where, as ancestors (the *warumu*, the living dead), they were able to influence the living, to a nether world where they no longer retain an influence on the community. They are banished to a kind of oblivion, a void explained in the Chagga creation myths as the result of the bad conduct of the original Chagga people who had the gift of eternal life revoked by God (Lema 1981). Those who are remembered are eventually erased and inserted into the "not remembered" category of mregho once their last living descendants have perished.

I contend that the fundamental element in mregho instruction is the transmission of the experience of time and how it should be understood. Gender divisions/combinations and genealogies of ancestors (the living dead) are two possible ways to contemplate the dual properties of time (Leach 1961). One is circular. Living things are born, grow up, procreate, and die, but the spiritual or vital force that connects them continues in the fashion of seasonal cycles of death and rebirth. Alternatively, time is linear. Death has a corporeal finality and even the ancestors, the living dead, cease to participate in the vital connecting force once their heirs die and they are no longer remembered. Mregho instruction seeks to resolve the problem of linear time (death and forgetting) by means of circular time (generativity and remembrance).

The power in mregho performance lay in the mystique of the texts that *created* ("When the old man sings he creates you") the initiate through symbolic rebirth and transformed him into a person. The texts also recreated culture through an exegesis of history and rules of community from the domestic level outward to the level of the chiefdom. I suggest that the radical decentering and reintegration of the initiate's understanding of time and its meaning in his social relations called for in these lessons were aided through the attachment of texts to inscribed objects. While the sticks themselves derived power only through their attachment to mystical utterance, they visually ordered for the initiate a new understanding of the past and a prediction for his future. The sticks acted as dominant symbols, analogous to the human body and analogous to a microcosm of the universe. They are an example of what Turner (1967) refers to as *sacra*: objects/symbols that use the body's attributes as a template for the communication of gnosis. While the magic of the texts transforms the social person, the template of the stick teaches neophytes to think with some degree of abstraction about their cultural milieu. The lessons on mregho are then "reinscribed" in the memories of the initiates. As Gutmann's informants put it, "the teachings are pushed deeper into their thinking."

THE RECONTEXTUALIZATION OF
MREGHO TRADITION

I became aware of revived interest in the traditions of initiation by Chagga intellectuals, primarily from the former chiefdoms of Old Moshi and Marangu, in the late 1980s. First, there was talk of young men requesting the services of elders in circumcision and mregho instruction and controversy over the revival of clitoridectomy. The motivations of the young men were unclear, but preliminary interviews in the districts where clitoridectomy was regaining popularity indicated that the practice was being reinstated at the insistence of grandmothers, who reasoned that the operation would discourage premarital sexual activity, thus minimizing the distractions to schoolgirls who needed to concentrate on their studies so as to land good salaried jobs. The second thing to come to my attention was that local intellectuals were systematically collecting mregho sticks and conducting interviews with surviving elders who had some knowledge of how to perform the ritual. One of these intellectuals attempted to enlist my aid in applying for funding for a research project on the subject and another had submitted his raw interview data to a major publishing house in the hope that it would be accepted as a book manuscript. Chagga intellectuals have now accumulated the knowledge of memory from witnessing performances and conducting interviews and have many of the written records of these rituals. The question prompted by this revival of interest in mregho is: why initiation and why now? As a tentative answer, two recent events may explain the revival of interest and use of these traditions.

Sexuality and Risk

The first event is the AIDS pandemic. The Kilimanjaro region ranks third in the nation in HIV infection and AIDS-related deaths. Owing to its high proportion of educated workers and acute land shortage, Kilimanjaro is a region characterized by out migration, particularly male migration. The common pattern has been for young men to work until in their thirties, when they have accumulated enough money to organize a lavish wedding and build a modern house on purchased or inherited land on the mountain. They then marry and leave their wives to tend the farm while they return to salaried jobs in urban areas. Delayed age of marriage and long-term separations increase the likelihood of numerous sexual contacts, thus increasing the possibilities of HIV transmission. The Chagga are aware of the modes of heterosexual transmission of the virus and their accommodation to this information has been to encourage earlier marriages. Clitoridectomy, which theoretically dampens female desire, and the revival of lessons about the moral and physical dangers of improper combinations and sequencing in sexual activity, might also be seen as part of a preventative solution.

Many of the lessons of mregho deal with questions surrounding sexuality, procreation, and growth, and a number of informants made the explicit connection between attempts to revive mregho teachings and initiation ceremonies in general with the specter of the AIDS epidemic. Whether it is only those elements that deal with the spiritual and moral dangers of sexuality that are selected for initiation revivals in this new context remains to be seen.

Memory and the Changing Political Field

While the event of AIDS represents a specter of chaos and death, another event, the introduction of multiparty politics, affords a vision of growth and opportunity. The link between multiparty politics and the revival of interest in initiation is tenuous, but suggestive. Chagga intellectuals are emphatic that the strongest mregho traditions survive in the area known as Kibosho, a former chiefdom that reached its apex in the immediate precolonial period, but lost its bid for power during the era of indirect rule. It is considered a backward area these days. I was curious as to why

Kibosho was singled out as the major locus of Chagga cultural memory. I would have guessed that another division representing a contemporary success story might have been considered the cultural center. The answer I received inevitably involved the recitation of a historical narrative about the battle involving the former chiefdom of Kibosho and its rival, Machame.

In the nineteenth century, the Machame people had committed treachery against their neighbors in Kibosho. The chief of Machame plotted to overthrow his rival by inviting Kibosho youths to participate in the Machame initiation ceremonies. His army then turned and slaughtered the Kibosho youths when they were naked and unarmed, thereby wiping out one generative half of the Kibosho population and an entire generation of future warriors. Kibosho became a tributary chiefdom to Machame, until the terrible revenge of the Kibosho chief Sina one or two generations later. Sina pillaged Machame through military cunning. His father had sent him to Machame as a young child and he had received initiation instruction there. The knowledge he had of the court and its defenses enabled him to attack with stealth and to crush the chiefdom entirely. Sina was the last and perhaps the most talented chief to utilize military might and cunning to expand and consolidate an empire of many political units beyond his borders. He brought Machame and a number of other chiefdoms to the west under his control and grew prosperous through their tribute. He reserved his harshest punishment for Machame: Machame people were henceforth forbidden to conduct initiation rituals and to use mregho.

But Sina's hegemony was not to last. He was outwitted by the diplomatic dexterity of rival chiefs in Marangu and Old Moshi who created powerful alliances with the Germans, and later by the ingenuity of the chief of Machame who was favored by the British. The history of Machame was effectively invented during British rule to sanitize its past and to justify its preferred status. Infrastructural development is highest in this part of Kilimanjaro, which received a disproportionate share of the local government budgets in the colonial and postindependence eras. The envy and hostility by which people of Machame are regarded by other Chagga are evident in comments about their "progress" and the observation that no trace of Chagga culture survives there.

At a more abstract level, then, perhaps a revived interest in Chagga cultural memory, via initiation, signals the possibility of settling old scores, equalizing opportunities for progress, and asserting moral norms for regulating competition. The new era of multiparty politics promises an opening of the field of competition and a shifting in the rules and routes to power. Two themes that run through all Chagga historical narrative are the political assets of cunning and patience: cunning to outwit your competition and the patience to wait until the time is right.

Inscription and Truth

Finally, there is the question of how Chagga intellectuals who are actively collecting sticks and text and who are familiar with the literate history and ethnography of their culture view the project they have undertaken. The question is complex, but at least their consciously stated motive is clear: they primarily want to use mregho to prove that the Chagga had developed a written language in the precolonial period. Much of their effort has gone into developing a transcription system for the notches on the sticks. Why is transcription important to them?

First, proof of a common notational system throughout the mountain in the precolonial period would authenticate claims that the Chagga were culturally unified through written language. Second, it would legitimate Chagga claims for indigenous intellectual achievements separable from their alliances with foreigners (Swahili and European). Both claims were briefly recognized during the later phases of colonial rule when the Chagga were consolidated under a paramount chief and had their own national flag. Such claims were discarded during the era of ujamaa socialism (the single-party regime) when the chieftancy was abolished and Chagga political ambitions were curbed at the national center. Might Chagga attempts at unification and claims to a capacity for rule have been reactivated by the opening of the political field? Real material benefits for the Kilimanjaro region, in the form of infrastructural development (roads, water supply systems, electrification, schools, clinics) and job patronage, are at stake as the single party system gives way to alternative platforms of choice and if the Chagga assert a visible claim to political power at the national level. The recent proliferation of new "improvement" associations throughout the mountain clamoring for registration as political parties suggests this may be the case.

CONCLUSION

Chagga intellectuals active in mregho research discuss these sticks as a book and each lesson inscribed as a chapter. They would like to write a book about this memory book, to preserve what should not be forgotten. What is the significance of equating mregho sticks with books? Are the narratives of mregho really chaptered in the linear sense of a written account? In answering this question it is useful to return to the question of how the construction of memory is related to the act of inscription and the attachment of oral narratives to material objects.

The brief example presented earlier of the call and response performance of mregho between the meku and mwitsi illustrates that something quite complicated and even puzzling occurs in the transmission of knowledge through mregho. The sticks are in one way mnemonic devices and a form of sacra, but they are more than that as well. Mregho begins with an opaque and mysterious song, followed by an interpretive response during which a puzzle is unraveled in conjunction with pointing to an object map. Unraveling the puzzle and pointing are accompanied by a debate/elaboration that serves to reinforce both that which is known (and now to be learned in a new way) and that which is previously unknown to initiates. The performative context of mregho suggests that it is the layering of texts that enables elders to discuss dangerous things with young men: sexuality, hierarchy, political treachery, rules of warfare.

Many of these lessons about dangerous things are a form of knowledge of things that inhere in relationships with people (rules governing relations between agnatic/affinal kin, men and women, parents, children and siblings, commoners and nobles). The rules and the consequences for transgressing them are laid out. But the dangerous lessons also contain a form of knowledge about how to do things. Mregho texts begin with a description of the function of each body part, but then layered within these are further lessons about how to cure illnesses that afflict each part of the body, the steps for ritual preparation at each successive stage of life, and etiquette for every different type of social encounter. This skill knowledge also carries explicit and implicit warnings about the destructive consequences of failure to perform ceremonies, sequence ritual preparations correctly, or breach good manners.

That a loosely constituted group of Chagga elders currently would like to reconceptualize mregho sticks as books at this point in time when the norms of family life, community, and definitions of the political field are highly in flux seems more than coincidental. What is clear in this exercise is a recontextualization in which two types of knowledge, the memory of things (inhering in relations with persons) and the memory of how to do things (skill knowledge), are inserted into a different genre: memory about things (e.g., historical and ethnographic "facts"). Memory about things is propositional knowledge (Fentress and Wickham 1992). It is contingent and temporary and can be detached from the person who possesses it. It is essentially the memory that is seen as objective and therefore considered to have greater power to assert truth claims. If mregho sticks are actually books, then their power is, as one elder put it, "equal to that of the bible,

both of which I keep under my bed to remind me of what I need to know."
A focus on the process of recontextualization suggests that chaptering the
narrative of mregho is a radical agenda (to equate an indigenous corpus
of ritual knowledge with the Christian bible) embedded in a conservative
maneuver. The perils and possibilities of change would seem to require
more than the reification of an authenticated collective memory.

NOTES

Funding for the research project upon which this chapter is based was granted
by the Hewlett-Mellon and Wenner-Gren foundations. Research affiliations in
Tanzania were provided by the University of Dar es Salaam and the Cooperative
College, Moshi, during the years 1990–1991. I am grateful to these institutions
for their support and want to acknowledge with special thanks the help of Messrs.
Foya, Meney, and Ntiro. Fr. Kiesel of the Lutheran Church Archives in Moshi
provided me with copies of Gutmann's manuscripts on mregho and Marealle's
manuscript on Chagga culture. This chapter grew out of two earlier versions
presented as papers at the American Anthropological Association meeting in
San Francisco (1992) and at Northwestern University's Institute for Advanced
Study and Research in the African Humanities in 1993 and reprinted in the journal
Passages, no. 7 (summer 1994). Critical comments from Karen Barber, Jacob
Climo, and Marea Teski have helped me to strengthen the analysis presented here,
but I take full credit for the errors that may remain.

1. A project such as this raises immediate questions about the problem of
translation. For example, Winter (1979) calls attention to Gutmann's idiosyncratic
and often ambiguous translations of certain key Chagga concepts. His theories
of social evolution and his particular model of folk psychology appear to have
been influential in his word choice. Chagga intellectuals, working with contemporary
oral Chagga texts translated into Swahili, sometimes find themselves influenced
by previous analyses based on English translations of German translations of
archaic Chagga oral texts. In the long run, the only possible solution to such
translation difficulties is a collaborative effort between social scientists and local
intellectuals who possess a good working knowledge of the different Chagga
dialects and who can return to the original sources and check their translations of
key concepts with a number of living elders. Translation problems aside, my
understanding of mregho, then and now, is framed by a substantial body of
literature on Chagga ethnography and history (e.g., Moore 1976, 1986; Rogers
1972; Stahl 1964) and my own fieldwork in Kilimanjaro, which took place over
the decade between 1983 and 1994.

It Only Counts If You Can Share It

Molly G. Schuchat

First I would like to share two incidents that incorporate a past and its memories with a more recent event, connections made possible by voice-to-voice communication.

In 1946, as the culmination of my freshman year at Vassar College, I spent several weeks in Tennessee and Alabama immersed in the field trip component of a multidiscipline course on the Tennessee Valley Authority. It was a very significant exposure, enlisting me in the cause of regional development and at the same time making me shockingly aware of the full horrors and outrages of segregation as a continued blot on this great land of ours.

There were twenty of us students, two professors, and the Greyhound Bus driver, visiting rural electrification sites, dams and their reservoir parks, cities, the fertilizer plant at Mussel Shoals, and the still almost secret Oak Ridge town. Of the last I only recollect a maze of wire fences and wooden sidewalks over the mud.

But the dams I recollect in great detail. They were thrilling, with their majestic, powerful spillways and their huge round turbines down low inside the power stations. The interiors themselves were very moving, each with a wall where aluminum letters spelled out the triumphant proclamation: "Built for the People of the United States of America."

But flanking and circumscribing that proud statement were a pair of water fountains built into wall niches with their chiseled signs "White" and "Colored." This, more than explicit behaviors (although there were many), was my most searing visual memory of that expedition and what was terribly wrong with the region.

This was my only personal experience of "the midsouth" until 1991, when I spent a term at a historically Black college in Mississippi, a state in which I had never before set foot and which I had regarded as a backwater to be avoided at all costs. I found that it is not, and there are many continuing changes in that still mostly rural world.

During this recent term in the South, my husband and I took a day trip to visit Shiloh Battlefield in nearby Tennessee. It was not far from Pickwick Landing Dam, near the Alabama border, and we continued on there. We parked beside the spillway and walked into the same power house I had visited forty-five years before and faced the same aluminum sign, "1935—Built for the People of the United States—1938," the same interior bridge from which we looked down on the same turbines below. We turned and there were the two fountain niches on either side of the entrance door, but the "colored" and "white" designations chiseled into the walls above had been removed and the fountains, too, replaced by potted plants. The combination of recognized return and dramatic symbolic change was stunning!

My memory-view had the two fountains adjoining the proclamation, instead of on opposite walls of the power house lobby. The current reality is that drinking water is available from a metal cold water dispenser located in a corridor off the lobby, between the men's and women's rest rooms (there used to be four rest rooms, too).

Fundamentally, it was not selective memory being shown up but a change in technology and the mores of the region and the nation that affected me. Thrilled though I was, and sharing this with my husband, who had heard about the "symbol of the divisions in this great land of ours" over many years, the triumph of truth and memory was only confirmed that evening when I spoke on the phone with a college classmate in upstate New York. Together we had shared that TVA course and been introduced to "real" southern culture so many years before. She was equally jubilant at this fantastic manifestation of the changes we, of course, "knew" had taken place: We had seen TV; we had read articles and books. But as Flo said, "If you hadn't reached me right away, it would have lost so much meaning."

The second memory incident involves my husband, who was recommissioned and served on a destroyer—the U.S.S. *Bache*—during the Korean War, before we were married. Over the subsequent years he had frequently recounted a number of his war and sea stories, and several of his shipmates had visited us.

One night in the fall of 1969, listening to the evening news, Mike was startled to hear that the *Bache* had foundered on the rocks off the Island of Rhodes in the Aegean Sea and that the crew had abandoned ship and sought refuge at the Rhodes Yacht Club. Hardly had he begun to digest this shocking information when the phone rang, the first of an incessant number of calls exchanged well into the night.

"Mike, get back aft and get those pumps working," he was ordered by a voice not heard for seventeen years but instantly recognized. Subsequent calls made and received were to share congratulations on how well the abandon ship bill, written by Mike, had actually worked. On that and other matters, all were assured by the former executive officer and each other that "nothing could be pinned on us!"

A chain of fellow sailors got in touch with each other to mourn the end of their ship, always a terrible tragedy, and recall their time together knowing that now, for sure, it really was just memory. Not unnaturally, the decision was also made to have a reunion in person the following month.

Although I commiserated and shared that evening's news, obviously the tragedy and triumph were over the phone, where old meanings were brought up to date by new events that did not change the past but abruptly extended commonalities into the present. The subsequent physical reunion was a pleasure, but again, just old tall stories, recalled in tranquility, not the "reality" of that long night.

These examples illustrate both the reality of personal memory and the meaning of social life. The journey to the present is too vast to grasp by one's own actions alone, but by anchoring one's image to others' images, it is possible for it to become more than a movie or a photograph, but rather a continuing or renewed dialogue. Perhaps, being an anthropologist interested in communication and memory, I ruminate more about the conjunction of history and personality than I otherwise might. But they lend poignancy to a discussion of necessary interaction that is different from recall and review. It may be why the majority of TV tapes and home movies stay on the home library shelves, unlooked at. They recall the past, but need a comparable or culminating event to make that recall meaningful. Reunions are fine but they are time-out rather than renewed reality.

The relationships invoked in these two incidents are different from those familial ones that Jacob Climo discusses in his studies of distant familial communication (Climo 1992 and this volume), relationships commencing with life's beginning and the model from which subsequent ones are developed, gradually enveloped in an over-arching and more encompassing world. The present stories relate to shared young adult experiences with people who are not relatives, nor do they have continuing work or place relationships. However, they do relate to significant occasions and/or relationships from those early adult years, fixed in time and place. They may entail "flashbulb memories," unusually detailed and durable memories of the circumstances under which very surprising and emotionally arousing experiences or insights occurred (Conway 1993, citing Brow and Kulik).

Recent behavioral science research reports how the present paints the past, revealing people's propensity to forget parts of their lives that no longer fit with their current images of themselves. However, by checking memory of the past with others, more and clearer memories are made available (see Goleman 1987; Freeman, Romney, and Freeman 1987).

My TVA memory and the transferred location of the water fountains is reminiscent (!) of the account by Ulric Neisser of John Dean's testimony of conversations with President Nixon. Dean was Nixon's counsel who "spilled the beans" to the Senate Watergate committee. Meanwhile, Nixon had been secretly taping all his Oval Office talks. So Neisser compared Dean's later account with the Nixon tapes. He found Dean's testimony was often wrong on details but right on the substance (Neisser 1982). So, too, with my recollection.

For both self-correcting mechanisms and reinforcement of original perceptions and misperceptions, there is nothing like both instant and/or continued contact, a subject to be returned to later. As to the efficacy of tape recording interchanges to validate recall, let us also not forget the 18.5 minute ellipsis in the Nixon tapes!

The twentieth century has permitted us to keep in contact with each other and to interact through time as no time before in Western culture. The electrical signals activated by Samuel Morse traveled through wires, but radio is broadcast through space using electromagnetic waves. With Edison's phonograph, sounds could be saved as squiggles on a foil-wrapped cylinder and played time and again. Radio, TV, and tape recording made it clear that pictures as well as sounds could be transmitted and stored using patterns of electromagnetism. Therefore, when it was discovered that electromagnetic waves emanate from the brain, the idea of storing information in some physical medium had become less mysterious.

Now, so much more is being discovered and discussed concerning the brain, recording, and recall. This leads to attempts to put together theories of memory that draw from biology, psychology, computer science, physics, and philosophy, with the goal "to explain not only how we store individual facts but how we weave them together into a world view" (Johnson 1991:15, quoting Gary Lynch).

The renewed interchanges I am talking about revolve around telephone communication, although they could have as easily been any other interactive communication medium on our new technological highway. It is the immediacy of the interaction that is important in relation to the significance of the events old and new.

Postman laments that the decline of the Age of Typography and the ascendancy of the Age of Television dramatically and irreversibly shifted the content and meaning of public discourse, "since two media so vastly different cannot accommodate the same ideas." As the influence of print wanes, the content of politics, religion, education, and anything else that comprises public business must change and be recast in terms that are most suitable to television. He adds that "speech, of course, is the primal and indispensable medium. It made us human, keeps us human, and in fact defines what human means" (Postman 1985:8–9).

But the memory on TV screens does not connect us in the way that speech does, and the view from TV may not connect us at all unless we have been there before and can see ourselves there. Moreover, unless we share that with someone who was there *then*, it is still an empty memory. Looking at the places where one shared an experience that entered the bloodstream, so to speak, does not have real meaning unless shared with whoever else's bloodstream it entered.

Myerhoff wrote, "It is now commonplace to recognize the relativity of experience" (1992:313). Gergen invokes her work and that of earlier toilers in the vineyards of phenomenology ranging from Alfred Schutz to Thomas Kuhn:

As we see, although the intellectual origins differ, both the contextualist and the constructionist reach similar conclusions. Social actions, as matters of common concern, owe their existence to the social process whereby meanings are generated and events indexed by these meanings. There are no independently identifiable, real-world referents to which the language of social description is cemented. (Gergen 1986:145)

Or as Jonathan Friedman (1992) asserts: "The past is always practiced in the present because subjects in the present fashion the past in the practice of their social identity."

It was just before December 7, 1991, that I renewed acquaintance with Pickwick Landing Dam. Driving home on the highways and the back roads, we listened to the radio, where all comments, national and local, seemed fixated on remembering Pearl Harbor, fifty years before: Nostalgia, nostalgia, nostalgia, and bombs and betrayal.

One hopes it will be less persuasive and pervading than much of the mid-south's preoccupation with the Civil War, although even that may have begun to be replaced by more recent conflicts. All during our Southern sojourn in 1991, we saw American rather than Confederate flags flying from homes and autos, most often bound up with yellow ribbons, a rite transformed to celebrate victory in the Persian Gulf rather than the humiliation of hostages in Iran or at any other place or time.

In relation to Pearl Harbor nostalgia, I suppose the media's focus was not so much on "a day that will live in infamy" as on the depression and discouragement so many felt as Japan and Germany seemed to be "winning" now, so many years after their defeat, as their money and their markets were more buoyant than ours in the United States. There was current reevaluation of the past, but not closure and resolution.

Hobsbawm has argued that where the old ways are alive, even in personal memory, "traditions need be neither revived nor invented" (1983:8). But in a fascinating discourse among the Hajj, Lavie, and Rouse concerning "The Fantastic Journey" (The Hajj, Smadar, Lavie, and Forest Rouse 1993), the anthropologist hypothesizes that the Hajj is able to point out to her the transformation of a variety of Bedouin customs into an artificial (colonial textual) tradition because, for him and the others of his generation, the old ways "exist only as fragments of experiential memory that no longer cohere into a culture of spontaneous everyday life" (375).

In the mid-south towns through which we drove that Saturday in December, it was also the day for the local Christmas parades, joint efforts of the county schools—which provided the floats and children, and the stores on the square and on the edge of town—which provided the gifts and gathering places at parade close. The gifts were the same and the gatherings as inclusive as those in bigger cities in the United States and around the world.

But this was the first such parade for Holly Springs in many years, featuring a new generation coming to the fore. It seemed to be celebrating a coming together of the races for a public display of common consumption. A new generation, which has moved beyond the bitterest times of civil rights rebellion, and with the old Civil War defeat *almost* erased by the new Gulf victory.

In *How Societies Remember*, Connerton suggests that "a rite revoking an institution only makes sense by inadvertently recalling the other rites that hitherto confirmed that institution" (1989:9). The past does not just get recreated. For each set of memories, a satisfactory feeling of closure is produced by shared acknowledgment of change.

Perhaps before the days of our interactive electronic highway, we needed to get together to do it (see Da Sola Poole 1977), but the immediacy of these media *may* permit it in the present. Immediate gratification of the need to share perhaps then displaces a later, face-to-face meeting, when again it becomes just another event recalled in tranquility, not action and memory together.

Almost thirty years ago, Berger and Luckmann, in *The Social Construction of Reality* (1967), discussed "the intersubjective sedimentation of significant human experiences in memory, when several individuals share a common biography, experiences of which become incorporated in a common stock of knowledge." Although couched in quite different language from what sailors would use, this certainly describes the experiences of the crew of the Bache.

What seems to me to be the currency in cultural anthropology is what is common: what random acts and beliefs of individuals are truly felt to be shared and continue to reverberate through the community. And if they reverberate into existence, does that mean that there is a common or continuous culture outside of individual experience?

Jonathan Friedman (1992) avers that the past is always practiced in the present, not because it imposes itself, but because subjects in the present fashion the past in the practice of their social identity. Thus, the organization of the current situation in the terms of a past can only occur in the present. Of course, I borrow these ideas, in and out of context, to bolster my own thinking about our mechanisms to create collectivity.

Today we not only have the radio to listen to, or the telephone/fax with which to communicate over space, we have CDs and interactive TV and multimedia worlds. The information highway permits, nay demands, instantaneous communication, but how will we find this to differ from the depersonalized communication between sales clerk and consumer and other segmented relationships?

We need braided ropes, not strings, to connect to each other and to things outside ourselves. Obviously, family provides one such braided strand, as does the traditional idea of community. But in the current world, where individuals do transcend their communities and people in fact circulate worldwide, the more strands to tie us together, the greater the likelihood of our having a "future." There has to be a reason beyond plain recall to hold us together, to develop that possibility.

Cressy (1989), for instance, points out that some writers hammered on the urgency and importance of holding past events in memory. He cited both the Spanish Armada of 1588 and the Guy Fawkes Gunpowder Plot of 1605 as examples used to instill attentiveness to the past as the foundation for godliness in the seventeenth century present, and the future, too. The story of the Armada, Cressy then reminds us, has been retold more recently (as in the "Invasion of the Falklands") for current cultural-rallying purposes.

Phenomenology means we bring our own pasts and when they coincide, something more than propinquity binds us together. Still, remembering by the calendar does not quite gibe with experiences today when we are drowning in dates and data. Numbers on the page do not bring forth experience the way a repeat of our own history does.

Reflections on the social role of memory recall Josiah Royce's 1913 lectures where he wrote that each can say of an individual past event or deed "that belongs to my life, or occurred or will occur, to me" (1968:248–49). When several can so say, they form a community with reference to a particular past or future event. "How rich this community is in meaning, in value, in membership, in significant organization, will depend upon the selves that enter into the community and upon the ideals in terms of which they define themselves, their past and their future" (249).

Stewart (1988) insists that the idea of nostalgia (all those radio references to the fiftieth anniversary of Pearl Harbor, the music of the 1950s, and many items in between) rises to importance as a cultural practice as culture becomes more and more diffuse . . . as culture takes on the power of "distance that comes of displacing speakers" (227–41). Handelman tells us that the purpose of ritual is the small- or large-scale transformation of both the actor and the audience. He mourns that there are fewer authentic moments of catastrophic time, but only a world of many small victories and defeats, few absolute or final resolutions (1990:266).

Current popular attempts to retrieve memory, shaping the past on the air waves, picking up undirected voices, is not sharing, and this assault on the mind can easily lead to paralysis rather than action.

Casey (1986), writing on William Earle's work on memory and the past, says that Earle posed an alternative to the *passive* philosophies of Plato and Aristotle, stressing, rather, the *active* nature of memory. Earle said a genuine gap between the past and the present does exist, but that that is not the last word. "The gap must be bridged by the self that presided over both occasions, the same and identical self" (Casey 1986:185). I suggest that to enter culture, memory requires an *interactive* process, minimally two same and identical selves. Perhaps differently from psychology and philosophy, anthropology has always stressed the *sharing* that creates culture as well as the transmission that gives it viability.

To descend from memory and retreat from passionate encounters with their transforming ability for those who share a high moment of common view, let me finish by mentioning a study by Briody and Baba (1991).

They analyzed differences in the repatriation experiences of persons returning to their American company offices after overseas assignments.

The researchers agree that the world is rapidly becoming a global marketplace (I take it that this global market is bigger than the global village, because there is more interaction between locals and outsiders). They suggest that the only organizations in a position to compete with worldwide rivals are those with global implementation strategies in place. They make empirical comparisons between organizations they describe as decoupled from the international arena and those whose systems are what they call either coupled or supercoupled systems models. Of the three models they describe, supercoupled systems may hold the greatest promise for a competitive advantage:

They are the ones associated not only with a pro-global ideology and a cross-national organizational structure, but also with unrestricted exchanges of personnel, technology, resources, and products, all of which are central to global development. It is the simultaneous presence of all of these elements that is the foundation for the supercoupled system. The performance effectiveness of such a system is dependent on both internal organizational factors (e.g. employee knowledge and skills, product quality) and external environmental conditions (e.g. product supply and demand, government regulations). (Briody and Baba 1991:340)

In other words, continuing to interact, as well as to communicate the fact of activity at one or another location while at a distance is the way to maintain the urgency of working together even while at this distance. I do not think that Briody and Baba are suggesting that reading each other's E-mail in one's own good time in different offices is enough to make for a continued sense of community.

It is not just the changed perspective from the present for the remembrance of things past, as Proust demonstrated, but the opportunity to have the past interact with the present intersection that creates culture or community, whichever you wish to call it.

ACKNOWLEDGMENT

Let me express gratitude for the very helpful exchanges with the late philosopher Michael Marsh, who broadened my thinking and enlarged my viewpoint.

METAMORPHOSIS

The journey to the present is too vast to grasp by one's own actions.

Molly G. Schuchat

Memories of Violence, Monuments of History

Antonella Fabri

> The wrath of the disappointed creditor, the community, throws (the debtor) back again into the savage and outlaw state against which he has hitherto been protected; it thrusts him away—and now any kind of hostility may be vented upon him. "Punishment" at this level of civilization is simply a copy, a *mimus* of the normal attitude toward a hated, disarmed, prostrated enemy, who has lost every right and protection.
>
> Nietzsche, *On the Genealogy of Morals*
> (1967 (1887) II, 9:71)

This passage grasps a key aspect of the relationship between the Maya people and the nation-state in Guatemala, a country where the practice of ethnocide has characterized the government's policy toward the indigenous population.[1] The reasons for the violence are related to the ethnic, economic, and sociopolitical conflicts that have shaped the contemporary relations in Guatemala between Indians, ladinos, and the nation-state. Despite the establishment of a democratic government with President Vinicio Cerezo in 1986, violent repression is still one of the dark features of Guatemalan society perpetrated by the army against people who are labeled as enemies of the state. The relationship between the Mayas—who constitute about 60 percent of the total Guatemalan population—and the ladinos—the dominant minority of Spanish descent—is one of debtors and creditors.[2] Indians are accused by the dominant, ladino society of slowing down progress and modernization of the country. They are portrayed either as tourist objects that bestow an attractive image on the nation-state, or as a negative and subversive force that needs to be either domesticated or eradicated. These two main images shape the government's discourse on Maya identity and, consequently, Guatemalan official history.[3]

The interplay between memory and history and the role of resistance in testimonial narratives constitute the focus of this chapter. This analysis of violence is based on oral testimonies related in Spanish by Maya refugees displaced both in the United States and in Guatemala City. Testimonies are viewed as fragments of the official history that have been silenced and concealed in order to construct a "monument," that is, a totalizing and enclosed narrative of history. My thesis is that the testimonial narrative, by recalling the fragmentation of the bodies of the victims of violence, constitutes a disruption of that official effort to construct a monument of history. In other words, the ghosts of the victims, that is, the debtors' fragmented bodies that appear through the voices of the survivors, fragment the constructed unity of official history.[4] Testimonial narratives suggest two levels of signification: First, they rephrase the past according to the experiences of a vast majority that has been excluded from official history and bound by silence. Second, they provide a means to express the memories previously incarcerated in the body. Thus, the recounting of the trauma is for the victims of violence a form of recuperation of the history of their people (see Caruth 1991).

Massacres, tortures, and disappearances represent the most common techniques utilized by the "institution of violence" to maintain its control.[5] Misleading information in the Guatemalan press, silence, defamation, fear, and negation also constitute powerful mechanisms of repression. Widespread terror has been used in an effort to prevent people from communicating and from maintaining a sense of community. In this context of fear, gossip may result in a death sentence; old disputes between neighbors may lead to false accusations and executions by the army (Warren 1993). Therefore, silence has often been adopted as a mechanism of defense and survival. Victims of terror are forced to forget the episodes of violence.[6] But pain is a feature of the human body that reemerges in different forms and is often transformed by the victims into practices of resistance.[7]

Maya voices fragment and disrupt the antithetical images of the Indian constructed by official history: the good and the subversive (see Pearce 1965; Hulme 1992). The "good Indian" belongs to the realm of the exotic: a kind of identity that denies indigenous people "coevalness of time" (Fabian 1983), that is, an image overshadowed by what is left of the ancient

Maya civilization, a reenactment of a debris of the past, or a stage for the tourist industry. The "subversive Indian" is the "savage" who, as such, justifies the destruction of those who oppose national progress. Therefore, ruins become a trope of Maya identity since they represent the history of "subhumans" who make subversion their own strategy. Both the negation of counternarratives and the superimposition of images represent a denial of presence and voice to contemporary Mayas. The places to which Mayas are confined today are anachronistic and inhuman, since they are located in either museums and ruins or in "model villages."[8] It is no coincidence that the Guatemalan national hero is the Maya K'ichi' warrior Tekun Umán, who embodies the image of the "good Indian" because he fought the Spaniards but eventually succumbed to them. Indians become heroes only when they are dead. Otherwise they are considered subhumans, subversives, an embarrassment for the country and therefore targets of violence (Cojtí Cuxil 1991). Such a vision of the Indian constitutes the foundation of Guatemalan official history: If the Indian cannot be integrated, *it* has to be eliminated.

Previously, the resistance of our ancestors against the invasion was considered "wild" and "irrational" and for that reason the destruction of so many towns was justified as an act of pacification of those who are called "savages, idol worshippers and cannibals." At present, and after five hundred years, the same system of social control and deprivation continues. So that when our towns rise and claim their rights, the deprived peasants are immediately accused of being "communists, subversives and revolutionaries." (My translation. Montejo 1992:8)

Fragmentation, displacement, and incarceration characterize forms of dominance that are deployed in Guatemalan society at both physiological and psychological levels. The dismemberment and displacement of bodies that lie visible on the streets are to remind people of the pending terror. But the silence imposed on witnesses of violence does not repress the memory of experienced horror. In this "culture of terror" (Taussig 1987), the victims of such overwhelming brutality strive to reconstitute history through memory and, through it, a sense of place and belonging amidst the disrupted, or fragmented, geographies, communities, and familial ties.[9]

Memory, in its process of forgetting and yet salvaging the past, construes new levels of interpretation and representation of reality; that is, a text that is antagonistic to the official history in its own reconstruction of the past.[10] The writing of history is based on a clear differentiation between past and present and between the object of inquiry, set off in time and secluded from the present, such as museums, and the writing and researching subject (see De Certeau 1986:4). History, then, stands as the act of legitimation that sanctions the separation of times, authority, and, ultimately, death, since this kind of writing presupposes a work of fragmentation of the past into discreet and representable segments. Alterity is thus swallowed in the process of writing history, for it posits itself as the point of necessary departure and death in order to enable history to be further written. But is it possible to write a history that includes alterity—otherness, memory, even—without "cannibalizing" the Other, or radicalizing differences? De Certeau in *The Writing of History* observes:

The other is the phantasm of historiography, the object that it seeks, honors, and buries. A labor of separation concerning this uncanny and fascinating proximity is affected. . . . Modern Western history essentially begins with differentiation between the present and the past. . . . This rupture . . . assumes a gap to exist between the silent opacity of the "reality" that it seeks to express and the place where it produces its own speech, protected by the distance established between itself and its object (Gegen-stand). The violence of the body—[the social body, the body of knowledge, the Other body]—reaches the written page only through absence. (De Certeau 1988:3)

The Western notion of historiography assumes a linear model of progress and development. In order to come to an understanding of events of the past a selection must be made, thus excluding or "forgetting" whatever cannot be included in the broader scheme of "authoritative" history. But what is left behind reemerges. This can be observed in the case of Guatemala, where the past is recuperated and reinterpreted in the testimonies. These narratives not only stand in opposition to the official history, but also represent the expression of a conception of time and rationalization of events that contest the official narrative. In other words, narratives of violence stand as testimonies of a notion of time where progress does not exclude the past, since the past is actually reabsorbed in the life of the present, as a memorial for those Others and as a point of connection with a multilayered spatial construct to which historical events belong.

The perpetrators of violations of human rights have always downplayed and denied their actions.[11] President Cerezo's request to the relatives of disappeared people to forget the past seems to be ingrained in the national idea of progress and modernization. In the national ideology of modernization the past needs to be left behind and "monumentalized" in order to make the country improve and advance. So, the time and space of violence are displaced and omitted from Guatemalan official history or, at the most, acknowledged as past, concluded events that should not interfere with the present. At the same time that the vast majority of Guatemalans are excluded as subjects of their own history, episodes of violence, though pervasive and integrated in everyday life, are transported into a different level, that is, "metaphorised," as the original meaning of the Greek term "metaphor" indicates (see van den Abbeel 1992:xxii).

The Foucauldian notion of "other" space, or heterotopia, indicating a space disjoined from any other context and located on a level that is both outside and still immersed in everyday life, can be applied to the violence of Guatemalan official history as well as to testimonies of the victims of violence.

[Heterotopias are] places that do exist and that are formed in the very founding of society—which are something like counter-sites, a kind of effectively enacted utopia in which the real sites, all the other real sites that can be found within the culture, are simultaneously represented, contested, and inverted. Places of this kind are outside of all places, even though it may be possible to indicate their location in reality. (Foucault 1986:24)

In the Guatemalan context, violence represents a spectacle of reality in the sense that while it mirrors reality it obeys different rules of space and time. Thus, the episodes of violence become sealed in and transferred to another space which, like a museum, is just a spectacle of the real.[12] The space of crime is appropriated by the official history, which continuously denies and conceals it by portraying it either as an episode of street violence or as a revolutionary conspiracy.[13] Clandestine cemeteries, model villages, and refugee camps can be viewed as heterotopias, that is, as spaces that swallow or cannibalize the bodies of the enemies in order to domesticate and appropriate them. These properties of the nation-state constitute a place in which victims become absorbed and constituted as subjects. Hence, the spaces of violence become the economy of victims' identity, "sacred" places where "unclean" bodies are kept under surveillance and witnesses are made to confess their uncommitted crimes.[14] Such spaces of pain and deprivation become, therefore, the victims' "natural" places that identify them as subversives (Taussig 1987:7).

The exclusion and segregation of the Mayas from the Guatemalan-ladino nation originates at the level of language. The silence imposed upon the victims is related to their banishment from official history; it parallels the confinement of "deviants" to the periphery, their immersion into cultural anesthesia, or denial of representation. One displaced woman in Guatemala City affirmed that Maya people's limited knowledge of Spanish before they go to the capital is one factor that is held against them by the soldiers who surveil their communities: "[The soldiers] ask people for names and between the fear and the fact that we don't know Spanish well, we don't understand what they're saying and we answer that we don't know, that we cannot understand, hear them." Once in the new place, as a displaced person, she reexperiences the frustration and the fear of being "caught" or discovered in her identity of an indigenous, Maya-speaking woman: "I was afraid that they find out where I come from, from which village. They used to ask me where my village is, and more and more questions, but I couldn't answer because I did not speak Spanish then. So, I didn't say anything to them."

Language, as it is conveyed by this informant, represents a mark of identity of indigenous people, just as their traditional clothing, or *trajes* which, as it is indicated in the following quote, lowers the status of Maya people:

We are poorer and poorer: sure, we have our trajes, we have our language, we may speak our language, and our clothes are very pretty, but this is not just what indigenous people experience in their own flesh. With all this dismay caused by the murders of the indigenous people . . . no matter how things turn around, we are the ones who lose all the time.

The silence imposed by terror upon the Maya people is broken in testimonies that allow the victims of violence to express their sense of estrangement and the embodiment of their painful conditions. The same informant, who has been displaced in Guatemala City since the 1980s, looking back at her past says:

[The memory of the past] evokes too big of a history. It summons the growth, the suffering, many things that encourage me to struggle. In the 1980s with the repression, the army reached our communities at night, shooting, threatening people. Since people are very humble and poor there, at that time they slept in little houses which we could not abandon because they belonged to us. I was afraid to leave the house, I was scared because never in Guatemala has it been heard, seen a soldier in the community; soldiers who shoot in the streets and ask us for names, us who don't speak Spanish and can't quite understand what they say.

The lives of displaced people are characterized by movement and deprivation of a center, a "home"; this nomadic experience also implied a continual fracturing and a dissemination of identities. In this context, testimonies represent a means to insert the narrators in the flow of history, and a mirror that reflects their condition. Although Spanish, the language of the testimonies, represents the context of domination for Maya people, it is also a ratification of their moment of presence in history. Stated another way, the adoption of Spanish implies both the power of domination and the appropriation of that site of power by the repressed. Like Caliban, the archetypal figure of the Colonized in the Western tradition who was forced to speak the language of his master, indigenous people use Spanish to orient themselves in their space (see Hulme 1992; Greenblatt 1991). Spanish, as a ghost of hegemony, inserts itself in the fracture of power since it enables marginalized people to raise their voices. The language of the colonizer is therefore adopted by the colonized as a means to articulate *differánce* and supplementarity, that is, to create the space for fractures and differences that destabilize the authorial narratives of official history and identities.[15]

The testimonial narrative, even if repressed by official history, is already part of history because it is the expression of time as articulated through and by memory. The position of authoritative or official representation of history is double but not ambivalent. The narratives of violence are either used to justify the state's techniques of repression or deleted from the official records of history. In the first instance, testimonies come to reiterate the righteousness of violence against those who are accused of disrupting the harmony of the nation-state and thus present the image of the Other as the one interfering with state politics. In this context, therefore, the testimonies reflect back to the narrator his or her identity as a subversive and "cannibal."[16] In the second instance, testimonies are deleted from the official records, thus indicating that the state has erased its crimes along with personal and communal recollections of the occurred events. Furthermore, even when the government has to confront the evidence of human rights violations, such episodes of violence are treated as events of the past that need to be put behind and relegated into a history of no-return. For this reason, then, the memories engraved in the bodies and minds of the survivors are either kept separated from the public sphere or destroyed, in order not to contaminate the truth created by the official records.

To the witnesses of violence, testimonies offer a chance to reappropriate the denied space of memory and reterritorialize their misplaced identities. Narratives of violence become the practice of a process of consciousness-raising among the victims who ultimately acquire a voice and a visibility through the narration of their own stories. Testimonies enable a rupture of a self-encompassed truth that bestows on the survivors who narrate these stories the power to supplement and thus resist the truth of official history. In other words, the writing of these narratives and their transposition into texts create a fracture in another writing, that is, the official history. It is this fracture that underlies the power of representation and its innumerable possibilities to construe truth and reality. The constitution of another and still another truth points out the lack or the gap that is ingrained in any system of knowledge. In this context, testimonies represent a disturbance of the "official" constitution of presence. In the postcolonial condition, truth is disseminated with the consequence that the transcendental site of representation, or presence, is disrupted, "troped," and subverted.

The testimonial genre can be considered a resistance literature and a counterdiscourse. In testimonies, memory exists and functions as a system of writing, since it opens a space for representation and inscribes Otherness in the supposed site of wholeness. Testimonies are translations of the writing of the mind, or memories and interpretations—transpositions or transcriptions of oral stories which, once transposed into literary texts, individualize and create presence. However, at the same time, the multitude of representations and presences thus newly created lead necessarily to further fragmentation. This "rhizomatic" process extends the limits of the official, self-contained representation of the real and contends even more the illusion of the absence of fracture as claimed by and represented in the official history.[17] The rupture of truth created by official history parallels another disruption initiated by the process of writing and/or recounting one's own experience, namely a disruption at the level of identity. In other words, the testimonial narrative points out that identity as an all-encompassing and self-contained whole exists only at the level of desire, because there is no identity without fracture, especially in the postcolonial condition. Therefore, testimonies as written witnesses disrupt the concept of integrity and produce identities as ruins and fragments.

THE SILENCE OF PAIN

Physical pain has no voice, but when it at last finds a voice, it begins to tell a story, and the story that it tells is about the inseparability of these three subjects, their embeddedness in one another. (Scarry 1985:3)

The fracture conveyed in the testimony parallels another fracture, the one operated at the level of the body. The suspension of the body from a social life that is organized through pain may be related to the suspension of the voice of the victim.

It is the intense pain that destroys a person's self and world, a destruction experienced spatially as either the contraction of the universe down to the immediate vicinity of the body. . . . Intense pain is also language-destroying: as the content of one's world disintegrates, so the content of one's language disintegrates. (Scarry 1985:35)

The experience of the survivors of violence is constituted by the internalization of pain, since silence incarcerates the individual into the body, which is thereby reduced to its materiality; at this point the body of victims becomes their own enemy. According to reports, survivors of violence often blame themselves rather than their aggressors. Victims experience isolation from their community and even from their family, which in Guatemala are the primary nuclei of support. Pain is isolating and its external objectification and catharsis are often unreachable without the help of doctors and psychologists.

Among the forms of violence and torture practiced by the Guatemalan military is the disappearance of people. The absence of their loved ones has the power to annihilate those who remain. Rosa, a Maya woman whose husband disappeared, remarks:

For this reason now I feel sick, tired. It affects me to realize that I cannot reflect upon what happened. The pressure makes me suffer of a disease that mostly affects displaced women. It's the nerves, the aching head, the pressure, the history and its rationale that won't ever be forgotten because we saw it with our own eyes, with our own face. Thus, one cannot leave this history in the oblivion.

What Rosa conveys is both the intensity of pain in her body which "rebels" against her to the point of making her feel sick, and the power of liberation that her voice acquires from the pain felt. The body becomes a receptacle of pain, divided into aching organs that "choose" to have a life of their own. In other words, the articulation of pain enables an individual to recover part of the space that had been lost by the retrenchment of the subject into the body. In the case of "disappearances" this commonly happens to persons who are left behind. They experience a suspension and paralysis that numb the senses and immobilize them in a time and space that is other than everyday. This removal of time is thus internalized by the survivors as a simulation of death and as an experience of uprootedness and chaos (Feldman 1991:137). Only the breaking of silence allows a person to recuperate her body and its space. Antonio Martinez, director of Chicago's Marjorie Kovler Center for the Treatment of Survivors of Torture, has reported emotional conflicts, flashbacks, and nightmares as the most common symptoms of the survivors of torture.[18] The experience of terror cuts individuals off from their natural, social environment; while people avoid the victims for safety reasons, the victims avoid people who might remind them of their traumatic experience. The experience of terror becomes, therefore, the organizing focus of all other relationships; silence, fear, and mistrust become the norm, that is, the achieved goal of the institution of violence.

Many people recur to local medical centers with the hope of relieving their pain. But medicines and doctors, or the effort to forget—as it is stated in this testimony—cannot heal the victim, because terror is everywhere.

Even though I take many medicines, I cannot forget this wound, this history, the time when they killed my brother. They left him beheaded, with his arms cut off. The head couldn't be found, we found only pieces of his body. And when I got home the soldiers asked me questions: where I came from, what kind of job I had, my address. They asked me for my children and more and more questions. . . . And they warned me against my words.

The sight of torture is itself a torture, and so are threats. When terror is shown or staged it has a great power of deterrence. The institution of terror embodied by the Guatemalan army alternates the hiding with the displaying of evidence, but the aim does not change, since its goal is to isolate and silence individuals. During my fieldwork in Guatemala I learned that in spite of the proliferation of clandestine cemeteries in the village of one of my informants, the corpse of a "subversive" was once left hanging in the center of the village for several days. No matter the type of "ritual," silence is still part of a practice of dominance and control in Guatemala.[19] Neither victims nor witnesses can speak or express their pain, which remains internalized, embodied. The ceasing of communication even among the members of the same family is a measure of safety. But pain and its experience become first of all associated with guilt. "Children have to tell lies about the disappearance or arrest of their parents," says Antonio Martinez (1992). Concealing evidence of torture by inflicting wounds to parts of the body that would not be visible without clothes on, also has the effect of silencing witnesses. Hence, whether visible or not, pain cannot leave the body of the "criminal."

Victims' narratives are labelled by the official history as the confessions of "deviants," which ultimately reinforces the sense of guilt and shame of individuals who experienced torture. For example, women who were raped by soldiers during village raids were also ostracized by their communities: "Since being raped is perceived as a stigma, these women won't ever marry; they have a bad image, and their children a bad name. While the widow is still respected by the community, the woman who has been violated is not."[20] Furthermore, going public with one's own story might endanger the whole community, as if the victim were both a deviant and a political subversive. Thus, Maya women who have been raped by soldiers are marginalized by people in their communities.

Silence is both a technique of control and a safety strategy. Isolda, a thirteen year old girl, explained to an interviewer that

Several men and women with babies on their backs were kneeling in the plaza next to the church, "worshipping and praying"—in her words—when a helicopter appeared in the sky. She heard "loud pops" and saw fire pouring down on the people. Frightened, she ran home to tell her father what she had just seen.

And when the interviewer asked Isolda what her father told her, she replied:

He told me not to tell anyone what I had seen and that if the soldiers ever asked to never admit I had been baptized as a Catholic . . . because the Government soldiers think all Catholics in our village support the guerrillas and would kill us. (Boothby 1985)

Bearing witness to episodes of violence also has repercussions on the general well-being of individuals. Many cases have been reported that describe how people, especially children, were suffering from an increased susceptibility to minor infections and psychological problems related to control, learning and social abilities. "These were young beings who had simply seen too much" (Boothby 1985).

The breaking of silence means condemnation to death, as in the case of the members of GAM—an organization of the relatives of disappeared people—who are portrayed by the government as "a bunch of communists." A refugee woman who now lives in Florida asserts:

It is too dangerous to open one's mouth, the people of GAM, for example, are determined to die. People cannot talk, one has to be silent because those who speak are dead. . . . The army doesn't want us to speak, doesn't want people to know about the assassinations. The quieter, the better. When the soldiers call "metiches" those who talk, those who stick their noses into the army's business, [they refer to] indigenous people. Those who are innocent keep their mouths shut as if all the violence and the abuses were natural acts.[21]

People who speak about atrocities are accused of being either subversives or liars, as is exemplified by the case of Sister Diane Ortiz. She was abducted from a convent in Guatemala in November 1989, taken away in a National Police car, then raped and tortured. The government placed the blame on Sister Diane and dismissed her accusations as "a fabrication, a lesbian love twist" (Martinez 1992).

THE VOICE OF PAIN

"If something is to stay in the memory it must be burned in: only that which never ceases to hurt stays in the memory." . . . Man could never do without blood, torture, and sacrifices when he felt the need to create a memory for himself. . . . Pain is the most powerful aid to mnemonics. (Nietzsche 1967 [1887]:II, 3)

"While the first legacy of la violencia was silence" (Warren 1993:32), the aftermath of silence is the textualization of memory, part of which is the genre of testimonial narrative. Nietzsche's quote stresses the relation between memory, history, and pain, since memory is created by inflicting pain and history is the residual of collective suffering.

The testimonial narrative entails the reconstruction by the victims of violence of their sensory experience. The previous section of this chapter discussed how silence represents one modality of torture which causes individuals to lose their sense of the world. In contrast, the victim's reconquered place of the senses entails a learning process or a catharsis of pain. In other words, the violence of the state apparatus "compresses" pain inside the body until it is utterly consumed, thus reducing the body to a black hole that swallows pain to the point of endangering the whole system.[22] But the body of the victim is sometimes able to heal itself through reenactment, verbalization, and textualization of the inflicted pain. In this way, the recounting of that sensory experience creates the story of the whole community that has been numbed. These narratives become a mimesis of the body and its pain, or "black holes" since they are conceived by the state apparatus as monstrous stories of deviance and "cannibalism" which history needs to forget and monumentalize. If torture has impeded the participation of the Other in civil society and has excluded those bodies through the silence of pain, the testimonial narrative recuperates that history as if it were recomposing the body's fragmented pieces. In the practice of violence the body is partitioned, dislocated, silenced and concealed, deprived of any sensory capability. It is not a coincidence that many of the tortured bodies have the tongue extracted and many of the vital, operative organs—such as genitals, hands, and head—taken off the trunk and dispersed somewhere else. The broken unity of the body reflects the fragmentation and annihilation of families, of communities, and of that part of society that cannot be integrated within the nation-state. Bodies in pieces, disseminated on the streets, enhance terror and fear; as in a museum, these bodies are dissected and exposed, deprived of any context, and secluded for fear of contamination. Further, this theater of terror operates as a museum. As in a museum those bodies rest in a self-contained space and are classified in the desired or "proper" structure, which also represents the spectacle of power.

Aeschylus, in the *Agamemnon*, identifies pain as a main factor in the constitution of the person; in Catholic ethics, pain is transformed into experience and guilt. Once victims succeed in breaking the silence, they are able to articulate their place within society and achieve a rationale of their history. Personal memory, in the form of articulation of pain and reenactment of the experience, becomes a repository for the collective memory and a basis for a communal historical consciousness (see Seremetakis 1991; Pandolfi 1991). It is in this context that the testimonial narrative raises the question of resistance as well as of the translation of the annihilation of the body and of the erasure of its physical/social dimensions into a form of empowerment and counterdiscourse.[23] The testimonial narrative represents a form of catharsis and resocialization through the reenactment of pain, which is thus purged from the body (see Taussig 1987:368). The recollection of that history, paraphrasing the words of a victim of violence, entails an act of courage because fear has stifled the expression of those memories. While forgetting implies the erasure of one's own past, memory can lead to the integration of the past into the victim's present and future life.

Many survivors of torture have pointed out the cathartic effect of narrating their traumatic experiences. Although signs of torture might not be physically visible, narration makes the wounds visible and audible. Thus, memories of the past become reorganized and the nightmare of the episodes of violence recontextualized. However, testimonies also attest to the victory of power, that is, the presence of the state in that body, which is visible only through its segmentation. The body then becomes a topography, a text and a map, a mirror of torture and *the* sign that there exists a whole apparatus behind torture.[24] The reenactment of pain through narration allows individuals to explore the will and power of the state on their bodies so that the dismembered body becomes, paradoxically, but also consequently, the spectacle of power. In other words, the body is "acted upon" to be reduced to a mirror of itself, to a repository of power (see Foucault 1978).

To conclude, the testimonial narrative in its relation to history as a totalizing narrative raises several questions: Is this writing like a Kafkian penal colony? Is it a floating signifier that is put in motion by desire but remains self-enclosed and self-referential? Does testimony resituate the individual in history, or does it, rather, construct an identity on ruins and fragments of other times, identities, and spaces? Furthermore, is the historical memory transposed onto the testimonial narrative in order to be isolated from the historical continuum, hence paradoxically included but isolated from history, without relation to external, or present, and past context? I suggest that, like the fragment, testimony resists totality and totalization. It constitutes a counternarrative in the form of a fractured mirror of the state and its power, since it reflects its monstrous identity—a ghostly, cannibalized representation. Hence, testimony typifies a metonymic representation of history, a trope and substitution that provide the victims with another frame of knowledge. Ultimately, it seems that it constructs a space for the memory of pain and a therapy for a trauma which operates as the primal scene of repression.

The testimonial genre seems to partake of postcolonial discourse as a representation that links and differs the Other to the state. In this condition, the individual is fixed into an origin of disruption and ruins, which provides fragmentation in terms of identity and representation but also a place for a counterdiscourse where universalization is no longer possible. Once the center is dismantled by the proliferation of histories, identities, and representations, only fractures, fragments, and ruins remain. Thus, the monumentality of the official construction of history, along with its attempt to overcome the dissonances of representations, is dismantled. Representation is always rearticulated, fractured, disseminated, and subverted. Difference, in a Derridian sense, seems to be the articulating principle of identities that offer the "margins" a strategy of resistance. The disruption of space fragments identities and presences but also creates meaning in their dispersal and displacement. Meaning is in the margin, not in a distinctive locale but diffused, and therefore available to anybody who wants to represent it.

In conclusion, counterdiscourses lie on the crack or fracture of any form of domination, thus enabling the margins to resist. Testimonies turn the inscriptions that are written on the body of the victim by the institution of violence into a representation of fractures of monumental history. Although the institution of violence has created deaf and numb bodies, it has not succeeded in suppressing "differences." The writing of testimonies enables the victims to insert themselves in temporal and spatial frames that differ from the linear construction of official history. The reconstruction of time and memory present in testimonies struggles against the imposition of silence and forgetting. This new fragmentation represents a prelude to the constitution of a counterdiscourse that contests and yet supplements the monument of history. The power of testimonies does not exclusively lie in their contestation of truth, but, rather, in their effort to disseminate and fragment the knowledge enforced by the state. Only in this way can memory be a countermemory.

NOTES

A preliminary version of this chapter was presented at the Annual Meeting of the American Anthropological Association (San Francisco, December 2–6, 1992) in the session "Memory, Generation, and Culture" organized by Jacob Climo and Marea Teski. This version greatly benefited from the generous commentaries and suggestions of Jacob Climo, my mentors at the University at Albany, Gary H. Gossen and Helen Elam, and my colleague Quetzil Castañeda. I am also grateful to Peter Upton for his support during my research in Indiantown, Neil Boothby for allowing me to use his data, and John W. Upton for his assistance in the final revisions. Finally, I wish to express my gratitude to those people in Guatemala and Florida for sharing their stories with me and making this analysis possible.

1. The most brutal expression of the Guatemalan government's violence occurred in the 1980s. According to Human Rights Commissions, since 1980, political violence has resulted in 100,000 civilian deaths, 40,000 disappearances, 450 villages destroyed, 250,000 orphans, 45,000 widows, over 100,000 refugees, and one million internally displaced people (Barry 1992). The army campaign against guerrilla activities in the highlands was started and promoted by General Lucas García, who became president through electoral fraud in 1978, Ríos Montt, who seized power in a military coup in 1982, and general Oscar Mejía Victores, who was in power between 1983 and 1985. When the Christian Democrat Vinicio Cerezo won the election in 1985, he established hopes for a democratic government. However, after he took office, in January 1986, human rights violations and the counterinsurgency campaign continued. During the presidency of Jorge Serrano Elías (1991–1993), disappearances and killings increased, especially in the period surrounding the president's self-coup. To date, with Ramiro De León Carpio, former human rights ombudsman, as president, Guatemala is still a country where the army's abuses and techniques of repression perpetuate a state of terror (major sources: Jonas 1991; Barry 1992).

2. The term *ladino* refers to the Guatemalan population of Spanish descent who emerged as an ethnic group between the sixteenth and the nineteenth century (Adams 1990:153). On ethnic relations in contemporary Guatemala, see also Warren (1978) and Hawkins (1984).

3. Guatemalan official history refers to the media's and government's records of episodes related to political violence, which are usually reported either as lawful repression of subversive and criminal attacks for the sake of the citizens, or as occurrences of ordinary violence.

4. The bodies of people who had been kidnapped were often found dismembered, with the most atrocious signs of torture. One of the reasons for

this fragmentation is to spread the fear and to keep the population passive (see Figueroa Ibarra 1991:41). For a discussion on the use of terror by the colonizer as a mechanism of control see also Taussig (1987:51–73).

5. The expression "institution of violence" is used in reference to the development of specific technologies of power deployed and maintained by the state. This use of institution derives from Foucault (1980:141). A similar concept of institution has had more recent anthropological development (see De Certeau's "institution of the rot" [1986:35] and Taussig's "culture of terror" [1987]).

6. The widespread use of clandestine cemeteries testifies to perhaps the highest and most poignant practice of repression and concealment of evidence of crimes of the Guatemalan military apparatus.

7. It is worthwhile mentioning that the testimonies collected during my time spent in Guatemala were not always solicited. On many occasions people would ask me to record their personal experiences with the hope that somebody in my country could eventually support them to put an end to their miserable conditions.

8. Model villages are settlements built and monitored by the military and occupied by the rest of the people whose villages have been destroyed by the army. On the subject of model villages and their relation to the army's strategy of control see Manz (1988).

9. Fragmentation starts at the level of the family with the disappearance or death of the closest relatives. Many displaced people and widows mention sorrow and deprivation that derive from the prohibition against performing funerary rituals for their victims. Out of fear, people confine themselves to their homes; in many cases they do not work at their lands and they even avoid talking because any word could be used against them and turn into a death sentence. Under this condition, many people decide to leave their communities to find safer and anonymous places.

10. De Certeau argues that memory consists of two opposite, yet complementary operations: forgetting and remembering. While the former is an action against the past, the latter is an action by a past which, like a ghost, returns to the present. "What was excluded re-infiltrates the place of its origin—now the present's 'own' [propre] place. It resurfaces, it troubles, it turns the present's feeling of being 'at home' into an illusion" (De Certeau 1986:4). Memory, as expressed in the testimonies of the survivors of violence, bridges the gap between the personal and social spheres since it helps the individual to find a place in history and to reconstitute a sense of community. Furthermore, especially for displaced people, memory and its textualization represent home, that is, a tangible place of belonging.

11. Continuous threats and attacks on journalists, human rights activists, and social workers are still occurring, as is the destruction or disappearance of court records for cases under prosecution.

12. The concept of museum is used to convey the idea of an enclosed space that, estranged from the context of everyday life, becomes a monument of and to history with the purpose of sealing a historical period and laying the basis for an

"untainted" future. In this context, the history of a particular museum piece is transformed into a representation of itself and transposed into the level of "hyperreal."

13. This is exemplified by the way the government handled the homicide of Myrna Mack (September 11, 1990), a prominent Guatemalan anthropologist who was investigating the displacement of the rural indigenous population caused by the counterinsurgency campaigns. Mack's murder, at first declared a street crime, was reopened thanks to national and international pressures. The National Police first concealed the reports that determined that Mack was under its surveillance and later altered the findings of that report.

14. In the refugee camp in Nebaj, people undergo psychological treatment, which consists of "making her perspectives change," as one of the local commissioners explained. Ironic is the name given to this refugee camp: "La Pista," or "The New Life."

15. The Derridian concept of differánce indicates the complex articulation of Maya identity that emerges in the testimonial narrative. This particular form of identity defers to and is intercalated with other representations; it therefore represents a moment or a splinter within other forms of self-constitution (see Derrida 1982:3, 13). Differánce "makes the opposition of presence and absence possible . . . produces what it forbids, makes possible the very thing that it makes impossible" (Derrida 1976:143). This quote warns against the danger of names and definitions that risk to overshadow other meanings and nuances. The term *Maya*, for instance, has been used as a device of colonization against the Guatemalan Indians, that is, as a means to homogenize and hide the existence of multiple Maya identities. Maya people, and so their identities, are not homogeneous but, rather, different from and supplementary to each other; this is also indicated by the existence of twenty-two Maya groups and languages only in Guatemala.

16. Today's portrayal of indigenous people echoes the view of colonial writings, expressing the absence of humanness and "alterity" of native people. Bernal Diaz del Castillo declares: "I must say that most of the Indians were shamefully ridden with vice: . . . they were almost all given to sodomy. As far as the eating of human flesh is concerned, it may be said that they make use of it exactly as we do with butcher's meat" (1960 [1575]). The Guatemalan newspaper *Prensa Libre* reported in an article about the discovery and exhumation of clandestine burials: The civil patrols [the system of militarization of civilians in the countryside to monitor the presence of guerrillas] of this place have threatened several people because of the exhumations carried out in the area. According to the statements of the [victims'] families, the patrollers told them that they should cook the victims' bones with tomatoes and onions and use them as food; and that even more blood should be shed after the departure of the delegation that has initiated this work" (August 14, 1991:8). In the newspaper *El Grafico*, a cartoon appeared ("El Chispazo de Hoy") mocking a statement by a Maya representative who claimed that indigenous people should be included in the government. It

depicted indigenous people as half naked, carrying loads on their heads, and speaking broken Spanish—in sum, as creatures of the past and dysfunctional human beings (August 15, 1991:9).

17. According to Deleuze and Guattari, a rhizome is what escapes unity and imitation since each part, although unique in itself, is still part of a greater whole. In the rhizome, multiplicities do not sum each other but, rather, they elude order and categories, thus creating a total heterogeneous reality. The rhizome constantly deterritorializes and displaces itself by moving into different directions and by eluding any central point of return (Deleuze and Guattari 1987:7).

18. Other common symptoms reported at the examination of Guatemalan survivors of torture include headache, gastrointestinal problems, cardiopulmonary problems, chest pain, vertigo, menstrual irregularity, sleeping disorders, tiredness, impaired concentration and memory, and sexual problems.

19. In this respect Warren mentions that "styles of violence changed from making the public a witness to death, when bodies were purposely dumped beside major roads in the late 1970s during the Lucas García regime, to the hidden burials and clandestine cemeteries of the early 1980s during Ríos Montt's presidency. But the fact of torture and desaparecidos continued" (Warren 1993:31).

20. Interview with a refugee Maya woman. Indiantown, Florida, 1993.

21. Interview, Indiantown, Florida, April 1993.

22. I refer here to the annihilation of the body caused first by violence and then by sickness, and to the "creation" of a discourse of deviancy that subjectifies the victim.

23. The autobiography of Rigoberta Menchù (1984) is a clear example of empowerment through writing. She utilizes the testimonial genre in order to ingrain her own trauma in the collective history of terror that has affected hundreds of thousands of Guatemalans.

24. One victim of torture was asked to draw herself during her session of psychological therapy. The drawing portrayed a naked body covered almost entirely by an eye encapsulated in a square (photo reproduced in the program of the Symposium on Torture in Guatemala, Washington, D.C., 1992). Furthermore, victims of torture often report that the place where violence is inflicted is always monitored by someone else who is "behind the scenes."

Representation and Valuation in Micmac Prehistory: The Petroglyphs of Bedford, Nova Scotia

Brian Leigh Molyneaux

INTRODUCTION

People often say that knowledge of the past is a scarce and valuable resource that must be preserved. What a society remembers and how it stores its memories, however, depend on what individual and social groups see as their own heritage (see Salmond 1982). A group may preserve ideas in oral and literary traditions and store images and other objects in special places, but its knowledge of the "past" is actually knowledge of something that only exists—now—in the mind; no matter what the origin of ideas and objects, they exist in the present and it is here and now that they are used. The study of the past is therefore always a social act concerned with present realities, and so archaeologists and other specialists in the past work in a domain of social relations—even if they are not aware of it.

The difficulty in translation of ideas sacred to archaeology to other social groups and cultures reveals the social nature of this science. Some people object to the idea that the study of material remains is the best way to determine what really happened in history because they have their own ideas of time and historical reckoning, and of the best ways to approach these matters. In North America such conflicts may be intense, because archaeologists are usually not of the same culture as the people they study. Native people had to put up with archaeology for generations, but now that they are beginning to take back control of their cultures after hundreds of years of domination, archaeologists must also learn to adapt.

The problem of conflicting interpretations of the past as it is experienced by archaeologists and native people is shown clearly in situations where they are brought together in disputes over land. What follows is an account of the fight to save a small petroglyph site (BeCw-2) and surrounding lands in Nova Scotia from development. The questions to be explored are why the interpretations of specialists from both groups sometimes conflicted—why individuals could stand on the same rock and see something different. The main goal, however, is not to convey the obvious fact that interpretation is socially relative, but to argue that there are dangers in such freedom if the interpretations do not take into account and agree on what is actually found on the site—the evidence of the eyes.

Both archaeologists and native people place value on the past, and this value relates both to their analytical traditions and to the important matter at hand: the struggle for aboriginal rights. The problem is that both groups seem to value some parts of the past more than others, and it is this issue that poses the danger to the preservation of cultural heritage.

There are two significant effects of such valuation. What is seen as the important past may be routinely studied and talked about, written about, or represented in modern situations—what we call history. An ancient rock painting, for example, may be represented in different ways to reinforce modern social or political identity. The problem is that this act, in effect, tears the image from its roots in the landscape and its wider relations with other cultural and natural things. As a symbol or icon, the image may have a new meaning and a new and important purpose, but it is now an object, no longer bound to the original, and at risk of becoming a commodity, an item of trade, in the business of communication (see Molyneaux 1989, 1994).

If some parts of the past are neglected because they are seen as less useful than others in some modern agenda, they also run the risk of being lost to future generations when needs might change. At risk in such valuation is a just recognition of the contributions of all our ancestors to the present—not simply the ones whose ideas and images are used as symbols for modern social and political aspirations.

In order to show the effects of valuation on interpretation, I will criticize specific interpretations of this petroglyph site in Nova Scotia by archaeologists and anthropologists—including myself—and also some other people involved, including some native people. Most will remain anonymous. Through this criticism, however, I will attempt to point the way to a resolution to the conflict of traditions so that we can all learn better ways of dealing with the past in the present.

THE DISCOVERY

The Micmac people have carved images in the rocks of the Kejimkujik Lake area of south-central Nova Scotia since prehistoric times. In 1983, a resident of the town of Bedford, further north along the Atlantic coast near Halifax, discovered some new petroglyphs at a place called the Barrens, a patch of undeveloped land on the edge of town.

Figure 1
Micmac "Star" Petroglyph

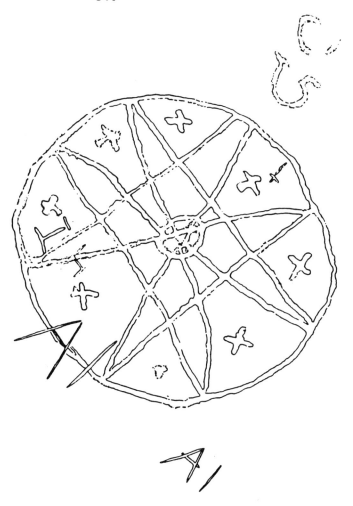

Note: The broken lines are indistinct parts of the actual petroglyph.

The Barrens is dominated by a series of remarkable quartzite ridges that run in parallel arcs across the face of a hill overlooking the sea. The ridges are unusual, looking like waves, with a sloping front, a rounded crest, and a vertical back, and they are separated by damp, wooded swales. The area survives only because at least until now, developers could not remove the rock economically and so build the kind of subdivision that covers the rest of the hill.

There seems no doubt about the Micmac origin of one of the petroglyphs: an eight-pointed star contained within a circle (see Figure 1). It resembles Micmac designs found in quillwork embroidery (Whitehead 1982) and other media, and Micmac people have said it is a celestial symbol linked to their religious beliefs (see also Rand 1894). Another image, a human-like form joined to a vulva, recalls carvings with sexual themes on the Kejimkujik Lake petroglyph sites (Molyneaux 1982). Because of the nature of the art, and the striking nature of the setting, local Micmacs and ethnologists have interpreted the place as sacred, the site of a shaman's rituals (Whitehead n.d.).

For several years the few people who knew of the discovery tried to the keep the location of the petroglyphs secret, but the intention of a developer to build a new subdivision in the area, destroying the Barrens as a whole, provoked a flood of publicity, and people took sides according to whether they were in favor of the plan or not. Many local residents supported the Micmac in their quest to save the petroglyphs, as they appreciated the Barrens as a wilderness area and were impressed by the presence of an important Micmac site in their neighborhood. Other townspeople rejected the interpretation of the petroglyphs as Micmac, choosing to believe that they were the work of neighborhood boys. During this time, many more visitors came to the site, and local residents and Micmac people reported some other possible petroglyphs. Fresh graffiti appeared in several places, some of it dangerously close to the weathered and difficult-to-see petroglyphs.

In order to gain further information about the petroglyphs and the Barrens, especially as to the extent of petroglyph carving in the area, the Town of Bedford and the Nova Scotia Museum set up an archaeological survey (Molyneaux 1990). I had intended to conduct this work as an empirical survey—a search for, and description of, what was on the rocks. But a specific event in the media coverage of this issue altered the course of the project: an artist and spiritualist from the Maliseet tribe of New Brunswick claimed on public radio that she had learned through fasting that the petroglyphs were pre-Columbian and that the circle petroglyph was not a celestial sign but a sweat lodge, marking a place of ritual fasting. Because of this act, the archaeology of the Barrens ceased being an "objective" survey of what was on the rocks; it became a journey into a long history of social conflict, of values, beliefs, ideals, and agendas in which the actual information on the rocks was secondary.

THE RESULTS OF THE ARCHAEOLOGICAL SURVEY

The results of the survey were unexpected and troubling. In spite of the great promise of a vast area of unexplored rock, there were no additional petroglyphs in the Barrens (Molyneaux 1990). For some of the towns-people and press, this meant that the value of the site was diminished because it lacked the scale of a great discovery—although others thought that if the site was a sacred place, it did not necessarily require, or invite, any more marks than it had.

One of the three petroglyphs, a stick figure throwing a spear, originally included with the others as of Micmac origin, proved to have been made in the 1970s by a local boy who also carved his initials and the date near the image.

These initials created even more of a problem. The boy cut them in with a steel chisel, but in less than twenty years weathering has made them difficult to see in ordinary light; they were overlooked when the carvings were discovered. Metal-cut initials from the 1920s show even more pronounced signs of weathering, including the rounding of carving edges. This rapid deterioration showed clearly that the aged appearance of the Micmac petroglyphs could not be used to even roughly date them, and it cast doubt on the original, confident notion that they may have been fashioned with stone tools. Little difference could be seen between the physical character of these carvings and nearby initials that were also gouged and scraped into the rock.

The other petroglyphs reported since the original discovery proved to be natural features of the rock. An ethnologist reported a possible "angel" figure on a slope farther along the same ridge, and other people found crosses and other patterns of shallow grooves in several places, identifying them as stick figures with upraised arms. These were actually features associated with the formation and weathering of the quartzite and the effects of glaciation.

It was at this point that the first collision of empirical and other forms of knowledge occurred, for there is no reason why images seen in rocks must be made by human hands. Natural forms commonly have cultural significance, as evidence of supernatural or historic events, as shown by the many sites of transformed beings across the world (see, e.g.,

Molyneaux 1987; Layton 1992). And indeed, the sight of these long rocky pathways crossing this hill above the sea struck all the supporters of this petroglyph site, whether Micmac or white, as remarkable. Some of the older residents in town—none of whom knew of the petroglyphs— recalled another place where they had seen many carvings, including animal tracks, holes, and circles. We found this site on the last day of the survey, cut off from the rest of the ridge by a highway. It did indeed have numerous pits and hollows highly suggestive of tracks and other forms, but these proved to be the remains of inclusions of softer minerals in the quartzite that had eroded away. Still, these "ancient carvings" formed part of the oral tradition of this local, largely white community.

Part of the problem with the rapid developments surrounded the inter- pretation of the site, considering the imminence of a threat to destroy it, was that all the experts who were involved in the study and interpretation of the site took everything at face value. At first, everyone thought that all the petroglyphs were of Micmac origin and so all the unusual features of the Barrens became aspects of its sacredness. This general feeling was reinforced by the apparent wildness of this last patch of untouched land in an area that was, literally, alive with the sound of construction.

A final discovery, however, altered both this idea and the growing speculation about the scale of shamanic activity believed for the area. A short distance from the petroglyphs along the ridge, a large slope of smooth, bare rock runs down to a cranberry bog, surrounded by trees. From the ridge, the bog is oddly symmetrical and a large stone in its center reinforces this appearance. It seemed at first that a shaman must have used this strange and compelling place for inspiration, as indeed, the slope faces the path of the sun, an important part of Micmac spirituality (Rand 1894). During the archaeological survey, however, we discovered that someone had formed and shaped the bog by building a low dike of loose rock packed with soil around it. And in the woods nearby, we found the remains of several small buildings with drystone foundations, a well, and a root cellar.

It turned out that this was the home and workings of a hermit who had moved into the Barrens around 1935 from his family home in Bedford and lived there until his death. His relatives said that he had built a pond and planted cranberries in an attempt to farm them. The illusion that this was a ritual site was destroyed.

In spite of these problems, however, we made an exciting discovery. The Micmac people were barely mentioned in a book on the local history of Bedford (Tolsen 1979), except, typically, in the opening chapter, but there was one reference to the Barrens that may be highly significant to its interpretation. Within the memory of some of the older residents, a wooden "tram-line" had run down through the Barrens, carrying logs to the mills. The account (Tolsen 1979:259) goes on to say that "There were Indians up there, also, and Sinclair Myers remembers Joe Morris, the Indian who made arrows for the boys." Further investigation indicated that some elder townsfolk still remembered hearing of Micmac people living in the Barrens around the turn of the century. One man recalled his father describing how they used to take supplies to a camp on level ground near the hermit's cabin, but left them at the edge, fearing the smallpox that had taken hold there. Such a camp seems plausible, considering that the Micmac would have been prevented from camping in their traditional areas at the mouth of the nearby Sackville River.

We tried to find the "level ground" where the Micmac might have lived. During this search, we discovered a small patch of exposed rock on a buried ridge immediately below the hermit's place on which someone had carved a name, the date of June 21, 1908, and the place name, Shubenacadie.

In the census of Enfield R.C. Parish for 1897, the Indian Reserve at Shubenacadie listed a person with the same surname and one of the same initials and, although it may be coincidental, this man's twenty-first birthday would have been June 21, 1908 (Tony Edwards, personal communication)—the same date as the carving on the rock!

THE RULING AGENDA

While we pursued these vague memories of a Micmac presence in the Barrens, the petroglyph images became instruments in the broader struggle for control of individual and social rights. For the Micmac, the petroglyphs were a visible sign of their rights to the land; for the townspeople, they were a symbol of their right to be protected from overdevelopment; and for archaeologists and ethnologists, they were a rare piece of evidence of Micmac art in earlier historic, or even prehistoric, times that needed to be protected. A Micmac artist involved in the archaeological survey created several new works incorporating these images and others from Kejimkujik Lake in several modern media, and the celestial petroglyph became the logo of a local antidevelopment group, the Shaman Wilderness Society.

When the archaeological survey was complete and it became clear that its findings would support the Micmac position, whatever doubts there were about the age, meaning, and function of the petroglyphs, the emphasis shifted from saving the site to preserving it. In the ensuing months, an advisory group was set up, bringing together Micmacs, townspeople, and representatives of government, business, and academia, and they have since made a number of proposals for protecting the land and the petroglyphs to ensure that their integrity will be preserved.

It may seem inappropriate and overly academic to talk about problems in the successful outcome of this controversy, but one needs to recognize that winning the war does not eliminate the effects of the battle. In this instance, people imposed a value on the past in order to defend rights to cultural and material property, and in this struggle, they used the most visible and accessible information about the site, the petroglyph images.

This approach has both good and bad aspects. Images are ideal tools for ideological reinforcement, and it is the sign of creativity and a thriving culture when someone uses the past in new ways—no less so here than in Europe during the rediscovery of classical antiquity in the Renaissance. But with their high visibility and aesthetic and iconographic impact, the petroglyphs absorbed virtually all the interest of the various groups, at the expense of the troubling and less visible information surrounding their creation and use.

This is particularly unfortunate because of the existence of a small amount of supporting evidence of Micmac activity in this place: the Micmac presence on the Barrens in the area of the petroglyph ridge into the first part of the twentieth century; a man, Joe Morris, connected to this almost totally neglected aspect of Bedford's history, and possibly another Micmac, from Shubenacadie. Although this information does not compare in magnitude to the petroglyphs, it could provide some insight into the actual history of the Barrens and its petroglyphs, rather than simply supporting the prevailing notion of this place as a monument to timeless cultural ideals.

Who were they? What happened to the camp? Are there Micmac people who remember this time and place? Is it necessary to know any of these things, since many people feel strongly that their ancestors should be left at peace, and because this is such a small issue in relation to the struggle for aboriginal rights as a whole?

One important reason to search further is that someone from this late nineteenth/early twentieth-century Micmac camp, apparently so close to the petroglyphs, could have carved them. Another reason, important to society as a whole, is that if we lose sight of individuals, and the events and acts that animate their lives, we are in a realm where there are no realities, no actualities, only general trends and points of view. Such idealism was a dominant feature of anthropology and archaeology in much of this century, to the detriment of the actual lives and histories of native people, and it is still a common problem in our complex world, especially when it dominates social and political struggles (see Molyneaux 1994).

What is important here is that as idealist accounts are unconcerned with the details of actual situations, so idealism in the current political and social struggle may account in part for the misrepresentation or rejection of factual information about Micmac heritage by some participants—including Micmac people—in the Bedford controversy. It is not surprising that the prodevelopment faction simply ignored the evidence on the rocks; but the failure by some archaeologists, ethnologists, and native people to consider the actual markings of past Micmac artists is more problematic.

An ethnologist who had correctly pointed out the relation of the Bedford images to other aspects of Micmac culture, and an archaeologist, myself, thought at first that the petroglyphs were probably prehistoric because they seemed at first glance to have been made with stone tools. And one Micmac participant stated in a paper that the claim by archaeologists that Micmac petroglyphs in general were postcontact was a speculation, and cited other sources that saw them as the work of the "wiklatmu'jk," tiny, elf-like beings. On the contrary, archaeologists have based their interpretation on the fact that many Micmac petroglyphs depict trade goods, such as guns and European clothing, sailing vessels, Roman Catholic altars, and other symbols, and images captioned and dated in Micmac script (Molyneaux 1982; 1985). Images without these historic references simply cannot be dated.

The intention here is not to dispute facts but to reveal a genuine intellectual and social dilemma that all people interested in the development of a more representative multicultural society must face: the difficulty with reconciling empirical and social knowledge. The problem is particularly clear in the examples above, because both the native and white specialists came to their conclusions using both kinds of knowledge. Indeed, the Micmac author states in one paragraph that the petroglyphs cannot be dated and then in the next paragraph, interprets them according to oral traditions and traditional Micmac religious beliefs.

This is an argument that the evidence of the eyes is as important as the evidence of the heart. If the Maliseet spiritualist who interpreted the Bedford petroglyph image as a sweat lodge had looked carefully at what she had identified as a clearly carved door, for example, she would have seen that it was in fact the letter A of a pair of initials carved on top of the petroglyph.

Such inconsistencies may be understood at one level because of the often justified rejection of archaeology and its information by native people. Archaeologists have earned disrespect by their isolation and disinterest in the realities of the people they study, and so their findings are rejected.

But there is another reason for having concern about such disinterest in empirical evidence from the past; by distorting or ignoring what has actually existed, one devalues any real past, or any real contribution by the ancestors—such as those individuals whose names and images have survived, carved on the rocks of the Barrens. Indeed, in all the words of expert submission and recommendation and media coverage since the archaeological survey, there are no words for the Micmac people who may have lived on the Barrens in the late nineteenth and early twentieth centuries. It seems that both specialists and other participants in this controversy focused on what many of them saw as an image from the distant past at the expense of the scattering of evidence in the Barrens about the acculturated past within our reach—but a part of history that may have also produced these petroglyphs.

This is not a criticism of the interpretation of the petroglyph as an important symbol or the petroglyph site as a sacred place. It does not matter how old the petroglyphs are or what details might be there or not—the Micmac discourse is expressed in terms of the land that was once all theirs, and people who have lived there since deep in the past. All these memories, this recognition, symbolized in these images in the rock, make the site sacred. But the Micmac of the nineteenth and twentieth centuries are part of this legacy, and so they, too, should be recognized.

THE LANDSCAPE OF KNOWLEDGE

If there is a lesson in all of this, it is that we must come to terms with the fact that memory is not only a complex overlay of interpretations and agendas, but also a landscape with physical dimensions. Parts of the earth have always been storehouses of memory, as the physical features of a place are tied to some mythological or actual event, remembered (see, e.g., Rappaport 1987). But there is also a part of memory that is silent, outside words, that is about doing, about movement and action in the world. Pilgrimage shows the significance of the physical journey; consider a sacred place, Adam's Peak in Sri Lanka, that is revered by Buddhists, Moslems, Christians, and others. Each has a different account of what great supernatural being left a footprint on the peak and each brings different prayers and offerings to leave at the top, but they are united in their desire to climb the rugged path to the summit. With all the controversy swirling around the Barrens and their modest scatter of petroglyphs, and the competing interpretations and interests of people of different cultures and backgrounds, the only thing that is perfectly clear about the images here is their sheer physical existence—you can feel the grooves with your fingers.

From the view above the Barrens rocks, however, native and nonnative specialists disagree because they see the world differently and pursue different agendas. As a result, their ways of knowledge about the material world are also isolated from each other. If we are to understand more about this shared world, we must find a way to make use of the insights of each form of knowledge, so that the silent evidence of the eyes, the physical experience of this strange and compelling place, can exist without being overwhelmed by the opinions and interpretations of experts from either culture.

The isolation of knowledge resources is an essential aspect of a society, part of the distribution of power and control of resources as a whole, but it is also influenced by physical access. Institutions preserve actual material evidence of the past, but this material is kept in places outside networks of social relations and realities—in museums, libraries, laboratories, and other storage places. An institutional setting is like a foreign country: many people crossing the boundary may be denied access to images, objects, or other information because they are not allowed to do research, are unfamiliar with the places and procedures, or find things within such environments that they think should not be seen or talked about, such as information about the dead or about religious objects or rituals.

Even if physical access to collections and research materials is not a problem, the path to an understanding of the past may be predetermined and suffused with implicit value. Indeed, the conventional structure of narrative literature and the physical structure of a book, whether historical account or field report, may provide implicit reinforcement for the valuation of the past. First of all, texts tend to link physical description and interpretation together through pages of writing as if one leads directly to the other. Second, in the physical environment of a chronological narrative the reader usually meets the distant past first, and then leaves it behind for increasingly more familiar territory as pages are turned. This symbolic and physical separation of the past from the present may cause a person to treat the distant past as wonderful and sophisticated—or deprived and primitive—as compared to the near present, in which the complexities of life are more clearly represented. The result may be that the individual neglects one for the other, in spite of their equivalence as things in the present that refer to the past—like the recent past of the Micmac.

There are now alternative forms of writing and organization that do away with the long and straight trail represented by a paper report or book.

Hypertext computer programs allow texts, static and moving images, and sounds to be incorporated into what the mind understands as three-dimensional structures. In such electronic environments, information is arranged in different levels, across the field of vision (the computer monitor screen) and in layers that can be examined individually, instead of in a set sequence of paragraphs and chapters. Each idea or picture is independent of the others around it. In such an electronic environment, readers can follow paths of their own choosing, instead of a single trail set by someone else.

The potential benefit of structuring and displaying knowledge in this way is that it allows any individual—a native researcher, for example—to organize, display, and control information according to his or her interests and priorities, rather than those of, for example, a nonnative archaeologist, ethnologist, or historian.

This creation of a more open informational landscape may help to save the fragile evidence that has been left to us from the past, perhaps shifting interest from the material object, all too often a political tool, to the discourse about its interpretation. That way the petroglyphs can simply be.

Working to solve the problem of the actual situation of production—who made the petroglyphs at the Barrens and why—remains, but such issues are outside the languages of tradition and interpretation, because the petroglyph makers are gone. That is a different issue, one between science and the earth.

Because what remains of the valued cultural past continuously erodes or fades away or is forgotten, it may seem to be a simple step to say that the "past" should be protected at all costs and memories institutionalized. But many people around the world would prefer that their ancestors' bones be allowed to lie undisturbed—and that memories should fade as the grass is allowed to grow up around the tombstones of an English cemetery. This solution may be difficult for those dedicated to the past, but it is a necessary part of memory, too.

NOTE

This chapter is a version of a paper I presented at the "Creating Shared Pasts: North American Oral Tradition and Archaeology" session at the annual meeting of the American Anthropological Association in San Francisco in December 1992. I am grateful to Randall H. McGuire and Larry J. Zimmerman for including me in their session. I am indebted to Jacob Climo, Michigan State University, for his interest in my paper and for offering to publish it in this volume. The project described was funded by the Nova Scotia Museum and the Town of Bedford.

I thank Robert Ogilvie, Ruth Whitehead, and Joan Waldron of the Museum, and Donna Davis-Lohnes of the Town of Bedford Planning Department for their organization and assistance with the project. Teresa McPhee, my field assistant, provided an artist's and a Micmac's perspective to a difficult but rewarding task. Tony Edwards, a Bedford local historian, introduced me to many of the towns-people; he also provided essential historical data. Louis Morris generously introduced me to the daughter of Joe Morris, and I am indebted to her, Ms. Patricia Morris, for telling me of the life of her father. Finally, I would like to express my gratitude to those kind people in Bedford who allowed me into their homes to talk about the Barrens: Mr. and Mrs. George Christie, Mr. Edward Boutilier, Mrs. Eileen Mitchell, Mr. and Mrs. Arthur Beach, Mrs. Mary Joudry, Mr. Dave Pasley, Mr. Mark Pasley, Mr. and Mrs. Stan Johnson and their son, Josh, and Mr. and Mrs. Donald Ross, whose son, Michael, found the petroglyphs in 1983.

VICARIOUS MEMORY

The key to understanding vicarious memory lies in the realm of emotions; such memories evoke powerful feelings in individuals, which link them to important group events they did not experience directly in their individual lives—but which impact greatly on their identities and connect them profoundly to their heritage and culture.

Jacob J. Climo

Prisoners of Silence: A Vicarious Holocaust Memory

Jacob J. Climo

I began writing this chapter when I first learned that the Holocaust was going to be commemorated in a public ritual. I am one of many Jews who believe that everything about the Holocaust needs to be told. For many years after the war, Holocaust survivors were silent about their experiences and the general public did not know much about it. They didn't speak sooner for many reasons. Survivors in Israel were often silent. Intense nationalism during the early years of the state created a hostile atmosphere; sometimes survivors were accused of passively allowing the Holocaust to happen. In some accounts survivors tried to conceal their experiences from their children to protect them, but when they reached adolescence the children insisted on knowing and the parents told them. In part, public rituals arose from the influence of Primo Levi and Elie Wiesel, especially from Wiesel's ability to bring into public view his role of witness (Wiesel 1958, 1970). Becoming a witness in Auschwitz enabled him to survive there, and in relating his testimony to the world so faithfully he helped define and assist in the search for meanings of the Holocaust for Jews and non-Jews throughout the world.

But when I first learned the Holocaust was going to be commemorated in a public ritual, although I knew intellectually that public disclosure was necessary, I was overcome with powerful feelings of emotional pain and anxiety and a strange sense of loss, betrayal, shame, and urgency, as if some secret of my own past had been revealed by a stranger, without my knowledge or consent. When I began to confront these feelings (because I couldn't avoid or repress them) I didn't have a clue about their source.

This chapter arose out of my search for the source of those strange yet urgent feelings I could not explain. It is a personal narrative, my effort to explore my memory of how I became aware of the Holocaust and its emotional impact on my childhood in America. With time and distance from these childhood events I am able to construct a bridge between the past and the present. Yet the painful emotions my memories still evoke in me attest to the power of the past in the present, and especially to the power of vicarious memory, a concept that refers to strong, personal identifications with historical collective memories that belong to people other than those who experienced them directly.

I present my vicarious memory of the Holocaust in narrative form. But it is first necessary to examine the concept of vicarious memory and its correlate, vicarious identity, because I suspect it can explain many strong emotional commitments people make to rituals and collective experiences they learned about but did not experience directly. As in my case, an individual can integrate a vicarious memory into his or her identity by maintaining a strong attachment to a person who experienced it directly or from a person who integrated it into his or her own identity as a vicarious memory. Through strong emotional attachments, vicarious memories may be passed from one generation to the next as a parent passes his or her personal experiences to a child. Or they may be passed over many generations as collective memories of groups that share a common historical identity and the process of its redefinition through time.

Much anthropological literature supports the concept of vicarious memory. For example, hunger may be remembered and passed along from parents to children without formal rituals or explanations. Paul Fussell (1983) identifies Minnesota as the geographic center of obesity in America and explains that the past generation of European immigrants to that region suffered from chronic hunger in Europe; overeating by the next generation is both a vicarious memory of hunger and a cultural response that proclaims without words, "Look at our size, we are not hungry (as our parents once were)."

Some vicarious memory and identity may arise through an individual's choice and discovery, without parental modeling or influence. Young children, for example, may argue about the professional baseball or football teams they identify with personally. Hence, an eight year old boy can remember and relate with pride that his team played in the World Series twenty years ago. Listening to his pride one might imagine he had been there himself. His memory of the team's past accomplishments, even before his own life began, has become real for him and the memory of actions that came before him are integrated as part of his identity.

It is not surprising that much vicarious memory is learned in childhood, because in rearing children parents have an opportunity to transmit the meaning of their own identities and experiences, both vicarious and direct, to their offspring. In a recent paper (Climo 1990) I showed how story-telling by elderly grandparents can be used to transmit ethnic and family identities to young children. My example was a ninety year old man's narration of a family story that took place when he was four years old. He recounts these family events as a story his mother told him about the first move in his lifetime, events that he experienced directly but was not old enough to remember first-hand. His story then lies in a gray zone, between personal and vicarious memory.

Some vicarious memories may be taught overtly as part of culture. The Hagadah, at least several hundred years old, is the legend Jews read out loud during the traditional Passover seder, the festive family meal. It retells the story of the Jews' exodus from Egypt, from slavery to freedom. The Hagadah says explicitly that each individual in every generation is expected to regard himself as if he had gone personally out from Egypt. In the narrative, each son in the context of a dialogue with his father is judged on his empathy and ability to identify personally with the collective experience.

And vicarious memories may be learned covertly. In my field research in Mexico I often witnessed women praying in tears to a picture on a family altar of the Madonna and Child. As a young daughter witnesses her mother's identification with the Madonna I suspect she absorbs its meaning and feels similar emotional attachment and identification with the memory of Mother Mary's suffering and with her own mother's identification with that suffering.

Modern technology can facilitate the construction of vicarious memories. Paul Stoller (1992) explains that for the Songhay people of Niger cinema-tographer Jean Rouch has become a "cinematic Griot," a kind of bard whose ethnographic films from decades past trigger the vicarious memories of current generations of Songhay as they witness people of the past, including some deceased relatives and friends, performing rituals and ceremonies that have important collective meaning to them.

In reconstructing my childhood I can now identify some of the processes involved in the formation of my vicarious memory of the Holocaust. As a child I began to identify vicariously with the Holocaust as a consequence of strong emotional attachments to teachers and friends and through what I now understand was a forbidden, collective conspiracy of silence concerning the Holocaust by the Jewish community of my childhood. Since then I have become aware of other forms of conspiratorial silence:

for example, that which surrounds children regarding sexual abuse or the silence around nursing home residents regarding death (Shield 1988). But then I was unaware. During my childhood I was a prisoner of silence, caged by my identification with powerful memories I had experienced vicariously.

A fragile bird, I sat silently in my cage as the door swung open. My eyes transfixed on the fresh air outside, I imagined myself flying out and up into the warm sun of freedom. But I remained in the prison, motionless and silent. Like an arrow in the sheath, I could not find the courage to speak.

I grew up in a community of Holocaust survivors. Although my parents were American-born, most of the important models of my youth—teachers, neighbors, local merchants, and parents of my friends—came to America after the war as refugees. The healthiest among them came to pick up the pieces of their lives or begin again.

A Bar Mitzvah boy, I often walk home with cantor Greenberg from our temple. I can see Isaac Greenberg's opened mouth, his golden teeth gleaming. He is shouting defiance, taunting the Nazi executors, his smile singing in his deep baritone voice, "These are my golden teeth. You wanted them but you could not get them and you never will." As the cold wind rips through our coats his eyes are also glistening. He walks with one arm down, his hand at his side. With his other hand he grasps the collar of his dark wool coat, holding his scarf in place while protecting his throat and voice so he can sing and thus survive. I walk beside him holding my coat collar the same way. His pace is continuous, he never slows down or speeds up, he acknowledges none of the elements, none of the obstacles; there is no cold, no wind, no buildings or markers, no sidewalk, no distance yet to walk, no defeat. He walks as if he will never stop and I learn from him that he never will stop.

Many survivors brought a special kind of mental anguish, which they developed through persecution. It was a raw, human desperation, a passionate drive for freedom, an unquenchable need to be cared for; their needs were far beyond my comprehension. In one of my earliest memories I am at my grandmother's house asking my mother about the young woman sitting at the kitchen table eating very intensely. She is so engrossed in it that she never bothers to look up or greet us. I ask my mother who she is and what she is eating. Her name is Magda. She is a refugee boarding at my grandmother's and she is eating beef fat. Why, I ask, would anyone eat meat fat? The thought of it made me nauseous. Mother explained that during the war the Jews couldn't get any meat to eat. Magda was making up for the war years all at once. She didn't look different from an ordinary person, just hungrier.

I did not realize that many survivors remained enslaved to their past and that their slavery would have a direct impact on my life. In those early postwar years, being a student of survivors meant learning to keep the darkest secrets of one's torment silent, locked deep within the soul. It was a collective conspiracy to keep it there forever, thus hiding the pain but also denying that deep inner yearning to be free of it. The community may have felt morally stronger for it, but we carried the burden too long and too far. Even I, who learned it second-hand, used my knowledge to conceal feelings, and so remained enslaved to my fear.

My childhood was instilled with Holocaust images and fears, even Holocaust games if such a thing is imaginable. One game is escaping from home quickly without anyone noticing because the Nazis are coming. Did you remember to take the cash? Did you bring the fake passports so we can cross into Canada? The border guards won't recognize us because our English is perfect. When he asks you where you were born say very casually, "Oh, Cleveland." It's the truth after all. Isn't it?

Another game is hiding our identity in public, a game I play with my sister when we ride the train to visit our aunt in New York. We fool the other passengers. They speak to us about Christmas and we smile and nod at them, pretending Christmas is also an important part of our lives. Then they unwrap ham sandwiches for lunch and offer us some and we politely refuse without revealing who we are. My eyes catch my sister's eyes and in that sparkling light that recognition ignites and in the clatter and clang, the train running along its rails, we sustain the illusion, and so survive another trial.

We also play the survivor-tastes-food-for-the-first-time game: as our father pounds his fist on the table shouting "Food is life," we pretend it is our first food after the camp is liberated and who cares what it tastes like; and so we survive. And I play the game of emotional and physical deprivation, which includes not crying out in the night, so the Nazis will not hear me and know where I am hiding. And I play the game of not complaining when I am hungry or thirsty or when my feet are frozen from the ice. These games are endless practice. But for what?

In those years people didn't speak openly about the Holocaust and certainly not to children. It was barely ever mentioned. Even parents rarely or never spoke about their experiences to their children. Some say it was a desire to protect the children. But it was also the inability of most people to put their humiliation into words. It was too soon. Yet it hovered over their daily lives like a dark cloud of pain and dread. And it was passed along to me through unspoken gesture and mood. The most powerful learning in childhood is what we see adults do and what we feel they are feeling rather than what they tell us. In this way they unknowingly transmitted their pain and fear to me.

It was a singular force in the lives of most of my Hebrew teachers and many of the parents of my friends. It was their deep secret—an unspoken reality that imposed itself on everything in their lives and on every child they knew. Yet, as American children we could not understand why our Hebrew teachers were so different.

Mr. Guzik was a young rabbi in Poland just before the war. When he came to America after the Holocaust his life was only a piece of what it might have been. He saw the Nazi soldiers murder his wife and small children. He never remarried. He only went on living because of his unflinching faith in God. But he never managed to rekindle his spirit because he never left the scene of the murder.

Mr. Guzik could not control the students. His class was always in chaos. The noise was never-ending and several times during the hour more aggressive teachers would come in to quiet the students. Guzik could never raise his voice above a soft fragile plea for quiet; it was really his plea for peace. Somehow all of us knew that the noise inside him was so much greater. Our noise could not compete. Besides, to him, the noises we children made were the sounds of Jewish life. Try as he might he could not object to or interfere with that noise of Jewish life. He needed our life-noise to balance the noise inside him of Jewish death.

One gloomy winter afternoon a few years before his untimely death he looked out the window at the darkening sky and stopped the class. He told us he remembered such a day in Poland after the Nazis killed his family. He hid out with the Polish partisans in the woods.

His body survived but his spirit never left the Holocaust. While we read and learned from the Bible we could feel its drug-like effect on him. Only while concentrating on the readings would his mind drift into a tolerable world, freed from the horrible chaos and noises planted deep inside him. No student ever asked about that noise. It was so loud even we could hear it from within him. After all, he was our teacher. We could feel the noise from him. Who would think to inquire about the most obvious reality?

Mr. Sarnoff was another teacher, a survivor who repressed the most important horrors in his life. I copied him by repressing my own growth and by burying my sadness. Shortly after my Bar Mitzvah my father returned to the orthodox synagogue where his father had been a charter member. I was enrolled in the synagogue's after-school high school. When I entered the school Rabbi Baumgarten gave me a test; I had to read and translate a few lines of the Chumash, the Old Testament, and Rashi, the medieval rabbi whose commentaries are fundamental to Jewish understanding of the scriptures. I had never studied Rashi, and his script is printed distinctly so I couldn't even read it. Rabbi Baumgarten smiled at me while he explained that my education in the conservative synagogue wasn't good enough, even though I had been one of the best students there. It was a deep blow to me when he put me in a grade where most of the students were younger. That became the source of my disruptive behavior. The teacher I persecuted most was Mr. Sarnoff, because he was new. He was originally from Czechoslovakia, and had come to the city to study for his Ph.D. He used to write important sayings from the Rabbis and the Ethics of the Fathers on the board. We teased him unmercifully about his accent. I was often exiled to the hall for long periods. The last straw was when he said, "No more disturbtions" and my friend and I burst out laughing and corrected him. His face and neck turned red; he was totally humiliated.

My parents had one pat answer to any problems in Hebrew school. In their minds all of my problems arose because I didn't have enough time in class. So when Rabbi Baumgarten called about my behavior they decided to hire Mr. Sarnoff to tutor me in the Talmud, Jewish law. The plan was that private lessons would help me develop greater respect for him and I wouldn't be disruptive in the class.

I walked to his apartment on Superior Park Drive every Saturday afternoon. That was the first time I ever saw anyone make coffee from tap water; since it was the Sabbath he couldn't heat the water on the stove so he let the tap run until it was hot enough to make instant coffee. Then he sat at the table sipping the coffee loudly with obvious delight and stared at me intensely while I read and attempted to translate and understand selected passages from the Talmud.

The Talmud text consists of rabbis discussing the scriptures over many centuries, presenting their differing interpretations of the meaning of the sacred scrolls for the everyday life of Jews. The laws and problems of human life are regarded as timeless, so the discourse has no recognized historical context. The discussion often opens with a question or problem. For example, the rabbis ask how late they can begin the evening service to fulfill the requirement to pray every night. This discussion that follows may begin with a rabbi who lived, say, a thousand years ago and his comment will be answered by another rabbi who lived four hundred years ago. The discourse proceeds as if all the rabbis are sitting and standing around a single, large rectangular dining room table as it floats through the sky, where time and space are subordinated to the universal conflicts and dilemmas of the human condition.

Mr. Sarnoff's presentation of the Talmud involved a mixture of selections, including parts he felt every Jew simply had to know, and parts I realized were subtly yet obviously addressed to me as a disruptive barbarian who needed to be civilized. I didn't learn very well and we didn't go very far. We had to repeat some sentences for weeks. Even I was surprised how quickly and systematically I could forget the meaning of the Hebrew words from one week to the next.

I learned better when the portion had a direct application to me. Mr. Sarnoff told me that the rabbis were very concerned that we must understand the meaning of the commandment not to kill. Unlike some other commandments that involve mundane acts like stealing, keeping the sabbath, and bearing false witness, killing seemed like such an extraordinary act. But according to one rabbi it isn't: a man commits murder if he causes another person to become so enraged in public that his face turns red. I knew immediately that one was for me. Mr. Sarnoff had light brown hair, almost blonde, and very deep blue eyes. His complexion was fair and when we laughed at him in class that day his face had turned red. Until then it was part of the fun of disturbing the class. Now I could think of myself as a murderer.

Those lessons were colored by my unspoken thoughts about Mr. Sarnoff in the Nazi death camps. But he set up clear borders and I could never ask him about it directly. My most sustaining thought was that what I needed to know most about him I could not ask, and what he most needed to tell me he could not say. The most important things about him remained unspoken, and even then I could feel a barrier between us.

Mr. Sarnoff taught me something important on those Shabbat afternoons. It was about his own sense of discipline and the strength of his will to survive in spite of his enemies' efforts to murder him and destroy his spirit. The Talmud classifies people according to the degree and duration of their anger. The worst and most dangerous person is the man who becomes angry with very little provocation but cannot let go of his anger; instead it takes hold of him and the anger is sustained for a very long time. Of course, the kind of person we should strive to be grows angry very slowly—trying to imitate God—while his anger passes quickly. The remaining two types are intermediary. One man becomes angry slowly but also forgets his anger slowly. He is burdened. The other man becomes angry easily and forgets it easily; he is a foolish and shallow man.

I never asked Sarnoff what type he was. I somehow understood he was profoundly angry and it wasn't because of me. I realized my father was foolish; his anger was easy to arouse and slow to assuage, and I was sad about that because in my heart I also felt that my father was sensitive and profound. I knew I understood very little about myself and my own feelings.

On one occasion my sister and I drove into the parking lot of Sarnoff's apartment building and took a picture of his car. It was a 1955 two-toned Chevy, turquoise and white. Even then everyone seemed to love that car and to know instinctively that it would become a classic. My sister had a crush on Sarnoff. She met him in the synagogue one Saturday morning when he came to pray. He was eligible but quite a bit older. But my family didn't mind; they liked him very much.

Sarnoff and Beccie went out a few times in the evening after Shabbat and he liked her. One evening he told her that he needed a more mature woman, one who would understand him when he woke up at night screaming, reliving his nightmares in Auschwitz. His job as a fourteen year old boy in the camps was to shovel the ashes of dead bodies from the ovens and take them away in wheelbarrows. He had been abused sexually by the Nazi guards and those memories still haunted him.

I often thought about him involved in forced homosexual acts with the Nazi guards. I wondered if being abused in that way had made him into a homosexual. But I could never ask him about his experience. And he could never tell me about the horror he knew when he was my age. I could feel him suffering as I suffered, from an inability to speak about his pain. Sarnoff and I remained prisoners of silence.

Many aspects of culture such as ritual and narrative, or in the case of the Holocaust, the retelling or the silent communication of events to children, may provide the vehicle for vicarious memory and its logical outcome, transmitting collective identity. The key to understanding the importance of vicarious memory lies in the realm of emotion; such memories evoke powerful feelings in individuals, which link them to important group events they did not experience directly in their individual lives but which impact greatly on their identities and connect them profoundly to their heritage and culture.

Having brought to light my vicarious childhood memories of the Holocaust, I am now able to confront and examine my intense and complex emotions when I first learned that the Holocaust had become a public event—why I felt loss, betrayal, abandonment, and urgency, and why I knew intellectually that it needed to be commemorated in public. Putting the Holocaust on the calendar as a public, collective event contrasted sharply with my memory of silence and secrecy. The loss I felt was the sharing I had experienced as a child; sharing an unspoken, secret experience with adults had bonded me in silence to the generation of Holocaust survivors. The public speaking out about the Holocaust put an abrupt end to the secret nature of that bond, and I lost an important attachment of my childhood, something familiar and important to me. I felt betrayal in the sense that I was part of the conspiracy but not part of the decision to end it. Ending the silence at the same time forced me to reconsider the Holocaust in a new way. I could no longer regard it as an unspoken secret carrying intense but unfocused emotions that I could hide behind in childhood innocence. Making it public required me as an adult to consider it for the first time rationally and consciously as a real event; I had to confront it intellectually as an adult, not only emotionally as a child.

And for one of the few times in my life, I found myself crying out loud when I thought about the Holocaust. I was crying because I began to understand the nature of genocide and I was crying because as a child I had not cried but simply had accepted my reality without question. And I cried because I suddenly became acutely aware of the immense pain my Holocaust teachers had repressed and concealed from me, and because I understood for the first time that the conspiracy of silence was constructed to conceal their pain, so they could control it and it would not control them.

I believe my feelings of abandonment also represent a sense of accepting the responsibility to remember the Holocaust, a responsibility passed from one generation to the next: from those who had experienced it directly to those, like me, who had experienced it vicariously. For the generation of survivors, Holocaust fears and memories had encompassed their lives in the postwar years. Most felt little desire to talk about it; they wanted instead to repress it and get on with their lives. But their mannerisms, body language, attitudes, perceptions, and melancholia betrayed them and set the tone for transmitting their feelings to anyone near them, especially to children like me who were sensitive to them as people.

But for my generation, however real and vital to life, Holocaust memories and identities will always be vicarious. Understanding the Holocaust and its universal human messages about genocide and in particular Jewish terms, about the gaps in Jewish life caused by the destruction of European Jewry, requires talking and telling: putting overwhelming experiences into words and language so we can carry the message and the memory with us now and into the future.

Memories and
Their Unintended
Consequences

Iwao Ishino

It has been more than fifty years since President Roosevelt signed
Executive Order 9066, which authorized the incarceration of 120,000
Japanese Americans living on the West Coast at the beginning of World
War II. This incarceration took place without due process of law and
without formal charges of misbehavior. The federal officials who supported
this Executive Order attempted to justify it on the basis of "military
necessity." However, as postwar studies have shown, military necessity
was just an excuse. A study by a congressional commission in 1982,
for example, concluded that the placing of the Japanese Americans in
concentration camps was the result of "racial prejudice, war hysteria and a
failure of political leadership" (Commission on Wartime Relocation and
Internment of Civilians 1982).

However wrong the Executive Order 9066 was in 1942 and however
humanely the order was carried out in the ten wartime internment camps,
the long-term consequences of the order on both the interned people and
American society at large were incalculable. In this chapter I will discuss
some of these long-term consequences in the context of memories,
generations, and culture—the themes that run throughout the present book.
First, I will discuss why the survivors of internment camps repressed their
memories of camp life for two decades and what was done later to resurrect
their memories. Then I will address how these submerged memories
affected their children as well as the Japanese American community in
general. Finally, I suggest how the children of the camp survivors, who
came of age in the late 1960s and early 1970s, contributed toward the

formation of a new ethnic entity known as Asian Americans and sometimes as Asian Pacific Americans. The creation of the new entity was not
only the product of a common, shared need to fight racism among the
various Americans of Japanese, Chinese, Korean, and others of Asian
descent, but it also led to community activism and organized electoral
politics that were absent in the early years of post–World War II. But
before I get into these issues, a background statement on the Japanese
American community will be helpful.

THE PREWAR JAPANESE AMERICAN COMMUNITY

The Japanese immigration to the U.S. mainland began soon after the
Chinese Exclusion Act of 1882. From a population size of only 2,039 in
1890, the mainland Japanese community (excluding those in Hawaii) grew
to 72,257 by 1910 when it surpassed the Chinese population in size. For
the next twenty years, while the Chinese population remained virtually
constant, the Japanese nearly doubled, to 138,834 (Takaki 1989:180). This
population increase came, not from more immigrants arriving on these
shores, but from the second-generation children of immigrants. It is
interesting to note that the Japanese American community coined special
terms to recognize the differential memories and legacies that existed
between the generations—*Issei* for the immigrant group and *Nisei* for the
children who were born in this country.

Because of the prevailing attitudes toward people of Asian descent, the
Issei were not eligible to become naturalized citizens, even though
many had been residents for more than thirty years. (It was not until 1952,
seven years after the end of World War II, that the Issei became eligible for
naturalization under the Walter-McCarran Immigration and Naturalization
Act.) Moreover, the Issei, along with other foreign-born Asians in
California and other Western states, were prohibited by law from owning
land and from marrying non-Asians. By 1924, this anti-Japanese climate
on the West Coast was so pervasive that further immigration from Japan
was prohibited. This 1924 law and other discriminatory laws resulted in a
rather steep cultural gap between the Issei and Nisei generations. The Issei,
or first generation, not being able to become U.S. citizens, identified with
Japan, their homeland, while the Nisei, born and educated in the United
States, identified with this the only country they knew. However, many
Issei, not certain what the future might hold for their families, sent their
Nisei children to Saturday schools to study Japanese language and culture.
The Issei believed that if the anti-Japanese sentiments worsened, they

would have to return to Japan with their Nisei children. The language school training was seen as a form of insurance and preparation for that worst case scenario. In fact, some Issei sent their children to Japan for a Japanese education. These were called *Kibei*. According to Hosokawa (1969:296), there were some eight thousand Kibei in the United States on December 7, 1941, who had spent three years or more in Japan.

However, by the 1930s, sufficient numbers of Nisei had come of age to manage their own future and to exert influence on the community's future. By the time of Pearl Harbor, the Nisei constituted two-thirds of the Japanese American community. Perhaps in response to their growing recognition of this leadership in their local community and at the same time in full awareness of their minority status in the general American society, the Nisei formed an organization in 1930, known as the Japanese American Citizen's League (JACL). By 1934 some twenty-one chapters located in Washington, Oregon, and California were linked together into a national organization (Hosokawa 1982). The JACL published a weekly newspaper, *Pacific Citizen*, which served as the main voice by which the organization reached its membership and the larger society. (More will be said about this organization when the postwar situation is described.)

Serving the Japanese American communities on the West Coast were a number of newspapers like the *Rafu Shimpo* and the *Kashu Mainichi*. A recent study (Yoo 1993) of the Japanese language newspapers published on the West Coast in the 1930s reveals a number of interesting facts about this Japanese American community. First of all, the 1930s was the period of the Great Depression and job opportunities were limited, especially for minority groups. Accordingly, much of the community looked inward for its basic recreational, religious, and social life. Secondly, when the Sino-Japanese war broke out in 1937, the community was split ideologically. Many Issei writers took a pro-Japan interpretation on the progress of the war, while the Nisei journalists took a more critical view of the Japanese action in China. And finally, the newspapers reported a few incidents where Chinese Americans took out their frustrations on some Japanese Americans over this Asian war.

This same war was the reason for my first appearance on the pages of the local newspaper, the *San Diego Union*. A Chinese American friend, Jack Wong, and I were interviewed for our respective views on this Asian war, even though I was grossly uninformed about it. Perhaps what made this story newsworthy was that both Jack and I were in the high school R.O.T.C. unit.

In any case, by the time World War II came along, the majority of the

Japanese American community was composed of Nisei, as I noted above. Most Nisei were in their late teens and about one-fifth of them were married, mostly within the Japanese American community. Less than 1 percent had married outside of their racial or ethnic boundary. To put it another way, the Nisei was the generation that came of age in the late 1930s and early 1940s when the Japanese American community was closely knit and provincial in its outlook.

Though there were speculations that a war between the United States and Japan might lead to the incarceration of certain enemy aliens (i.e., the Issei), the Nisei did not believe that they would be affected because they were citizens. Their confidence in the rights of citizenship was shattered when the Nisei found themselves face-to-face with military orders for evacuation and internment following President Franklin Roosevelt's Executive Order 9066. Even though several Nisei used the courts to challenge the constitutionality of these military orders, most Nisei entered the internment camps without engaging in any form of mass protest. However, after the incarceration took place, a deep and long-lasting controversy emerged where one group of Nisei argued that the JACL had betrayed American principles of justice by urging its own constituents "to accept evacuation to U.S. Army-operated concentration camps" (Hosokawa 1982:190). The dissidents also argued that the JACL had too great an influence in persuading the military and government authorities that the Japanese Americans would obey these evacuations peacefully because they were loyal citizens eager to serve the war effort.

Much has been written about life in these concentration camps and much has been written about the historical circumstances that led to this unfortunate event (see, e.g., Uchida 1982, Spicer 1969). Here is a short description of the camps, or "Relocation Centers," which summarizes well my own thoughts about them:

It can be said safely that there were no happy Relocation Centers. All had their problems. At best, camp life was abnormal—subject to uncertainty, fear, frustration, anger, emotional pressures, great physical discomfort, resentment, and beset by an abundance of rumors that fed on boredom and bitterness. (Wilson and Hosokawa 1980:220)

Other than this short quotation, I shall not attempt to describe the experiences in the camps, because my purpose here is to examine what happened afterwards, that is, how the memories of camp life formed the basis for a series of events and collective actions that were unexpected at the time the uprooted people were leaving the camps.

MEMORIES OF THE "SILENT GENERATION," THE NISEI

It may seem natural for the Japanese American community today to be dedicating monuments and going on rather expensive pilgrimages to the former camp sites where they were held as prisoners during World War II. But from the vantage point of the immediate postwar years, the Issei and Nisei had no interest in revisiting the camps, much less in raising funds to dedicate monuments at these camp sites. The reason for their disinterest in these symbols of remembrance was fairly obvious to the former internees. They did not cherish reliving the suspicion of disloyalty and the feelings of being victimized by the wartime hysteria. Revisiting their former camps and placing monuments would have meant a resurrection of unpleasant memories that they had repressed or had forgotten.

Many *Sansei*, the children of the Nisei, have commented on the failure of their Nisei parents to discuss and explain what conditions were like in the camps. One Sansei (Nagata 1993:vii) tells about an incident of finding a jar of colored shells under the kitchen sink when she was six years old. Not getting a satisfactory answer from her Issei grandmother, she asked her mother. Nagata describes her mother's response:

"Oh, I made them in camp." "Was it fun?" I asked enthusiastically. "Not really," she replied. Her answer puzzled me. The shells were beautiful, and camp, as far as I knew, was a fun place where children roasted marshmallows and sang songs around the fire. Yet my mother's reaction did not seem happy. I was perplexed by this brief exchange, but I also sensed I should not ask more questions.

Then Nagata generalizes from this interchange:

As time went by, "camp" remained a vague, cryptic reference to some time in the past, the past of my parents, their friends, my grandparents, and my relatives. We never directly discussed it. It was not until high school that I began to understand the significance of the word, that *camp* referred to a World War II American concentration camp, not a summer camp.

Another Sansei has written (Hirasuma 1992:50) about her parents' failure to communicate with her about their internment experience at the Jerome camp in Arkansas:

By the time I was born, exactly a year after the bombing of Hiroshima, the family just called it "Jerome" or "camp." Time was separated between pre-camp and post-camp. "We knew them from camp." "That was before Jerome [camp]." "We had to buy a new one after camp." No one told me what camp was and I never asked. I just accepted its existence. Yet somehow I knew that camp was not a good place, whatever it was.

Indeed it was not until the late 1960s, nearly three decades after they were first incarcerated, that the Nisei began to drop their inhibitions about discussing the internment experience. About the only noteworthy event was a weekend workshop the UCLA Extension Department organized in 1967 to commemorate the twenty-fifth anniversary of Executive Order 9066 (Nakanishi 1993:18).

This silence or the unwillingness on the part of the Nisei generation to dredge up their memories about their camp experience has produced some critical responses on the part of their children, the Sansei generation. Many Sansei did not understand why their parents have remained silent. There was a language barrier between themselves and their Issei grandparents' generation, but there was no such barrier in the Nisei household. They spoke English.

In this context, consider an announcement inviting the public to participate in pilgrimage to the former Tule Lake camp, the last camp to be closed. The sponsors of this program explained:

We hope this journey [pilgrimage to Tule Lake] will allow us to heal the intergenerational wounds of Executive Order 9066. This is the time for you to talk with your children, parents and interested people about a painful subject in a safe and supportive environment." (*Rafu Shimpo*, July 6, 1994, 1)

This explanation is given for a pilgrimage taking place not five or ten years after the camps were closed, but in August 1994, some fifty years after the end of World War II.

Another type of unanticipated activity at the closing of the camps was the set of political activities dealing with Executive Order 9066 (E.O. 9066). This order that set in motion a series of events leading to the incarceration camps became obsolete when World War II ended. However, there was no formal statement of termination for E.O. 9066 and there were many civil rights activists who were concerned that the order had some life left in it. For example, the basic idea of incarcerating citizens under emergency conditions in E.O. 9066 was incorporated in the "Emergency Detention Act," Title II of the Internal Securities Act of 1950. During the urban race riots in sixteen American cities in 1966, some concerned citizens feared that this detention act would be activated and the "trouble-makers" placed in a camp such as the one at Tule Lake in northern California. Officially recognizing this threat only in 1968, the national JACL began a systematic campaign to repeal this Title II law (Nagata 1993:189). The campaign was spurred on by the Sansei activists—a part of the 1960s generation—who were critical of the JACL's World War II role of representing the Nisei to the federal government as a cooperative and "Quiet American" who could be led by the nose. This detention provision in the act of 1950 was repealed in 1971.

Soon after the successful campaign to repeal the Title II detention program was finished, JACL entered another campaign to obtain an apology for the errors committed by E.O. 9066. Taking advantage of a year of national celebration (that is, the Bicentennial Year of 1976), JACL requested from the president a formal statement regarding the termination of E.O. 9066. By some delicate lobbying efforts, this campaign was also successfully completed. On February 19, 1976, President Gerald Ford issued this proclamation (quoted in Hosokawa 1982:340–42):

February 19th is the anniversary of a sad day in American history. It was on that date in 1942, in the midst of the response to the hostilities that began on December 7, 1941, that Executive Order No. 9066 was issued . . . resulting in the uprooting of loyal Americans. . . .

We now know what we should have known then—not only was that evacuation wrong, but Japanese Americans were and are loyal Americans. On the battlefield and at home, Japanese Americans . . . have been and continue to be written in our history for the sacrifices and contributions they have made to the wellbeing and security of this, our common Nation.

The Executive Order that was issued on February 19, 1942, was for the sole purpose of prosecuting the war with the Axis Powers, and ceased to be effective with the end of those hostilities. Because there was no formal statement of its termination, however, there is concern among many Japanese Americans that there may yet be some life in that obsolete document. I think it appropriate, in this our Bicentennial Year, to remove all doubt on that matter, and to make our commitment in the future.

Still another unanticipated postwar activity by the "silent" Nisei was the resurrection of three court cases that challenged the military orders that excluded the Japanese Americans from the West Coast. In 1942 three Niseis—Gordon Hirabayashi, Minoru Yasui, and Fred Korematsu—were put in prison because they challenged these wartime orders. In the midst of World War II (in 1943) their test cases were reviewed by the Supreme

Court. The Court had decided that the exclusion order was a lawful exercise of the army's power and that due process of law was not violated (Nakanishi 1993; see also Wilson and Hosokawa 1980:252).

At the end of the war, many Nisei believed that their wartime record for serving in the military had proven their loyalty and their place in American society. It was not necessary to review these court cases because by so doing it would call the public's attention to them again. Besides, there was still a large part of the American public that did not know about the internment of the Japanese Americans, or if they did know, some of them accepted the very fact of incarceration as evidence of the need to be interned (Nagata 1993:188).

But other Nisei believed that these court cases should be reopened to inform the public about the injustice of internment and about "a story of democracy gone awry." This desire to reopen the court cases was reinforced by the fact that researchers discovered under the Freedom of Information Act government documents that indicated that Justice Department officials withheld vital evidence and issued false statements to the Supreme Court in the above-mentioned three cases (Irons 1989). By raising funds in the Japanese American community and conducting the research necessary to overturn the Court's decision, it was believed that the community would revive its memories about camp life and talk about it more openly than before. It would also serve to remove the suspicion of disloyalty placed upon the community by the Court's decision. Thus in 1983 *coram nobis* petitions were filed to remove the convictions of Hirabayashi, Yasui, and Korematsu, the three who were jailed for disobeying the curfew or evacuation orders. It may be noted here that in 1988 two of the petition cases were successful, while the third person's case (Minoru Yasui) was considered moot because he died in 1986 (Irons 1988; Nagata 1993:193).

But the most significant unanticipated consequence of the internment experience was the organization and implementation of the "Redress Movement." This movement hinged on the decision of the Japanese American community to seek a formal apology as well as financial redress from the federal government for the personal humiliation Japanese Americans suffered and for the property and businesses they sacrificed as the result of being imprisoned in the camps.

In the context of reparations, it might be noted that in 1948, President Harry Truman signed an "Evacuation Claims Act," which paid less than ten cents on a dollar for property that the Japanese Americans lost in the internment process. But this act was highly unsatisfactory because, lacking documentary proof, many could not file a claim. These documents were lost or destroyed in the wartime process of being uprooted from their homes. Regarding this act, Wilson and Hosokawa (1980:260) had this to say:

The Department of Justice, which administered the claims program, misunderstood the intent of Congress, which was to offer the evacuees some sort of compensation for their losses. The bureaucrats took the position that their responsibility was to challenge every claim.

Needless to say, achieving the broad aims of the redress movement would be especially difficult not only because it involved gaining the approval of Congress in a time of budget deficits, but also because this ethnic community, compared to other minority groups, had a very small constituency that carried little political clout in Congress. There were other factors to overcome if the movement was to succeed. Because the Japanese Americans were no longer living in the tightly knit ethnic communities of the prewar days, communication and coordination of the dispersed population was very difficult. There were also emotional barriers to overcome. Many Nisei felt that launching a public campaign to seek an apology and monetary redress at a time when they were seeking to be assimilated into American society was unwise. Also at the time that the campaign started, the general public was poorly informed about the internment, and textbooks in the public schools generally failed to mention the internment program (Nagata 1993:187).

Nevertheless, the movement did begin in the early 1970s as the result of some forward-thinking Nisei leaders. But it was not until ten years later that the first tangible progress in this strategy was achieved. This step came on July 31, 1980, when President Carter signed the law that created a Commission on Wartime Relocation and Internment of Civilians (CWRIC). The commission had three large goals: to review the basis for an impact of Executive Order 9066; to review the military directives requiring relocation; and to recommend appropriate remedies.

The commission provided one of the best opportunities for the members of the Japanese American community to retrieve their memories collectively and to give public testimony about their camp experiences. There were twenty days of public hearings that took place in nine cities. Congressman Mineta from California described the testimony given by the former internees as a "painful outpouring of memories" and a "great unlocking of passion" (Naito and Scott 1990:8).

The second major step in the redress movement was the enactment of the redress bill, known officially as the Civil Liberties Act of 1988. Before it was finally passed there had been two previous attempts that failed to obtain the requisite votes, one in 1983 and the other in 1985. The Japanese American community mustered its resources and its energies to lobby the legislative bodies in Washington, D.C. On one occasion, a Los Angeles–based group known as the National Coalition for Redress and Reparation brought to the Capitol a large volunteer group which spent five days lobbying.

Before leaving this discussion about the unexpected events in the postwar period, I want to note that the Nisei who served in the armed services of both the European and Pacific theaters during World War II contributed much to an improved public opinion about Japanese Americans. Before the war, some 3,500 Nisei were serving in the U.S. army, but when Executive Order 9066 went into effect the enlistment of Nisei was stopped and they were reclassified as "4-C," the designation used for "enemy aliens." The message was clear: Nisei were under suspicion that they were disloyal. Then, in the fall of 1942, the Japanese American Citizens League requested the War Department to open up the Selective Service responsibility to Japanese Americans. By January 1943, the War Department responded by agreeing to form an all-Nisei combat team, which eventually became known as the 442nd Battalion (Wilson and Hosokawa 1980). After the formation of this combat team and its heroic service in Europe, the Selective Service was opened to Nisei and eventually 33,300 Nisei served during World War II and in the Korean War. Included in this group were nearly four thousand Nisei and Kibei who served in the Pacific theater (Harrington 1979; Oda 1981). Two of these veterans became U.S. Senators—Daniel Inouye and Spark Matsunaga—and played key roles in the passing of critical congressional bills discussed above. A third veteran of the 442nd was Mike Masaoka who, more than any other Nisei, helped to shape JACL policies that influenced the sweeping legal and monetary gains that were unexpected when the camps were closed (Hosokawa 1982; Masaoka and Hosokawa 1987).

VICARIOUS MEMORIES AND
THE SANSEI GENERATION

These unanticipated outcomes following the end of the internment camps were described here largely in terms of the Nisei generation. What comes next are the contributions the Sansei generation made to the success of the postwar programs. As stated before, the Nisei were the direct victims of the incarceration and thus had first-hand knowledge for taking action in these postwar movements.

However, it was different for the Sansei. This generation was either too young to recall this experience or born after their Nisei parents left the camps. Yet, I believe that the Sansei played a unique role in restoring the submerged collective memories of their parents and in initiating the postwar activities just described. To support this thesis I rely on the concept of "vicarious memory," which my colleague Jacob Climo has suggested. He describes this concept as follows:

Every group and individual has a rich store of memories that are not personal and self-generated. These memories come from others—from families, groups, cultures, and nation. [Such memories] are often not remembered personally but things that others have told us about and . . . that somehow become important enough for members of the group to include in their collective memory. (Climo, personal note, June 1994)

To Climo's definition, I would like to add another feature of vicarious memories. In my view these "memories" cannot be claimed by just anyone wishing to do so. Rather, only those people who have particular ties to the people who had the original experiences and memories of those experiences can be said to have vicarious memories. Thus the Sansei children of those who were in the camps can claim vicarious memories of the camps because their personal lives have been affected by the camp experiences of their parents. Or, to put it another way, the Sansei are legatees of their parents' memories. The word "legatee" is used here to suggest that vicarious memories are those that can be bequeathed.

The notion of vicarious memory fits nicely with the history of the Sansei generation's involvement with the issues relating to Executive Order 9066, because most of them did not have personal experience in the camps. The vast majority were born after the camps were closed or after their parents had relocated. Furthermore, as previously indicated, their Nisei parents did not come out of their self-imposed silence about these matters until the late 1960s and early 1970s—about the same time that the Sansei were coming of age. Thus most of the ideas and images they have of the camps came from their efforts to construct their vicarious memories.

The development of the Sansei's vicarious memories was greatly aided by the establishment of the Japanese American Research Project (JARP), located at the University of California, Los Angeles. This project was initiated in 1982 by a small group of scholarly types within the Japanese American Citizens League (Hosokawa 1982:312–13). The project's aims were to conduct an in-depth sociological survey of the Issei and Nisei, to publish a scholarly history of Japanese Americans, and to assemble documents as well as oral histories of this community. The project was initially financed by private contributions and later by the Carnegie Foundation and the National Institute of Mental Health. A number of publications came out of this project and it was an important source of vicarious memories for the Sansei. Some of the basic publications from the project are listed below:

- *The Japanese American Community: A Three-Generation Study*, by Gene N. Levine and Robert Colbert Rhodes.
- *The Economic Basis of Ethnic Solidarity: A Study of Japanese Americans*, by Edna Bonacich and John Modell.
- *The Bamboo People*, by Frank Chuman (a study of the legal history of Japanese Americans).
- *Planted in Good Soil: Issei Contributions to U.S. Agriculture*, by Masakzu Iwata (unpublished manuscript).
- *East to America*, by Robert A. Wilson and William Hosokawa.
- *Nisei: The Quiet Americans; The Story of a People*, by William Hosokawa.

The last book in the above list was the most controversial—not so much for its contents, but for its title. One segment of the community, mainly the Sansei population, objected to the "Quiet American" designation because it tends to create a negative stereotype of Japanese Americans. Others, largely the Nisei, felt it was an appropriate designation, and it generally matched the interpretation of facts presented in the book. In any case, the controversy over the book illustrates very well the generation gap between Nisei and Sansei. It was the Nisei view that, if they kept their faith in American democracy, eventually justice and rationality would prevail. Patience and perseverance, many Nisei felt, were the requisites to their full assimilation into American society. In fact, this point of view seemed to have been supported by non-Nisei writers who looked upon the Nisei as a "model minority" (Takaki 1989:474–84).

The Sansei, on the other hand, argued that people do not achieve justice without a struggle and without confrontation of issues. Born and raised in a different political climate from that of their Nisei parents, they saw the image of the Quiet American and the Model Minority as detrimental to their own self-image and to their future.

Armed with the vicarious memories of World War II and imbued with the political rhetoric of the late 1960s, the Sansei generation played key roles in all the postwar unanticipated activities of the Japanese American community—such as the pilgrimages to the camp sites, the repeal of Executive Order 9066, and the complicated movement to secure an apology and monetary redress from the U.S. government. For example, it was a team of Sansei lawyers that petitioned the courts successfully to vacate in 1988 the *Hirabayashi, Yasui,* and *Korematsu* cases that went before the Supreme Court in the 1940s.

The Sansei generation persisted in learning about the camps even though their parents were reluctant to talk about it. The Sansei provided the stimulus for resurrecting their parents' memories and they provided the skills and training to organize the postwar activities. Sansei journalists and scholars did much to increase substantially the literature on the internment and its consequences. They initiated the *Amerasia Journal,* now in its twentieth year of publication, and the *Asian America,* a journal of culture and the arts, published since 1991. They interviewed their parents, they took advantage of the Freedom of Information Act to delve into government documents, and they researched the newspapers that catered to the Japanese American community of the period. Sansei in the educational field prepared a teachers' guide and histories of the internment camps so that this information may be placed in the classrooms.

One of the more detailed analyses of the Sansei's vicarious memories is known as "The Sansei Research Project," conducted in 1987 [Nagata 1993], just a year before the redress campaign was successfully completed. This national sample included a twenty-page questionnaire received from 740 Sansei (out of 1,250 mailed to potential respondents) and over forty in-depth interviews. More than half who completed the questionnaires also wrote additional comments expressing their personal and emotional reactions to the topics raised in the survey instruments. The author of the book, a Sansei, subtitled her book "Exploring the Cross-Generational Impact of the Japanese American Internment." I believe it is a most comprehensive analysis of the vicarious memories of the Sansei on the Nisei camp life.

The survey investigated these topical areas (Nagata 1993:65):

1. The nature of communication that has occurred between the Sansei and their parents about the internment experience
2. The level of interest held by Sansei about the internment
3. The level of knowledge Sansei have about the internment as a historical event
4. Sansei opinions about the movement to seek monetary redress from the government for former internees

Here are a few findings I have selected (Nagata 1993:209):

1. The researchers hypothesized that the age of parents at the time of their incarceration and their length of internment would influence Sansei responses. But the data did not support their hypothesis.
2. Sansei fathers were seen to be less communicative about internment experience than their mothers.
3. [In the sample, there were some Sansei who had neither parent and other Sansei respondents who had at least one parent in camp.] The Sansei who had a parent interned said they attribute to themselves a number of negative consequences including "feelings of low self-esteem, the pressure to assimilate, an accelerated loss of Japanese culture and language, and experiencing the unexpressed pain of their parents."
4. On the positive side of internment, many Sansei "admired their Nisei parents for their ability to succeed in life despite the injustices" and they "recognize that they now share in the responsibility to educate others about the internment and must themselves be vigilant not only of their own rights . . . but also of the rights of all minority groups."

This last statement alludes to attitudes and activities that engaged the Sansei generation in their adult years. As noted before, the Sansei were the generation that grew up in the late 1960s and early 1970s. Many of them attended college at a time when students in general were swept up in a whirlwind of civil rights issues and antiwar sentiments.

While the urban riots, campus strikes, and antiwar movements in the 1960s received much national press attention, there was very little space devoted to the rise of the Asian American movement during the same period of social upheaval. Sansei, as well as other Asian American students, were engaged in student strikes and sit-ins at various campuses around the country. But the student strike at San Francisco State College (now a "University") was so significant to the Sansei community that an entire issue of *Amerasia Journal* (15:1, 1989) was devoted to it.

Having now reached middle age in the 1990s, the Sansei are thinking about passing on their legacy to their children, the *Yonsei*, or fourth generation, some of whom are now reaching adulthood. The Sansei editor for this special issue of the *Amerasia Journal*, Glen Omatsu, had this to say:

It may be difficult for a new generation—raised on the Asian American codewords of the 1980s stressing "advocacy," "access," "legitimacy," and "assertiveness"— to understand the urgency of the demand by Malcolm X for freedom "by any means necessary," Mao's challenge to "serve the people," the slogans of "power to the people" and "self-determination," the principles of "mass line" organizing and "united front" work, or the conviction that the people—not the elites—are the makers of history. But they were the ideas that galvanized thousands of Asian Americans and reshaped our communities. And it is these concepts which must be grasped in order to understand the scope and intensity of our movement and what it created.

He continued to state the rationale for this special issue:

This issue of *Amerasia* is devoted to a reexamination of these themes. Our focus is not on recounting the past events themselves but on retrieving the legacies for our current situation. Our goal is to identify—especially for a new generation of Asian Americans—the lessons of an earlier generation.

It is noteworthy that Omatsu writes of the "new generation" as being Asian Americans, not as *Yonsei* or fourth-generation Japanese Americans. In the next and final section of this chapter, I discuss the significance of this new "codeword" and new generation.

ASIAN AMERICANS, A NEW SUBCULTURE

During the campus turmoil of the 1960s and 1970s, the Sansei generation, perhaps sensitive to their small population size (compared to the African American and Hispanic populations), began to form coalitions with other organizations, particularly those of Asian descent: Chinese Americans, Filipino Americans, Korean Americans, and so on. In due time, a social movement was formed and duly recognized as the Asian American Movement (see Wei 1993).

One example of a coalition group with Sansei membership was the Berkeley AAPA (Asian American Political Alliance), the first of many that sprang up around the country. William Wei (1993:21) has this story to tell about this Berkeley AAPA meeting:

It was at the second meeting that Larry Jack Wong [Chinese American] first brought up the internment of the Japanese Americans, saying, "Hey, you're Japanese. Why don't you people protest about the concentration camps?" Woo noted that a long discussion ensued and, ever the gadfly, he said, "Hell, the way things are going now, they might do that to us. So you're not doing this just for the Japanese, but for all other people."

William Wei continues this story:

Wong and Woo had touched upon a taboo topic, one that older Japanese Americans had sought to forget. After that tragedy was revealed to *sansei* (third-generation Japanese Americans) participating in the Asian American Movement, the internment during World War II became the issue among Japanese American activists and, for many of them, the sole reason for being involved politically. (Wei 1993:21)

The previously mentioned statement by Omura implies that a new community, known as Asian Americans, is now a viable and self-sustaining social entity. That is, the student activities of the period constructed a new subculture out of previously unconnected organizations.

Wei (1993:271–74) discusses this Asian American movement and its accomplishments under a number of specific points. The movement:

1. Produced a new identity by transcending specific Asian ethnic identities and focusing on a pan-Asian consciousness
2. Created a generation of activists who were willing to act for the collective benefit of their Asian American community
3. Attempted to change the caricature of Asians by producing new histories, literature, film, and art works that were more in tune with mainstream America
4. Became associated with the Asian American women's movement, a movement that faced the gender inequalities
4. Gave birth to a host of new institutions in higher education, for example the new academic field known as Asian American Studies
6. Sponsored community agencies in Asian enclaves of the country: welfare assistance, counseling services, recreational facilities, job placements, etc.
7. Validated, without intending to do so, ethnic pluralism and multiculturalism that is becoming a new vision of American society

In summary, then, this chapter has attempted to relate the post–World War II consequences of Executive Order 9066, consequences that were largely unintended and unanticipated. The chapter started out with the Nisei generation's memories of their internment camp experiences and why for two decades the Nisei were reluctant to discuss these memories with their children or to engage in collective action to "display" these memories. Next, the chapter focused on the eagerness of the Sansei generation to learn more about the camps and as a result created a memory bank that was identified as "vicarious memories." With these learned memories, the Sansei supported a wide range of collective activities that were unanticipated at the time the camps were closed, such as pilgrimages to former camp sites, congressional hearings on the reasons for internment, and a large-scale movement to seek redress and apology. The final section described how the Sansei generation, armed with these vicarious memories of interned citizens, were engaged in a social movement that culminated in a new ethnic identity known as Asian Americans and thereby added a new dimension to the growing multiculturalism of mainstream America. From the perspective of the aging Nisei generation, this Asian American identity was an unintended consequence of the camps.

Bibliography

Abrams, Philip. 1988 [1977]. "Notes on the difficulty of studying the state." *Journal of Historical Sociology* 1(1):58–89.

Adams, Richard. 1990. "Ethnic images and strategies in 1944." In *Guatemalan Indians and the State*, edited by C. Smith, 141–62. Austin: University of Texas Press.

Alonso, Ana. 1988. "The effects of truth: Re-presentations of the past and the imagining of community." *Journal of Historical Sociology* 1(1)33–57.

Anderson, Benedict. 1991. *Imagined Communities: Reflections on the Origins and Spread of Nationalism*. London: Verso Press.

Anti-Defamation League of B'nai B'rith. 1987. "Not the work of a day." *Anti-Defamation League of B'nai B'rith Oral Memoirs*. Vol. 6, B2–3. New York.

Arnold, Hans. 1991. "The 'century of the refugee,' a European century?" Aussen Politik. *German Foreign Affairs Review* 42:271–80.

Atiendo, Odihambo, E. S. Wanyande, and Peter Wanyande. 1991. *History and Geography of Kenya: Book Two*. Nairobi: Longman's.

Barry, Tom. 1992. *Inside Guatemala*. Albuquerque, NM: The Inter-Hemispheric Education Resource Center.

Battaglia, D. 1992. "The body in the gift: memory and forgetting in Sabarl mortuary exchange." *American Ethnologist* 19(1):3–18.

Baxter, P. T. W., and U. Almagor. 1978. *Age, Generation and Time: Some Features of East African Age organizations*. New York: St. Martin's Press.

Beidelman, T. O. 1971. *The Kaguru: A Matrilineal People of East Africa*. New York: Holt, Rinehart, and Winston.

———. 1986. *Moral Imagination in Kaguru Modes of Thought*. Bloomington: Indiana University Press.

Benedict, Ruth. 1943. *Race, Science and Politics*. 5th ed. New York: Viking Press.

Berger, Peter L., and Thomas Luckman, 1967. *The Social Construction of Reality*. Garden City, NY: Anchor Books.

Biographies File, American Jewish Archives, Cincinnati, OH.

Boelhower, William. 1987. *Through a Glass Darkly: Ethnic Semiosis in American Literature*. New York: Oxford University Press.

Boothby, Neil. 1985. *Mayan Indians in Exile*. Unpublished manuscript.

Borkin, Joseph. 1978. *The Crime and Punishment of I. G. Farben*. New York: The Free Press.

Briody, Elizabeth K., and Marietta L. Baba. 1991. "Explaining differences in repatriation experiences: The discovery of coupled and decoupled systems." *American Anthropologist* 93:322–44.

Brubaker, William R. 1989. *Immigration and the Politics of Citizenship in Europe and North America*. Lanham, MD: University Press of America.

Butler, Robert N. 1963. "The life review: An interpretation of reminiscence in the aged." *Psychiatry* 26:65–76.

———. 1970. "Looking forward to what?: The life review, legacy, and excessive identity versus change." *American Behavioral Scientist* 14:121–28.

Calvino, Italo. 1987. *The Literature Machine: Essays*. Translated by Patrick Creagh. London: Secker and Warburg.

Carothers, J. C. 1952. *The Psychology of Mau Mau*. Nairobi: Government Printers.

Caruth, Cathy. 1991. "Unclaimed experience: Trauma and the possibility of history." *Yale French Studies* 79:181–92.

Casey, Edward. 1986. "Earle on memory and the past." In *The Life of the Transcendental Ego*, edited by Edward Casey, 172–92. Albany: State University of New York Press.

Castles, Stephen, Heather Booth, and Tina Wallace. 1984. *Here for Good: Western Europe's New Ethnic Minorities*. London: Pluto Press.

Climo, Jacob J. 1990. "Transmitting ethnic identity through oral narratives." *Ethnic Groups* 8:163–79.

———. 1992. *Distant Parents*. New Brunswick, NJ: Rutgers University Press.

Cohler, Bertram, and Morton A. Lieberman. 1979. "Personality change across the second half of life: Findings from a study of Irish, Italian, and Polish-American men and women." In *Ethnicity and Aging*, edited by Donald E. Gelfand and Alfred J. Kutzik. Vol. 5, Springer Series in Adulthood and Aging. New York: Springer.

Cotji Cuxil, Demetrio. 1991. *La Configuracion del Pensamiento Politico del Pueblo Maya*. Quezaltenango, Guatemala: Asociacion de Escritores Mayances de Guatemala.

Coleman, Peter G. 1991. "Aging and life history: The meaning of reminiscence in late life." In *Life and Work History Analysis: Qualitative and Quantitative Developments*, edited by Shirley Dex, 120–43. London: Routledge.

Collingwood, R. G. 1961. *The Idea of History*. London: Oxford University Press.

Commission on Wartime Relocation and Internment of Civilians. 1982. *Personal Justice Denied*. Washington, DC: U.S. Government Printing Office.

Connerton, Paul. 1989. *How Societies Remember*. Cambridge: Cambridge University Press.

Conway, Martin A. 1993. "Review of Winograd and Neisser: Affect and accuracy in recall." *Science* 261:369–70.

Corrigan, Philip, and Derek Sayer. 1985. *The Great Arch*. Oxford: Basil Blackwell.

Coupland, Nikolas, Justine Coupland, and Howard Giles. 1991. *Language, Society and the Elderly: Discourse, Identity and Aging*. Oxford: Blackwell.

Coupland, Nikolas, Jon F. Nussbaum, and Alan Grossman. 1993. "Introduction: Discourse, selfhood, and the lifespan." In *Discourse and Lifespan Identity*, edited by Nikolas Coupland and Jon F. Nussbaum, x–xxviii. Newbury Park, CA: Sage Publications.

Cressy, David. 1989. *Bonfires and Bells: National Memory and the Protestant Calendar in Elizabethan and Stuart England*. Berkeley: University of California Press.

Daniels, Roger, Sandra C. Taylor, and Harry H. L. Kitano, eds. 1991. *Japanese*

Americans: From Relocation to Redress. Seattle: University of Washington Press.

Da Sola Poole, Ithiel. 1977. *The Social Impact of the Telephone.* Cambridge, MA: MIT Press.

Davies, Norman. 1982. *God's Playground: A History of Poland.* Vol. 2, 1795–Present. New York: Columbia University Press.

De Certeau, Michel. 1986. *Heterologies: Discourse on the Other.* Minneapolis: University of Minnesota Press.

———. 1988. *The Writing of History.* New York: Columbia University Press.

Deleuze, Gilles, and Felix Guattari. 1987. *A Thousand Plateaus.* Minneapolis: University of Minnesota Press.

Derrida, Jacques. 1976. *Of Grammatology.* Translated by G. Spivak. Baltimore: Johns Hopkins University Press.

———. 1982. *Margins of Philosophy.* Translated by A. Bass. Chicago: University of Chicago Press.

De Vos, George, and Lola Romannucci-Ross. "Ethnicity: Vessel of meaning and emblem of contrast." In *Ethnic Identity: Cultural Continuities and Change*, edited by George De Vos and Lola Romannucci-Ross, 363–90. Palo Alto, CA: Mayfield Publishing Company.

Diaz del Castillo, Bernal. 1960 [1575]. *Historia Verdadera de la Conquista de la Nueva Espana.* Edited by Joaquin Ramirez Cabanas. Mexico City: Editorial Porrua.

Doi, Mary L. 1991. "The transformation of ritual: The Nisei 60th birthday." *Journal of Cross-Cultural Gerontology* 6:153–63.

Dumont, Louis. 1985. "Christian beginnings of modern individualism." In *The Category of the Person*, edited by Michael Carrithers, Steven Collins, and Steven Lukes, 93–122. Cambridge: Cambridge University Press.

Dundas, C. 1924. *Kilimanjaro and Its People.* London: Frank Cass.

Eastman, Carol M., and Thomas C. Reese. 1981. "Associated language: How language and ethnic identity are related." *General Linguistics* 21:109–16.

Edye, Dave. 1987. *Immigrant Labour and Government Policy: The Case of the FRG and France.* Aldershot, U.K.: Gower Publishing Company.

Erikson, Erik H. 1968. "Life Cycle." In *International Encyclopedia of the Social Sciences*, Vol. 9, edited by David L. Sills, 186–92. New York: Macmillan and The Free Press.

———. 1975. *Life History and the Historical Moment.* New York: W. W. Norton.

Erikson, Erik H., Joan M. Erikson, and Helen Q. Kivnik. 1986. *Vital Involvement in Old Age.* New York: W. W. Norton.

Esser, Hartmut, and Hermann Korte. 1985. "Federal Republic of Germany." In *European Immigration Policy: A Comparative Study*, edited by Tomas Hammar, 165–205. Cambridge: Cambridge University Press.

Evans-Pritchard, E. E. 1951. *Kinship and Marriage Among the Nuer.* Oxford: Clarendon Press.

Fabian, Johannes. 1983. *Time and the Other: How Anthropology Makes Its Object.* New York: Columbia University Press.

Feldman, Allen. 1991. *Formations of Violence.* Chicago: University of Chicago Press.

Fentress, J., and C. Wickham. 1992. *Social Memory.* London: Blackwell.

Figueroa Ibarra, Carlos. 1991. *El Recurso del Miedo: Essayo sobre el Estado y el Terror en Guatemala.* San Jose, Costa Rica: Editorial Universitaria Centroamericana.

Foucault, Michel. 1978. "The eye of power." *Semiotext* 3(2):6–13.

———. 1980. *The History of Sexuality.* Vol. 1. New York: Vintage Books.

———. 1986. "Of Other Spaces." *Diacritics* Spring 1986:22–27.

Freeman, Linton C., A. Kimball Romney, and Sue C. Freeman. 1987. "Cognitive structure and informant accuracy." *American Anthropologist* 89:310–24.

Friedman, Jonathan. 1992. "The past in the future." *American Anthropologist* 94(4):837–59.

Furley, O. W. 1972. "The historiography of Mau Mau." In *Hadith 4: Politics and Nationalism in Colonial Kenya*, edited by Bethwell Ogot, 105–33. Nairobi: East African Publishing House.

Fussell, Paul. 1983. *Class.* New York: Ballantine Books.

Geertz, Clifford. 1973. *The Interpretation of Cultures.* New York: Basic Books.

———. 1983. *Local Knowledge: Further Essays in Interpretive Anthropology.* New York: Basic Books.

George, B. P. 1966. "Fairs and Festivals of Kerala." In *1965 Census of India.* Vol. 5, part 3. Delhi: Government Printing Bureau.

Gergen, Kenneth J. 1986. "Correspondence versus autonomy in the language of understanding human action." In *Metatheory in Social Science*, edited by Donald W. Fiske and Richard A. Schweder. Chicago: University of Chicago Press.

Giddens, Anthony. 1990. *The Consequences of Modernity.* Stanford: Stanford University Press.

———. 1991. *Modernity and Self-Identity: Self and Society in the Late Modern Age.* Stanford: Stanford University Press.

Gluckman, M., ed. 1962. *Essays on Rituals of Social Relations.* Manchester: Manchester University Press.

Golman, Daniel. 1987. "In memory: People re-creating their lives to suit their images of the present." *New York Times* (reporting research published by Lee Robbins in the *American Journal of Orthopsychiatry* and also by Gordon Bowers at Stanford University). June 23:C1, 9.

Gomori, George. 1972. *Dominant Themes in Contemporary East European Fiction: The Cry of Home, Cultural Nationalism and the Modern Writer.* Edited by H. Earnest Lewald. Nashville: University of Tennessee Press.

Greenblatt, Stephen. 1991. *Marvelous Possessions.* Chicago: University of Chicago Press.

GSN News. 1994. *Current Guatemalan Issues.* Edited by M. Moors. Guatemala Scholars Network.

Gutmann, B. 1922/23. "Die kerbstocklehren der dschagga in Ostafrika." *Zeitschrift fur Eingeborenen.* Sprachen Bd. 13 s. 81–109, 205–35, 260–302.

Haggadah, The. 1989. *The Deluxe Edition of the Maxwell House Haggadah.* New York: General Foods Corporation.

Hailbronner, Kay. 1989. "Citizenship and nationhood in Germany." In *Immigration and the Politics of Citizenship in Europe and North America*, edited by William R. Brubaker, 67–79. Lanham, MD: University Press of America.

The Hajj, Smadar, Lavie, and Forest Rouse. 1993. "Notes on the fantastic journey of the Hajj, his anthropologist and her American passport." *American Ethnologist* 20(2):363–83.

Halbwachs, Maurice. 1950. *La Memoire Collective.* Paris: Presses Universitaires de France.

———. 1992 [1925]. "The social frameworks of memory." In *On Collective Memory*, edited and translated by Lewis A. Coser, 35–189. Chicago: University of Chicago Press.

Hall, Dinah. 1992. *Ethnic Interiors*. New York: Rizzoli International.

Handelman, Don. 1990. *Models and Mirrors: Toward an Anthropology of Public Events*. Cambridge: Cambridge University Press.

Harré, Rom. 1986. "An outline of the social constructionist viewpoint." In *The Social Construction of the Emotions*, edited by Rom Harré, 2–14. Oxford: Oxford University Press.

———. 1989. "Language games and texts of identity." In *Texts of Identity*, edited by John Shotter and Kenneth Gergen, 20–35. London: Sage Publications.

Harrington, Joseph D. 1979. *Yankee Samurai: The Secret Role of Nisei in America's Pacific Victory*. Detroit, MI: Pettigrew Enterprises, Inc.

Hawkins, John. 1984. *Inverse Images: The Meaning of Culture, Ethnicity, and Family in Postcolonial Guatemala*. Albuquerque: University of New Mexico Press.

Herbert, Ulrich. 1990. *A History of Foreign Labor in Germany, 1880–1980*. Ann Arbor: University of Michigan Press.

Hirasuma, Delphine. 1992. "Reflecting on Camp Jerome." In *Teacher's Guide: The Bill of Rights and the Japanese World War II Experience*, edited by Rosalyn Tonsi, Chizu Iiyama, Christine Hiroshima, and Bess Ricketts. San Francisco: National Japanese American Historical Society.

Hobsbawm, Eric. 1983. "Introduction: Inventing traditions." In *Invention of Tradition*, 1–14. Cambridge: Cambridge University Press.

———. 1992. "Ethnicity and nationalism in Europe today." *Anthropology Today* 8(1):3–8.

Hobsbawm, Eric, and Terence Ranger, eds. 1983. *The Invention of Tradition*. Cambridge and New York: Cambridge University Press.

Holzberg, Carol. 1982. "Ethnicity and aging: Anthropological perspectives on more than just the minority elderly." *The Gerontologist* 22:249–57.

Homze, Edward L. 1967. *Foreign Labor in Nazi Germany*. Princeton, NJ: Princeton University Press.

Hongo, Florence M., Miyo Burton, Andrea Kuroda, Ruth Sasaki, and Cheryl Tanaka, eds. 1985. *Japanese American Journey: The Story of a People*. San Mateo, CA: JACP.

Hosokawa, Bill. 1969. *Nisei: The Quiet Americans*. New York: William Morrow & Co.

———. 1982. *JACL in Quest of Justice: The History of the Japanese American Citizens League*. New York: William Morrow & Co.

Hourwich, Isaac A. 1922. *The Economic Aspects of European Immigration to the United States*. New York: B. W. Huebsch.

Hulme, Peter. 1992. *Colonial Encounters*. New York: Routledge.

Irons, Peter. 1988. *Justice at War*. New York: Oxford University Press.

Johnson, George. 1991. *In the Palaces of Memory: How We Build the Worlds Inside Our Heads*. New York: Knopf.

Jonas, Susanne. 1991. *The Battle for Guatemala*. Boulder, CO: Westview Press.

Kail, Robert. 1984. *The Development of Memory in Children*. New York: W. H. Freeman & Co.

Kaminsky, Marc. 1984. "The uses of reminiscence: A discussion of the formative literature." In *The Uses of Reminiscence: New Ways of Working with Older Adults*, edited by Marc Kaminsky, 137–56. New York: The Haworth Press.

———. 1992. "Story of the shoebox: The meaning and practice of transmitting stories." In *Handbook of the Humanities and Aging*, edited by Thomas R. Cole, David D.

Van Tassel, and Robert Kestenbaum, 307–27. New York: Springer Publishing Company.

Kanogo, Theresa. 1987. *Squatters and the Roots of the Mau Mau.* Nairobi: Heinemann.

Karp, Florence Berman. 1983. *Roses in December: A Memoir of My Parents.* Pittsburgh, PA: Wolfson Publishing Company.

Kellogg, Susan. 1990. "Exploring diversity in middle-class families: The symbolism of American ethnic identity." *Social Science History* 14:27–41.

Kerner, D. O. 1988a. "Land scarcity and rights of control in the development of commercial farming in northeast Tanzania." In *Land and Society in Contemporary Africa*, edited by R. E. Downs and S. P. Reyna. Hanover: England University Press.

————. 1988b. *The Social Uses of Knowledge in Contemporary Tanzania.* Ph.D. Dissertation, CUNY.

Kertzer, David I. 1988. *Ritual, Politics, and Power.* New Haven, CT: Yale University Press.

Kramer, Lloyd S. 1988. *Threshold of a New World: Intellectuals and the Exile Experience in Paris, 1830–1848.* Ithaca and London: Cornell University Press.

Kundera, Milan. 1980. *The Book of Laughter and Forgetting.* New York: Alfred A. Knopf.

Kuper, H. 1947. *An African Aristocracy.* London: Oxford University Press.

La Fontaine, J. S. 1977. "Ritualization of women's life crises in Bugisu." In *The Interpretation of Ritual*, edited by J. S. La Fontaine. London: Tavistock Publications.

Lakoff, George, and Mark Johnson. 1980. *Metaphors We Live By.* Chicago: University of Chicago Press.

Layton, Robert. 1992. *Australian Rock Art: A New Synthesis.* Cambridge: Cambridge University Press.

Leach, E. R. 1954. *Political Systems of Highland Burma: A Study of Kachin Social Structure.* Boston: Beacon.

————. 1961. "Two essays concerning the symbolic representation of time." In E. R. Leach, *Leach Rethinking Anthropology.* London: Athlone Press.

Le Espiritu, Yen. 1992. *Asian American Panethnicity.* Philadelphia: Temple University Press.

Lema, A. 1981. *The Foundation of the Lutheran Church in Kilimanjaro.* Hong Kong: Minda Press.

Le Page, Robert B., and Andree Tabouret-Keller. 1985. *Acts of Identity: Creole-Based Approaches to Language and Ethnicity.* Cambridge: Cambridge University Press.

Levi-Strauss, Claude. 1955. *Tristes Tropiques.* New York: Atheneum.

Lewis, Bernard. 1975. *History: Remembered, Recovered, Invented.* Princeton, NJ: Princeton University Press.

Lowenthal, David. 1985. *The Past Is a Foreign Country.* Cambridge: Cambridge University Press.

Macgoye, Marjorie Oludhe. 1986. *The Story of Kenya: A Nation in the Making.* Nairobi: Oxford University Press.

Manz, Beatriz. 1988. *Refugees of a Hidden War.* Albany: State University of New York Press.

Marcalle, P. I. 1947. *Maisha ya Mchagga hapa Duniani na Ahera.* Marangu.

Martinez, Antonio. 1992. "International Symposium on Torture in Guatemala." Washington, DC: November 13–15, 1992.

Martinez, Antonio, and Mary Fabri. 1992. "The Kovlee Center: The dilemma of revictimization." *Torture* 2(2):47–48. Copenhagen: RCTIRCT.

Masaoka, Mike, and Bill Hosokawa. 1987. *They Call Me Moses*. New York: William Morrow & Co.

Matsumoto, Valerie. 1993. "Putting the camps into UCLA's curriculum." *Amerasia Journal* 19(1):139–52.

McGoldrick, Monica. 1993. "Ethnicity, cultural diversity, and normality." In *Normal Family Processes*, edited by Froma Walsh, 331–60. New York: The Guilford Press.

Meillassoux, Claude. 1981. *Maidens, Meal and Money: Capitalism and the Domestic Community*. Cambridge: Cambridge University Press.

Menchù, Rigoberta. 1984. *I, Rigoberta Menchù*. Edited by Elizabeth Burgos-Debray. New York: Verso.

Middleton, David, and Derek Edwards, eds. 1990. *Collective Remembering*. London: Sage Publications.

Minister of Information, Polish Government in Exile. 1990. Private Conversations, London.

Molyneaux, Brian. 1982. *Kejimkujik Resource Manual*. Halifax: Parks Canada, Atlantic Region.

———. 1985. "Floating islands: The Micmac vision of sailing ships." *Rotunda*, Summer: 6–11.

———. 1987. "Lake of the painted cave." *Archaeology* 40:18–25.

———. 1989. "Concepts of humans and animals in post-contact Micmac rock art." In *Animals into Art*, edited by H. Murphy, 193–214. London: Unwin Hyman.

———. 1990. *The Bedford Petroglyphs*. Manuscript report. Halifax: Nova Scotia Museum.

———. 1994. "Introduction: The represented past." In *The Present Past: Archaeology, Museums and Education*, edited by P. Stone and Brian L. Molyneaux. London: Routledge.

Montagu, Ashley. 1942. *Man's Most Dangerous Myth*. 4th ed. Cleveland, OH: The World Publishing Company.

Montejo, Victor. 1992. Brevisima Relacion Testimonial de la Continua Destruccion del Mayab (Guatemala). Providence: Guatemala Scholars Network.

Moore, S. F. 1976. "The secret of men." *Africa* 46:4.

———. 1986. *Social Facts and Fabrications: Customary Law on Kilimanjaro 1880–1980*. Cambridge: Cambridge University Press.

Morawska, Eva. 1994. "In defense of the assimilation model." *Journal of American Ethnic History* 13:76–87.

Mosse, George L. 1975. *The Nationalism of the Masses: Political Symbolism and Mass Movements in Germany from the Napoleonic Wars Through the Third Reich*. New York: Howard Fertig.

Murphy, Richard C. 1983. *Guestworkers in the German Reich*. New York: Columbia University Press.

Mutungi, Onesmus. 1977. *Legal Aspects of Witchcraft in E. Africa with Particular Reference to Kenya*. Nairobi: East Africa Literature Bureau.

Myerhoff, Barbara G. 1978. "A symbol perfected in death: Continuity and ritual in the life and death of an elderly Jew." In *Life's Career—Aging*, edited by Barbara G. Myerhoff and Andrei Simic, 163–205. Beverly Hills: Sage Publications.

———. 1980. "Life history among the elderly: Performance, visibility and re-membering."

In *Life Course: Integrative Theories and Exemplary Populations*, edited by Kurt W. Back, 133–53. Boulder, CO: Westview Press.

——. 1988. "Surviving stories: Reflections on *Number Our Days*." In *Between Two Worlds: Ethnographic Essays on American Jewry*, edited by Jack Kugelmass, 265–94. Ithaca, NY: Cornell University Press.

——. 1992. *Remembered Lives*, edited by Marc Kaminsky. Ann Arbor: University of Michigan Press.

Nagata, Donna K. 1993. *Legacy of Injustice*. New York: Plenum Press.

Naito, Calvin, and Esther Scott. 1990. "Against All Odds: The Japanese Americans' Campaign for Redress." Unpublished manuscript, Kennedy School of Government, Harvard University.

Nakanishi, Don T. 1993. "Surviving democracy's 'mistake': Japanese Americans and the enduring legacy of Executive Order 9066." *Amerasia Journal* 19(1):7–36.

Nakano, Mai. 1990. *Japanese American Women: Three Generations, 1890–1990*. Berkeley: Mina Press Publishing.

Neisser, Ulrich. 1982. *Memory Observed: Remembering in Natural Contexts*. San Francisco: W. H. Freeman.

Nickles, Thomas. 1989. "Justification and experiment." In *The Uses of Experiment: Studies in the Natural Sciences*, edited by David Gooding, Trevor Pinch, and Simon Schaffer, 299–333. Cambridge: Cambridge University Press.

Nietzsche. 1967 [1887]. *On the Genealogy of Morals*. Translated and edited by Walter Kaufmann. New York: Vintage Books.

Oda, James. 1981. *Heroic Struggles of Japanese Americans*. Los Angeles: KNI, Inc.

Ogot, Bethwell. 1972. "The revolt in the elders: An anatomy of the loyalist crowd in the Mau Mau rising, 1952–56." In *Hadith: Politics and Nationalism in Colonial Kenya*, edited by Bethwell Ogot, 134–48. Nairobi: East African Publishing House.

Okada, John. 1976. *No-No Boy*. Seattle: University of Washington Press.

Opitz, Peter J. 1991. "Refugee and migration movements." Aussen Politik. *German Foreign Affairs Review* 42:261–70.

Oriol, Michel. 1982. *Introduction in Social Integration of Migrant Workers and Other Ethnic Minorities: A Documentation of Current Research*. Edited by Matthias Herfurth and Huberta Hogeweg-de Haart, xi–xviii. European Coordination Center for Research and Documentation in the Social Sciences. Oxford: Pergamon Press.

Orlov, Dietrich. 1987. *A History of Modern Germany 1871 to Present*. Englewood Cliffs, NJ: Prentice Hall, Inc.

Padden, Carol A. 1990. "Folk explanation in language survival." In *Collective Remembering*, edited by David Middleton and Derek Edwards, 190–202. London: Sage Publications.

Pandolfi, Mariella. 1991. *Itinerari delle Emozioni*. Milano: Franco Angeli.

Pearce, Roy Harvey. 1965. *The Savages of America: A Study of the Indian and the Idea of Civilization*. Baltimore, MD: Johns Hopkins University Press.

Peltz, Rakhmiel. 1987. "Who is speaking Yiddish in South Philadelphia today?: Jewish language in urban America." *International Journal of the Sociology of Language* 67:145–66.

Popular Memory Group. 1982. *Making Histories: Studies in History—Writing and Politics*. Minneapolis: University of Minnesota Press.

Postman, Neil. 1985. *Amusing Ourselves to Death: Public Discourse in the Age of Show Business*. New York: Viking.

Rand, Silas. 1894. *Legends of the Micmacs*. New York: Longman's, Green.

Rappaport, Joanne. 1987. "Mythic images, historical thought, and printed texts: The Paez and the written word." *Journal of Anthropological Research* 43:43–61.

Räthzel, Nora. 1990. "Germany: One race, one nation?" *Race and Class* 32(3):31–48.

Raum, O. 1940. *Chagga Childhood*. London: Oxford University Press.

Rempusheski, Veronica F. 1988. "Caring for self and others: Second generation Polish American elders in an ethnic club." *Journal of Cross-Cultural Gerontology* 3:223–71.

Richards, A. 1956. *Chisungu: A Girl's Initiation Ceremony Among the Bemba of Zambia*. London: Farber and Farber.

Rist, Ray C. 1978. *Guestworkers in Germany: The Prospects for Pluralism*. New York: Praeger.

Rodriguez, Richard. 1983. *Hunger of Memory: The Education of Richard Rodriguez*. New York: Bantam Books.

Rogers, S. G. 1972. "The Search for Political Focus on Kilimanjaro: A History of Chagga Politics, 1916–52, with Special Reference to the Cooperative Movement and Indirect Rule." Ph.D. Dissertation, University of Dar es Salaam.

Rohl, J. C. G. 1970. *From Bismarck to Hitler: The Problem of Continuity in German History*. New York: Barnes and Noble.

Roth, Henry. 1991 [1932]. *Call It Sleep*. New York: The Noonday Press.

Royce, Josiah. 1968. *The Problem of Christianity*. Chicago: University of Chicago Press.

Salmond, Anne, 1982. "Theoretical landscapes: On cross-cultural conceptions of knowledge." In *Semantic Anthropology*, edited by D. Parkin, 65–87. London: Academic Press.

Sanjek, Roger. 1990. "Fire, loss, and the sorcerer's apprentice." In *Fieldnotes: The Makings of Anthropology*, edited by Roger Sanjek. Ithaca and London: Cornell University Press.

Scarry, Elaine. 1985. *The Body in Pain*. New York: Oxford University Press.

Schleunes, Karl A. 1970. *The Twisted Road to Auschwitz: Nazi Policy Toward German Jews, 1933–1939*. Urbana: University of Illinois Press.

Schmitter, Barbara. 1983. "Immigrant minorities in West Germany: Theoretical concerns." *Ethnic and Racial Studies* 6:308–19.

Schuman, Howard, and Jacqueline Scott. 1989. "Generations and collective memories." *American Sociological Review* 54:359–81.

Seremetakis, Nadia. 1991. *The Last Word: Women, Death and Divination in Inner Mani*. Chicago: University of Chicago Press.

Shield, Renee Rose 1988. *Uneasy Endings: Daily Life in an American Nursing Home*. Ithaca, NY: Cornell University Press.

Shils, Edward A. 1946. "Social and psychological aspects of displacement and repatriation." *Journal of Social Issues* 2(3):3–18.

Shotter, John. 1989. "Social accountability and the social construction of 'you.'" In *Texts of Identity*, edited by John Shotter and Kenneth J. Gergen, 133–51. London: Sage Publications.

Simic, Andrei. 1985. "Ethnicity as a resource for the aged: An anthropological perspective." *Journal of Applied Gerontology* 4:65–71.

Skorupski, John. 1976. *Symbol and Theory: A Philosophical Study of Theories of Religion in Social Anthropology*. Cambridge: Cambridge University Press.

Sollors, Werner. 1986. *Beyond Ethnicity: Consent and Descent in American Culture*. Oxford: Oxford University Press.

———. 1989. *The Invention of Ethnicity.* New York: Oxford University Press.

Sorrenson, M. P. K. 1967. *Land Reform in the Kikuyu Country.* Nairobi: Oxford University Press.

Spencer, P. 1970. "The function of ritual in the socialization of the Samburu Moran." In *Socialization: The Approach from Social Anthropology,* edited by P. Mayer. ASA Monograph 8. London: Tavistock Publications.

Spicer, Edward H., Asael T. Hansen, Katherine Luomala, and Marvin K. Opler, eds. 1969. *Impounded People.* Tucson: University of Arizona Press.

Stahl, K. 1964. *History of the Chagga People of Kilimanjaro.* London: Mouton and Co.

Stewart, Kathleen. 1988. "Nostalgia—A Polemic." *Cultural Anthropology* 3(3):227–41.

Stoller, Paul. 1992. *The Cinematic Griot: The Ethnography of Jean Rouch.* Chicago and London: University of Chicago Press, paperback edition.

Tachiki, Amy, Eddie Wong, Franklin Odo, and Buck Wong, eds. 1971. *Roots: An Asian American Reader.* Los Angeles: Continental Graphics.

Takaki, Ronald. 1989. *Strangers from a Different Shore: A History of Asian Americans.* Boston: Little, Brown & Co.

Tamura, Eileen H. 1994. *Americanization, Acculturation, and Ethnic Identity: The Nisei Generation in Hawaii.* Urbana and Chicago: University of Illinois Press.

Tateishi, John. 1984. *And Justice for All.* New York: Random House.

Taussig, Michael. 1987. *Shamanism, Colonialism, and the Wild Man.* Chicago: University of Chicago Press.

Thomas, Anthony. 1974. "Oaths, ordeals, and the Kenyan courts." *Human Organization* 33(1):54–67.

Thornburg, Hershel D. 1982. *Development in Adolescence.* 2nd ed. Monterey, CA: Brooks/Cole.

Tolsen, Elsie. 1979. *The Captain, the Colonel and Me: Bedford, N.S. Since 1503.* Sackville, Nova Scotia, Canada: Tribune Press.

"Trek to Tule Lake internment camp site slated." 1994. *Rafu Shimpo* 1. July 6, 1994.

Turner, V. 1962. "Three symbols of passage in Ndembu circumcision ritual." In *Essays on Rituals of Social Relations,* edited by M. Gluckman. Manchester: Manchester University Press.

———. 1967. "Betwixt and between: The liminal period in rites de passage." In *The Forest of Symbols,* edited by V. Turner. Ithaca, NY: Cornell University Press.

Uchida, Yoshiko. 1982. *Desert Exile: The Uprooting of a Japanese-American Family.* Seattle: University of Washington Press.

UNESCO. 1961. *The Race Question in Modern Science.* New York: Columbia University Press.

United Republic of Tanzania. 1988. "1988 population census: Preliminary report." Bureau of Statistics. Government Printer.

Van Den Abeel, Georges. 1992. *Travels as Metaphor.* Minneapolis: University of Minnesota Press.

Van Langenhove, L., and Rom Harré. 1993. "Positioning and autobiography: Telling your life." In *Discourse and Lifespan Identity,* edited by Nikolas Coupland and John F. Nussbaum, 81–99. Newbury Park: Sage Publications.

Walker, Mack. 1964. *Germany and the Emigration, 1816–1885.* Cambridge, MA: Harvard University Press.

Wallich, Henry C. 1955. *Mainsprings of the German Revival.* New Haven: Yale University Press.

Warren, Kay. 1978. *The Symbolism of Subordination.* Austin: University of Texas Press.

———. 1993. "Interpreted la violencia in Guatemala: Shapes of Mayan silence and resistance." In *The Violence Within*, edited by Kay Warren. Boulder, CO: Westview Press.

Waters, Mary C. 1990. *Ethnic Options: Choosing Identities in America*. Berkeley: University of California Press.

Weber, Max. 1979 [1894]. "Developmental tendencies in the situation of east Elbian rural labor." *Economy and Society* 8:177–205.

Wei, William. 1993. *The Asian American Movement*. Philadelphia: Temple University Press.

Weibel-Orlando, Joan. 1988. "Indians, ethnicity as a resource and aging: You can go home again." *Journal of Cross-Cultural Gerontology* 3:323–48.

———. 1991. *Indian Country, L.A.: Maintaining Ethnic Community in Complex Society*. Urbana: University of Illinois Press.

Whitehead, Ruth Holmes. 1982. *Micmac Quillwork*. Halifax: Nova Scotia Museum.

———. n.d. Micmac Petroglyph Site BeCw-2. MS. Nova Scotia Museum.

Wiesel, Elie. 1958. *Night*. New York: Avon Books, The Hearst Corporation.

———. 1970. *One Generation After*. New York: Pocket Books, a Simon and Schuster Division.

Wilson, M. 1957. *Rituals of Kinship Among the Nyakusa*. London: Oxford University Press.

Wilson, Robert A., and Bill Hosokawa. 1980. *East to America: A History of the Japanese in the United States*. New York: William Morrow & Co.

Winter, J. C. 1979. *Bruno Gutmann, 1876–1966: A German Approach to Social Anthropology*. Oxford: Clarendon Press.

Wolf, Christa. 1984. *Patterns of Childhood*. New York: The Noonday Press.

Woodward, Kathleen. 1986. "Reminiscence and the life review: Prospects and retrospects." In *What Does It Mean to Grow Old?: Reflections from the Humanities*, edited by Thomas R. Cole and Sally Gadow, 135–61. Durham, NC: Duke University Press.

———. 1991. *Aging and Its Discontents: Freud and Other Fictions*. Bloomington: Indiana University Press.

"Working up the Mau Mau frenzy." *Monthly News*, September, 4–7. Nairobi, Kenya.

Wunderlich, Frieda. 1961. *Farm Labor in Germany, 1810–1945*. Princeton, NJ: Princeton University Press.

Yates, Frances. 1974. *The Art of Memory*. Oxford: Oxford University Press.

Yoo, David. 1993. " 'Read all about it': Race, generation and the Japanese American press, 1925–41." *Amerasia Journal* 9(1):69–92.

Yücel, A. Ersan. 1987. "Turkish migrant workers in the FRG: A case study." In *Migrants in Europe: The Role of Family, Labor and Politics*, edited by Hans C. Buechler and Judith-Maria Buechler, 117–48. Westport, CT: Greenwood Press.

Index

About the Contributors

JACOB J. CLIMO is Professor of Anthropology at Michigan State University. He has done fieldwork in Mexico and Michigan and has written numerous articles on the local impact of Mexican national agrarian development, intergenerational communications, the life cycle, and old age. His recent book *Distant Parents* (1992) explores the distant adult child/elderly parent relationship in America through an examination of adult children's narrative constructions of their past and present emotional attachments to parents and their patterns of telephone calls and visits to maintain family ties.

ANTONELLA FABRI has worked extensively on issues of memory, identity, and oral autobiographies from the perspectives of both textual and anthropological analysis. During her fieldwork in Guatemala City, Fabri collected testimonies of displaced indigenous people and analyzed these personal oral histories in relation to violence and the emergence of a pan-indigenous national movement. Additional issues that she has covered in her work are discourses of identity, ethnicity, and space within critical contemporary theories. Her fieldwork expertise has also been applied to government-sponsored programs of research on problems of adaptation of Spanish-speaking communities in the United States. Fabri has taught at Skidmore College in New York, the University of Houston in Texas, and New York University.

IWAO ISHINO is Professor Emeritus of Anthropology at Michigan State University, where he served on the faculty for thirty-five years with specialization in Japanese Studies, Asian-American ethnicity, and applied anthropology. Born in San Diego, California, in 1921, he and his family (along with 120,000 other people of Japanese descent) were incarcerated at an internment camp at the beginning of World War II. While in camp he became associated with an anthropological study of camp life and this experience led to his appointment in 1944 as social science analyst in the Office of War Information. In 1949 he became an analyst in the Public Opinion and Sociological Research Division of the Occupation Forces in Japan, where he focused on issues of postwar Japanese adaptations including resettlement, social relationships, ritual kinship, and socio-economic adjustments of the peasantry. Ishino served as Program Director of Anthropology at the National Science Foundation in 1973–1974 and as Assistant Dean of International Programs at Michigan State from 1975 to 1980. His current research interest lies in the diffusion of innovative workshop practices back and forth between Japan and the United States.

DONNA O. KERNER, a sociocultural anthropologist, is currently an Associate Professor of Anthropology at Wheaton College in Norton, Massachusetts. A decade of fieldwork in East Africa, concentrated mainly in northeast Tanzania, has resulted in publications covering such topics as education and social stratification, land tenure, informal sector trade, food security, and gender and cooperatives. She is coeditor (with R. E. Downs and S. P. Reyna) of *The Political Economy of African Famine* (1991).

BRIAN LEIGH MOLYNEAUX is an archaeologist specializing in the study of art and material culture. He has conducted extensive fieldwork in Canada in rock art. He is a Research Archaeologist at the University of South Dakota. His current research is concerned with problems in the study of ideology using visual representations.

RAKHMIEL PELTZ directs the Yiddish Studies Program in the Department of Germanic Languages at Columbia University. Previously, he was Assistant Professor of Modern Foreign Languages and Literatures at Boston University. He holds doctorates in cell biology and Yiddish studies, and has published extensively in both fields. His area of specialization is the social history of Yiddish culture, currently doing fieldwork with elderly children of Jewish immigrants.

MOLLY G. SCHUCHAT has just retired from consultancies in mental health and family-related agencies in the Washington metropolitan area. In the fall of 1991 and 1993 she was a visiting professor at Rust College under an American Anthropological Association program of outreach to predominantly minority colleges. She has done food habits and tourism research in Hungary and China as well as the United States.

ANDREA L. SMITH is a doctoral student in cultural anthropology with a minor in history at the Department of Anthropology, University of Arizona, Tucson. Her M.A. thesis, entitled "Social Memory and Germany's Immigration Crisis: A Case of Collective Forgetting," was completed in 1992 and forms the basis of her chapter here. Her areas of interest include social memory and state formation in Germany and France, French colonialism in North Africa, and immigration, ethnic conflict, and racism in Europe.

RICHARD SWIDERSKI began his professional life by studying medicine. He entered anthropology doing fieldwork with Italian-American fishermen. He taught anthropology in American universities and then began a series of overseas research/teaching projects, which culminated most recently in Kenya. At present he is returning to medicine by way of epidemiology.

MAREA C. TESKI is Professor of Anthropology at the Richard Stockton College of New Jersey. She has written extensively in anthropology and gerontology, especially on aging in diverse ethnic communities and on the uses of memory in ethnography. She has done fieldwork with exile groups and with grandparents who are raising their grandchildren. She is interested in the concept and ethnography of generational responsibility and reciprocity.

ISBN 0-89789-409-X

HARDCOVER BAR CODE